THE
PRISON
COOKBOOK

THE PRISON COOKBOOK

PETER HIGGINBOTHAM

The
History
Press

Front cover illustrations: (upper) Gloucester prison kitchen; (lower) Rochester kitchen; both photographs reproduced with the kind permission of the Galleries of Justice.

First published 2010

The History Press
The Mill, Brimscombe Port
Stroud, Gloucestershire, GL5 2QG
www.thehistorypress.co.uk

© Peter Higginbotham, 2010

The right of Peter Higginbotham to be identified as the Author of this work has been asserted in accordance with the Copyrights, Designs and Patents Act 1988.

British Library Cataloguing in Publication Data.
A catalogue record for this book is available from the British Library.

ISBN 978 0 7524 5423 8

Typesetting and origination by The History Press
Printed in India by Replika Press Pvt. Ltd.
Manufacturing managed by Jellyfish Print Solutions Ltd

Contents

Weights, Measures and Money

Below are some older measures and monetary units found in this book, with their approximate metric or decimal currency equivalents. Common abbreviations are given in brackets.

Weight

1 drachm (drm)		1.8 grams (gm)
1 ounce (oz)	16 drachms	28.4 grams
1 pound (lb)	16 ounces	450 grams
1 stone	14 pounds	6.3 kilograms (kg)
1 hundredweight (cwt)	112 pounds	50 kilograms

Volume

1 fluid drachm (or dram)		3.55 cubic centimetres (cc or ml)
1 fluid ounce	8 fluid drachms	28.4 cubic centimetres
1 gill (or noggin)	5 fluid ounces	143 cubic centimetres
1 pint (pt)	20 fluid ounces	570 cubic centimetres
1 quart	2 pints	1.1 litres
1 gallon	8 pints	4.5 litres
1 peck	2 gallons	9 litres
1 bushel	8 gallons	36 litres
1 firkin	9 gallons	41 litres
1 hogshead (of beer etc)	(originally) 52.5 gallons	239 litres
1 pipe	(typically) 2 hogsheads	479 litres
1 tierce	⅓ of a pipe or 35 gallons	160 litres
1 puncheon	cask of 72–120 gallons	327–545 litres

Length

1 inch (in)		2.5 centimetres (cm)
1 foot (ft)	12 inches	30 centimetres
1 yard (yd)	3 feet	90 centimetres
1 mile	1760 yards	1.6 kilometres

Money

1 penny (*d*)		0.4 pence (p)
1 shilling (*s*)	12 pennies	5 pence
1 mark	13*s* 4*d*	67 pence
1 pound (£ or l)	20 shillings	1 pound

In terms of its purchasing power, £1 in the year 1750 would now (2009) be worth around £139. In 1850 £1 would now be worth around £83.

one

Introduction

The dietary has an intimate relationship with all the other elements of prison life. On its proper adjustment to the requirements of the average prisoner, and the manner of its application and administration, must depend in large measure the successful working of the whole prison system. (Departmental Committee on Prison Dietaries, 1899)[1]

'Food', commented one prison governor, 'is one of the four things you must get right if you like having a roof on your prison.' (National Audit Office, 2006)[2]

Putting people behind bars has a very long history. In a Bible story dating from around the seventeenth century BC, the book of Genesis tells how Joseph, a young Hebrew enslaved in Egypt, was consigned to the Great Prison at Thebes for attempting to seduce the wife of his master Potiphar. The prison was probably a granary where foreign offenders were held and required to perform hard labour.[3] Today, prison has never been so popular – across the world, more than 10 million people are currently locked up.[4]

Being in prison, though, has not always been seen as a punishment in itself. In the past, it was more often used as a means for holding people securely until their trial or until their sentence was carried out. In early Rome, for example, debtors could be held in custody by their creditors for sixty days. Then, if still unable to pay, their fate would probably be slavery or execution by such means as burning, hanging, decapitation or clubbing to death. Justice in ancient Athens largely favoured retribution in the form of punishments such as stoning to death or throwing an offender from a cliff, with prison mainly used to confine debtors or those awaiting trial or execution. The Greek philosopher Plato, in a remarkably prescient view, proposed three new types of prison: a general prison to confine lesser offenders for up to two years; a more isolated centre where more serious but reformable cases were held for at least five years; and a remotely located institution where incorrigible offenders were held for life, without contact with other prisoners or visitors.[5]

Whatever the reason for someone being in prison, it has rarely been intended to be a comfortable or pleasant experience. Rome's ancient Carcer, a group of prison buildings near the Forum, included quarry prisons and the subterranean Tullianum, where Saints Peter and Paul are said to have been held. According to the Roman historian Sallust, the Tullianum's 'neglect, darkness, and stench made it hideous and fearsome to behold'.[6]

Many ancient prisons were, by modern standards, quite small and the health of the inmates – let alone their comfort – was of little concern to those who ran them. Living conditions for those held in early English prisons were often little better. For a long period, they were privately operated with the inmates paying for their own food and accommodation. For those who could afford it, prison could indeed be a relatively painless experience, with a comfortable room and meals bought from the gaoler,

The so-called 'Prison of Socrates' in Athens where, according to popular tradition, Socrates was held while awaiting his execution. He refused the advice of his friends to try and escape and suffered the Athenian penalty of compulsory suicide by drinking a brew containing the poison hemlock.

The Tullianum in Rome, later known as the Mamertine prison. Originally, the only means of access was via a hole in the ceiling. Tradition has it that while the Apostle Peter was confined here, a spring of water miraculously appeared in the floor with which he was able to baptise his gaolers and forty-seven companions.

cooked themselves or sent in from outside. But for those with little or no money, especially those being held for non-payment of their debts, prison life frequently consisted of a bed on the floor of a dark and damp cellar and a diet of bread and water. Even those found totally innocent of their charges could sometimes remain in gaol indefinitely because they could not pay the necessary release fees.

From the 1770s, reformers such as John Howard, Elizabeth Fry and James Neild exposed the iniquities of the English prison system and campaigned to make prisons more humane, often harnessing the power of public opinion to persuade prison operators to grudgingly fall in line with gradual legislative reforms.

In more recent times, even after the state had taken over the running of the country's prisons in 1877, providing inmates with a bed of bare planks and a meagre diet of bread, porridge or gruel, and occasional potatoes, was still viewed as part of the deterrent value of a prison sentence. Faced with such treatment, it is perhaps not surprising that convicts at Dartmoor in the 1870s resorted to eating dead rats and mice, grass, candles, dogs and earthworms.

Attitudes gradually changed, however, and by the end of the nineteenth century, prison conditions, and particularly food, started to improve. The 1899 Departmental Committee on Prison Dietaries acknowledged that food was a core element in successful prison operation. A new national prison menu saw the inclusion of items such as beans, bacon, suet pudding, tea and cocoa, while the fare provided for prisoners who were sick soon included chicken broth, fishcakes, boiled rabbit, custard pudding and stewed figs. For inmates who misbehaved, however, the result would still be a spell on bread and water. At the same time, increasing concern for how food was prepared resulted in the introduction of training courses for prison cooks and the publication in 1902 of the first prison cookbook – the *Manual of Cooking & Baking for the Use of Prison Officers* – which is reproduced in full as part of this book.

From the 1950s, prison food began to change out of all recognition with the arrival of sausage, bacon and fried bread for breakfast, and of roast beef, roast potatoes, Yorkshire pudding, bread-and-butter pudding and custard on the dinner menu. Nonetheless, during the 1970s and '80s, 'inedible and monotonous' food was still reported as one of the causes of dissatisfaction which led to a rash of violent disturbances and damage to prison buildings costing many millions of pounds.

By 2005, prisoners could select their meals from a multi-choice menu featuring dishes such as grilled gammon, chicken chasseur, or minced beef lasagne served with garlic bread and salad, with options catering for vegans, vegetarians, and a wide variety of religious and cultural diets. Porridge, the prison's signature dish, had virtually disappeared. Clearly, the prison authorities had taken to heart the maxim of food (along with mail, hot water and visits) being the things you have to get right if you want to keep a roof on your prison.

The kitchens at Holloway prison in about 1901 when the *Manual of Cooking & Baking* was being compiled. Food was served in a two-piece metal 'pail' or 'tin-dinner-inner', with the base holding liquids and the upper part solid food.

two

Prison and Other Punishments

PRISON, TRIAL AND JURY

English law has sanctioned the use of imprisonment for more than 1,000 years. In the ninth and tenth centuries, legislators such as Alfred and Athelstan formalised the use of prison sentences, typically 40 to 120 days, sometimes accompanied by a fine, for a range of crimes including oath-breaking, theft, witchcraft, sorcery and murder. Establishing guilt for such offences might involve the accused undergoing the 'threefold ordeal': first, the ordeal of hot iron (carrying a pound weight of the hot metal for a certain distance); second, the ordeal of hot water (the retrieval of a stone hanging by a string in a pitcher of boiling water); third, the ordeal of the accursed morsel (swallowing a piece of bread accompanied by a prayer that it would choke him if he were guilty).[7] Survival of these ordeals with little or no harm, or with an injury that healed very quickly, was taken as a sign of innocence.

The Normans, following their invasion of England in 1066, introduced an alternative form of ordeal, namely trial by combat or 'wager of battle'. This could take place where, for example, an offender accused another person of being the instigator or an accomplice in the crime. The person thus accused, the 'appellee', could demand wager of battle against his accuser, the 'appellant'. If defeated, the appellee was liable to be hung; if he won, the appellee was pardoned. The right to wager of battle was last claimed as recently as 1818 by Abraham Thornton. After Thornton was acquitted of murdering a girl named Mary Ashford, her brother mounted a private prosecution, in response to which Thornton was granted his request for battle. However, the brother withdrew before any combat took place.

The roots of the modern English justice system were created a century after the Conquest when, in 1166, Henry II issued an Act known as the Assize of Clarendon. The Assize is often credited with laying down the origins of the jury system by setting up a grand or 'presenting' jury in each district which was to notify the king's roving judges of the most serious crimes committed there. Clause 7 of the Assize also provided a significant impetus to the use of prisons – it decreed that the sheriff of each county was required to erect a county gaol if none already existed, with the cost being met by the crown.

CATEGORIES OF OFFENCE

As the English system evolved, a classification of different types of offence became established. Although their precise definitions changed over the centuries, the main broad categories of crime were high treason, petty treason, felony and misdemeanour.

High treason was an offence against the monarch or the safety of the realm, originally defined by a statute of Edward III in 1350–51.[8] Treasonable offences included: 'compassing or imagining the king's death'; violating the king's wife or eldest daughter (but only if she was unmarried);

waging war against the king or aiding his enemies; slaying the king's chancellor, treasurer or judges; and counterfeiting the currency of the realm.

Petty treason was a treason against a royal subject, in particular the murder of someone to whom allegiance was owed, such as a master killed by his servant, or a husband by his wife.

Felony, a word which originally meant 'forfeiture', was a broad category of more serious offence which at one time was punishable by the forfeiture of land or goods, but for which death later became the usual penalty. The main types of felony were murder, rape, larceny (i.e. theft), robbery (i.e. theft with violence) and burglary. However, many specific offences were later added to the list: for example, stealing a hawk became a felony in the reign of Edward III.

Misdemeanours, in contrast to felonies, were less serious offences not involving forfeiture of property.

The traditional punishment for misdemeanours was whipping, the stocks or pillory, or a fine, while that for treason was death.[9] Felonies could be capital or non-capital depending on the particular offence – which ones received the death penalty changed over the centuries.

THE GROWTH OF PRISONS

During the twelfth and thirteenth centuries, the use of prisons became more widespread. By 1216, all but five counties had complied with the Assize of Clarendon and set up gaols which were often situated in the castles that existed in most county towns.[10] Increasingly, other large towns set up their own gaols, with castles again being a popular location.

In the capital, the Tower of London and Fleet prison were used to hold the king's debtors as well as 'contumacious excommunicates, those who interfered with the working of the law, failed appellants, attainted jurors, perjurers, frauds, and those who misinformed the courts'.[11]

In the main, though, imprisonment was still not regarded as a punishment in itself, but rather a means for keeping offenders in secure custody while awaiting trial or execution, or until they had paid a fine that had been imposed or a debt that was owed. Nonetheless, there was a steady growth of offences for which the penalty was a term in prison. The use of imprisonment for debtors to the crown, which began in 1178, was extended to all debtors in 1352. Other offences, such as aiding a prisoner to escape, prostitution and brothel-keeping, also became punishable by prison. Between the thirteenth and sixteenth centuries, a gaol term – typically ranging from forty days to a year and a day – became the penalty for around 180 additional offences, including seditious slander, corruption and selling shoddy or underweight goods.[12]

SPECIAL-PURPOSE PRISONS

Not all prisons were operated by the civil authorities. The stannary courts at Lydford in Devon and Lostwithiel in Cornwall judged cases involving tin-miners and had their own prisons.

In the royal forests, which in the medieval period numbered eighty and covered three tenths of England, 'forest law' applied. Introduced by William the Conqueror, forest law prohibited not only unauthorised hunting, but almost anything that might be considered harmful to the animals or their habitat, such as felling trees, cutting peat or even – in some cases – collecting firewood. Penalties for offenders included fines and imprisonment, with forest prisons being set up in 1361 at Lyndhurst in Hampshire, and in 1446 at Clarendon Palace in Wiltshire.[13]

A number of prisons were also established by the Church and religious communities. The Bishop of Winchester maintained a small prison for disobedient clerics from 860. By 1076, the punishments inflicted on the inmates included scourging with rods, solitary confinement and a bread and water diet. In 1107, construction began of a new palace, chapel and two prisons (one for men and one for women), on land owned by the bishop at Southwark, the area later becoming known as the Liberty of the Clink. In 1161, the bishop gained the right to license brothels and prostitutes in the Liberty. A 'Winchester goose' subsequently became a popular name both for one of the women and also for a venereal condition that was characterised by a swelling in the groin.[14]

In 1332, the Archbishop of York erected a large gaol at Hexham, three storeys high, with two dungeons.[15] It was used to hold transgressors from his estates in the ecclesiastical liberty of Hexhamshire. Part of the Lollard's Tower at Lambeth Palace was used by the Archbishop of Canterbury to detain free-thinking (and therefore heretical) followers of John Wycliffe, translator of the Bible into English. The Bishop of London also maintained a prison within the precincts of St Paul's Cathedral.

Monasteries and abbeys often included a prison amongst their buildings. At Fountains Abbey, three cells were constructed in the basement of the abbot's house. Each had its own latrine and the inmates were chained to an iron staple which was set into the floor. Excavations in the nineteenth century revealed some Latin graffiti which indicate that the cells were used for disobedient monks rather than lay brothers. The scribblings on one of the walls included the phrase *Vale libertas* ('Farewell freedom').[16]

BENEFIT OF CLERGY

The Canon Law of ecclesiastical courts and the Common Law of the king's courts sometimes came to conflicting conclusions about the appropriate punishment for a crime perpetrated by someone in holy orders. To resolve this situation, Common Law courts relinquished the use of the death penalty for some less serious capital offences if committed by a member of the clergy. Instead, a lesser punishment was administered, typically a whipping or short prison sentence.

In 1305, the Benefit of Clergy, as it came to be known, was extended to secular clerks who could read and write Latin. It was later broadened to include anyone with a tonsure − the monk's traditional shaven crown − and finally to anyone who was literate. When faced with the possibility of the death penalty, an offender could demonstrate his entitlement to Benefit of Clergy by 'calling for the book' − the Bible − from which he would read aloud. The usual text was the so-called 'neck verse': 'Have mercy upon me, O God, according to thy loving kindness: according unto the multitude of thy tender mercies blot out my transgressions.'[17]

Capital offences for which the death penalty could be evaded in this way were classed as 'clergyable' and their number steadily grew, with murder on the highway being included from 1512 and privily [secretly] stealing from the person in 1565. However, increasing abuse of the privilege led, from the sixteenth century, to an increasing number of existing offences being deemed non-clergyable. These included murder, rape, robbery, witchcraft and stealing a horse, later joined by the stealing of sheep or mail.[18]

A common ploy for claiming Benefit of Clergy by someone who was not literate was simply to memorise the neck verse. In one famous case during the time of Edward III, the accused man appeared to read equally fluently regardless of which way round the Bible was given to him − it transpired that he had been coached by two boys let in to visit him by the gaoler. Another ruse was to shave the defendant's head in the style of the tonsure, again with the gaoler's assistance sometimes being provided.[19]

Left: Oxford's county gaol, dating from around 1166, was built within the town's Norman castle and operated on the same site until 1996. St George's Tower survived the prison being rebuilt in the late eighteenth and nineteenth centuries, and dominates this 1940's view of the prisoners' exercise yard.

Below left: Lydford Castle, built in 1195, was the administrative centre for the Royal Forest of Dartmoor and included a prison amongst its facilities. It was also home to the Stannary Court, which ruled on matters related to tin mining in Devon. The court's strict laws stipulated that a miner found guilty of adulterating tin for fraudulent purposes would have three spoonfuls of molten tin poured down his throat.

Below right: A branding iron from Lancaster Castle. Anyone claiming Benefit of Clergy was marked on the thumb with a letter 'M' (for Murderer) or 'T' (for Thief) so that if he repeated such a crime, he would not evade execution again.

CAPITAL PUNISHMENT

Despite the gradual growth in the use of prison as a punishment, the sentence for most serious crimes remained the death penalty. Execution had an obvious attraction in that it permanently disposed of the offender and so removed any possibility of further transgression. In the case of treason and other political crimes, a dead opponent could not indulge in any further plotting. For more commonplace offences, execution – carried out in a highly public and bloody manner – was viewed as a valuable deterrent for those who might be tempted to break the law.

For the highest in the land, beheading was the usual mode of execution, with two of Henry VIII's wives, Ann Boleyn and Kathryn Howard, among the best known to suffer this fate. For lesser mortals, however, the most usual form of the death penalty was hanging. In some cases the punishment was that of being hung, drawn and quartered or – more accurately – being drawn, hung, disembowelled, beheaded and quartered. Such executions often began with the victim being drawn through the streets attached to a hurdle. The hanging that followed did not necessarily result in death. Someone left hanging would eventually expire from asphyxiation but to experience the full agony of execution required that they be cut down before death, revived, and then castrated and disembowelled, with the pieces being burned. The body was finally decapitated and cut into four quarters with the pieces sometimes being boiled or coated in pitch if they were to be displayed.

The addition to the hanging procedure of a 'drop' through a trapdoor seems to have first appeared during the eighteenth century, possibly at the execution, in 1760, of Laurence Ferrers 'the Murderous Earl', for the shooting of his steward. The extra distance dropped caused the victim's neck to break and resulted in a much quicker death. This development had already been pre-empted by Guy Fawkes, the last of the Gunpowder Plot conspirators to be executed in 1606 at Old Palace Yard in Westminster. Having climbed up the ladder to the scaffold and with the hangman's rope around his neck, Fawkes leapt off and broke his neck, saving himself from experiencing the pain of disembowelment and quartering.

VARIETIES OF EXECUTION

As well as beheading and hanging, a number of other forms of execution were used at different times in the past. Burning to death was often used to deal with those found guilty of religious heresy or witchcraft. It first appeared on the statute book in the 1401 *De Haeretico Comburendo* or Statute of Heresy. The first victim, in 1402, was William Sautre for, amongst other heresies, his denial of transubstantiation. During the reign of Mary I, nearly 300 Protestants were burned, including thirteen in a single day at Stratford-le-Bow.[20]

For many years, it was the practice for women convicted of treason or petty treason to be burned at the stake, while men who were guilty of these offences would be hung, drawn and quartered. It became the custom for those facing the stake to be strangled with a rope immediately beforehand so that their death would not be unnecessarily prolonged. Occasionally, this procedure went awry – as in the case of Catherine Hayes, who in 1726 was executed at Tyburn for the murder of her husband. The executioner was in the process of strangling her but the already lit fire scorched his hands, causing him to leave hold before she had become unconscious, resulting in an agonising death.

In 1531, Henry VIII instituted the punishment of boiling alive for those found guilty of murder by poisoning. The penalty was introduced after Richard Roose, cook at the Bishop of Rochester's palace at Lambeth, had poisoned a pot of soup – as a joke, he claimed – with the result that two people died. Roose was boiled to death at Smithfield the following year. This form of execution was abolished by Edward VI in 1547.

A rather different form of execution was applied to prisoners who refused to make a plea, without which a trial could not proceed. The legal remedy for this refusal was *peine forte et dure* or pressing to death, whereby the victim was stripped and placed on the ground under a board with rocks piled on top until he either died or agreed to plead. For someone clearly determined not to plead, death could be hastened by placing a sharp stone under their back.[21] The area in London's Newgate prison where this procedure was carried out became known as the Press Yard. Pressing was abolished in 1772 and prisoners refusing to plead were then treated as guilty.

MORE OFFENCES AND MORE ESCAPE CLAUSES

The number of crimes punishable by death increased dramatically during the eighteenth century, rising from around fifty offences in 1688, to 160 in 1765, and 225 by 1815 – a body of legislation which has come to be known as the 'Bloody Code'. In 1722, a single measure, the 'Waltham Black Act' which aimed to curtail a rise in poaching, added around fifty capital offences to the statute book, none of which could be evaded by claiming Benefit of Clergy.

An execution outside Newgate in 1806. Prior to their abolition in 1868, public executions attracted huge crowds, with the well-to-do paying large sums to hire rooms overlooking the gallows. In Dickens' *Oliver Twist*, Fagin was executed at Newgate where 'a great multitude had already assembled; the windows were filled with people, smoking and playing cards to beguile the time. Everything told of life and animation, but one dark cluster of objects and in the very centre of all – the black stage, the cross-beam, the rope, and all the hideous apparatus of death.'

Above: Although beheading by use of
a machine is usually associated with
eighteenth-century French physician Joseph
Guillotin, falling-blade devices were in use in
both England and Scotland several centuries
before. The Halifax Gibbet, shown here, was
in operation by at least 1541, and claimed
almost fifty victims over the next hundred
years.

Left: An illustration of highway robber William
Spiggott undergoing the press at Newgate in
1721. Spiggott withstood a weight of 350lb for
half an hour but finally agreed to plead after a
further 50lb was added. In due course he was
convicted and hanged.

Despite the increase in the number of capital offences, and the clampdown on the use of Benefit of Clergy, the number who were actually executed was rather smaller than might be imagined. Judges could dismiss cases or hand down milder sentences. Juries, too, could return a 'partial verdict' and convict defendants for lesser offences than those for which they had originally been indicted. A typical example in the case of grand larceny – stealing goods worth a shilling or more, and an offence which attracted the death penalty – was to return a verdict of petty larceny – stealing goods worth less than a shilling, and which involved a lesser penalty. To rationalise such decisions, the goods in question could be undervalued or the verdict linked to only one item of a larger theft. This sometimes led to absurd decisions, such as the case in 1751 where a home counties jury found the accused guilty of stealing eleven half-crown coins (£1 7s 6d) which were agreed to have a total value of 10d.[22]

Even where the death sentence had been passed, pardons and reprieves were common. Although a reprieve was technically just the postponement of a sentence for an interval of time, it often led to a full pardon. One potential reprieve for females facing the death penalty was known as the 'benefit of the belly'. A woman declaring herself to be pregnant would not be hanged until after the birth of her innocent child. However, the sentence was rarely then carried out and effectively resulted in a pardon. Although such claims of pregnancy were supposed to be verified by a midwife, it seems doubtful whether this was taken seriously. Between 1559 and 1625, 38 per cent of convicted female felons in one court circuit successfully claimed that they were expecting.[23] At Newgate, women awaiting execution were placed together in a large ward on the top floor from where the widespread and open soliciting for men to provide this means of reprieve was known to shock visitors to the prison.[24]

OTHER PUNISHMENTS

For offences not serious enough to warrant the death penalty, a wide variety of unpleasant physical punishments evolved. These included the pillory, the stocks, whipping and mutilation.

The pillory was a post against which an offender was made to stand for a few hours and suffer public display, ridicule, abuse or – if unlucky – physical assault. In its earliest form, the occupant was kept in place by having his ear nailed to the post. At the end of the allotted time, the ear was simply cut off. This allowed a crude form of record keeping – a second offence would lead to loss of the other ear and a third one to hanging.[25] Later versions of the device included a wooden frame with holes for clamping the head and hands of those placed there. The pillory was used for a wide variety of transgressions, especially 'public nuisance' offences, such as selling tainted or underweight food. Evidence of the offence was often attached to the pilloried person – a fishmonger selling stale fish might be adorned with a collar of his wares.[26] Use of the pillory largely ceased in 1815, although its use for perjury continued until 1837.

The stocks, as revealed by the Acts of the Apostles, were known to the Romans – Paul and Silas' gaoler 'thrust them into the inner prison, and made their feet fast in the stocks'.[27] Like the pillory, the stocks had holes for locking an offender's legs, wrists or head in place, but were often positioned near the ground to allow the occupant to sit. Although stocks were used to expose offenders such as vagrants or drunkards to public indignity, they could also serve as an alternative to prison to confine someone until being brought before a Justice. In Scotland, a comparable device known as the 'joug' consisted of a hinged iron collar attached to a wall or post. The name may be the origin of 'jug' – one of the slang terms for prison.[28]

Two men suffer the indignities of the pillory – the nearer one appears to have been hit on the forehead by one of the throng.

The 1530 Whipping Act decreed that vagrants were to be 'tied to the end of a cart, naked, and beaten with whips throughout such market town till the body shall be bloody'. A small concession was made in 1597 with the victim only being stripped to the waist. Whipping-posts, often combined with pillories, were also used for carrying out the punishment, although the cart tail continued to be used for vagrants and cases where the whipping was ordered to be carried out from one place to another. Whipping in public was abolished in 1817.

Perhaps the most gruesome form of physical punishment was that of bodily mutilation. In 1176, during the reign of Henry II, crimes such as robbery, false coining and arson could result in the amputation of the right hand and right foot.[29] Under the Brawling Act of 1551 (not repealed until 1828) the penalty for anyone convicted of fighting in a church or churchyard was to have one of his ears cut off – or, if having no ears, to be branded on the cheek with the letter 'F' for 'fray-maker'. Under Elizabeth I, punishments for seditious libel included the removal of the right hand. A writer named Stubbs had a cleaver driven through his wrist with a mallet. The event was witnessed by historian William Camden who recalled that:

Stubbs, when his right hand was cut off, plucked off his hat with the left, and said, with a loud voice, 'God Save the Queen!' The multitude standing about was deeply silent, either out of horror of this new and unwonted kind of punishment, or out of commiseration towards the man.[30]

three

Early English Prisons

London, as well as being the country's largest city and the seat of government, also boasted England's largest concentration of prisons. In 1623, John Taylor's verse-pamphlet *The Praise and Vertue of a Jayle and Jaylers* listed eighteen establishments then in operation. A century later, Daniel Defoe counted twenty-seven public gaols, together with a large assortment of 'tolerated prisons.'[31]

Some London prisons, such as the Fleet, Marshalsea, Clink and King's Bench, were under the direct control of the crown and used, first and foremost, for those who had committed some kind of offence against the monarch. Other prisons were run by the City of London – these included Newgate, Ludgate and the Counters (or 'Compters') at Poultry and Wood Street. Newgate was the general holding prison for criminals awaiting trial for offences committed in London and Middlesex. Ludgate was used for the detention of the city's freemen and freewomen who had committed misdemeanours, although it came to be used almost entirely as a debtor's prison.[32] The two Counters, operated by London's two sheriffs, dealt speedily with those offending against the city's ordinances, including those causing a breach of the peace, and also housed debtors.

THE TOWER OF LONDON

Pre-eminent amongst London's prisons was the Tower of London. The Tower, whose construction was begun by William the Conqueror, served as a fortress, royal residence, ordnance depot and mint, but was also used as a prison for more than 800 years. As the securest stronghold in the kingdom, its main function was the confinement of what were considered the most dangerous class of offenders – those accused of high treason.

The Tower's first inmate was Ranulf Flambard, imprisoned in the White Tower by Henry I after the suspicious death of Henry's predecessor William Rufus. Flambard was also the first person ever to escape from the Tower. In February 1101, a rope was smuggled in to him in a large flagon of wine which he invited his guards to share. After they became drunk and fell asleep, he climbed down the rope to the foot of the Tower, where his friends had horses waiting to make his escape.

In 1305, Scottish resistance leader William Wallace, now famous as Braveheart, was imprisoned in the Tower prior to his execution for treason by Edward I. He was one of the first to undergo the fate of being hung, drawn and quartered. His dismembered limbs were despatched separately for display in Perth, Stirling, Berwick and Newcastle.

Other well-known detainees at the Tower included the 'little princes' (Edward V and his brother Richard, the Duke of York), Guy Fawkes, Sir Walter Raleigh and Samuel Pepys. In 1820, after the failure of their plan to assassinate the entire British cabinet, the Cato Street Conspirators were held in the Tower. Their gang, led by Arthur Thistlewood, were the last persons to be beheaded by the axe in Britain.[33]

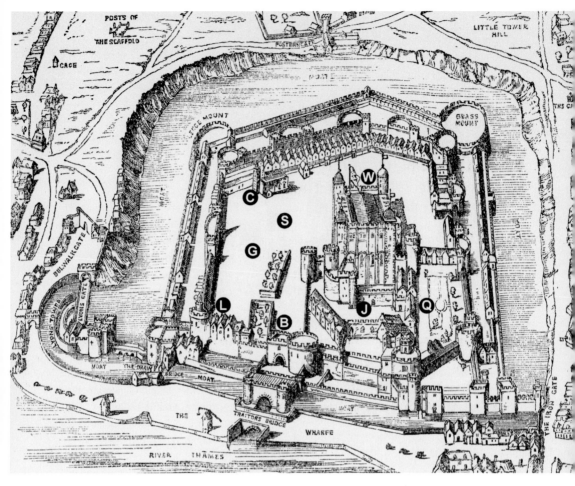

A nineteenth-century plan of the Tower of London showing the Bloody Tower (B), St Peter's Chapel (C), the Green (G), the Jewel House (J), the Lieutenant's Lodgings (L), the Queen's Lodgings (Q), the site of the Scaffold (S) and the White Tower (W).

THE FLEET

The Fleet prison was founded, probably in the late eleventh century, on the eastern bank of the River Fleet, just outside the Ludgate entrance to London. The prison was used by the king to hold those charged with offences against the state, including those of the highest rank.

In around 1335, a ten-foot-wide moat was built around the prison so that it was entirely surrounded with water. However, the prison's neighbours decided that the moat would make an excellent drain for the waste from their stables, lavatories and sewers. Within twenty years the moat was in a filthy state, a situation made worse in 1354 when a riverside wharf near the prison was let to some butchers as a place to deposit the entrails of slaughtered cattle. The moat soon became so congested with offal that it was possible to walk across it.[34]

The Fleet was later used to house debtors and bankrupts, and, as at some other prisons, payment of a fee to the gaoler could allow an inmate to reside in a designated area outside the prison – the Liberty of the Fleet.

MARSHALSEA

The Marshalsea (whose keeper was known as the Marshal) was erected in around 1329, at the north side of what is now Mermaid Court, off Borough High Street in Southwark. It originally held offenders who were members of the king's household but was later used for the confinement of debtors, pirates, mutineers and recusants – those refusing to acknowledge the established Church. Edmund Bonner, London's last Roman Catholic bishop, was imprisoned in Marshalsea for the final ten years of his life after refusing to swear the oath of supremacy to Queen Elizabeth.

In 1811, the Marshalsea was rebuilt a little way to the south of its original location, on the site of the White Lion prison. The father of twelve-year-old Charles Dickens was sent there in 1824 owing £40 10s. The prison later featured in Dickens' stories such as *Little Dorrit* and *David Copperfield*.

THE KING'S BENCH

The King's Bench prison was located near the Marshalsea on Southwark's Borough High Street. It originally held those being tried by the King's Bench Court, which dealt with offences directly affecting the king himself, and also those privileged enough to be tried only before the king. However, it largely came to be used for debtors and for those convicted of libel.

In 1755–8 the prison was relocated a short distance to Blackman Street, but had to be rebuilt after it was burned down during a riot in 1780. Thomas Allen, in his 1829 *History of the County of Surrey*, portrays an almost holiday-camp atmosphere within its confines:

> The prison occupies an extensive area of ground; it consists of one large pile of building, about 120 yards long. The south, or principal front, has a pediment, under which is a chapel. There are four pumps of spring and river water. Here are 224 rooms, or apartments, eight of which are called state-rooms, which are much larger than the others. Within the walls are a coffee-house and two public-houses; and the shops and stalls for meat, vegetables, and necessaries of almost every description, give the place the appearance of a public market; while the numbers of people walking about, or engaged in various amusements, are little calculated to impress the stranger with an idea of distress, or even of confinement.

In addition to the hospitable conditions within the prison, inmates of the King's Bench could purchase 'Liberty of the Rules', which allowed them to live outside the prison within an area about 3 miles across. Not surprisingly, the King's Bench was said to be 'the most desirable place of incarceration for debtors in England' – so much so that 'persons so situated frequently removed themselves to it by *habeas corpus* from the most distant prisons in the kingdom'.[35]

THE CLINK

By around 1500, the Bishop of Winchester's prison in Southwark's Liberty of the Clink had become known simply as 'the Clink' – a name that turned into a popular slang word for a prison. Although it was used for the detention of local breakers of the peace, the Clink was particularly employed for holding religious offenders, both priests and lay recusants.

The Oath of Allegiance, introduced under James I in 1606, allowed Roman Catholics to acknowledge their loyalty to the English king as head of the realm in what some viewed as a less objectionable way to that required by Henry VIII's Oath of Supremacy. In the years that followed, a number of priests who took this path, despite a prohibition by the Pope, were housed in the Clink,[36] notably the archpriest George Blackwell, who died there in 1613.

Left: From the 1630s until Hardwicke's Marriage Act of 1753, the Liberty of the Fleet was notorious as a venue for clandestine marriages. The proceedings, often held in taverns, were carried out by ministers – real or otherwise – who were themselves often debtors.

Below: The Marshalsea prison in 1819. The Marshalsea was largely demolished in 1849, although parts of the building continued to be used housing an ironmonger's, and later the Marshalsea Press.

The Newgate prison gateway in around 1750. The large rooftop 'sail ventilator' assisted the circulation of air around the building. Many prisons were dark and poorly aired, some even blocking a number of their existing windows up after the introduction of the window tax in 1696.

During the English civil war, the Clink was used as a prison for Royalists. The Bishop of Winchester's properties were sold off and the Clink was then used to house only a few debtors.

NEWGATE PRISON

Newgate was the main prison serving the City of London and the county of Middlesex. Founded in 1188, it was damaged by Wat Tyler and his followers during the Peasant's Revolt in 1381, but remained largely unaltered until its complete rebuilding in 1423 with funds from the estate of former Lord Mayor Dick Whittington. One improvement, in 1406, was the building of a tower specifically for women inmates who had previously been crammed into a small room, with the nearest privy being accessed through a men's section of the prison.

Newgate prison was rebuilt in the 1770s, and then again after being burned down in the Gordon Riots in 1780. This view shows it a few years before its demolition in 1902 to make way for the new Central Criminal Court building – the Old Bailey.

Newgate held a wide variety of inmates. Some were petty criminals, or those guilty of breaking the numerous ordinances governing life and trade within the city. These were usually given a fixed-term period of imprisonment ranging from a few days to a year and a day. In 1328, a thief received forty days in Newgate for stealing a tunic worth 10*d*, while in 1382 a man guilty of 'molesting' foreigners was confined for a year and a day.[37] Newgate was also used to confine those awaiting trial for more serious offences, habitual criminals, those with unpaid fines and debtors whose detention would continue indefinitely if they could not pay their creditors. However, the prison's reputation grew largely out of its use by the king and his Justices to hold all manner of dangerous and hardened criminals, heretics, rebels and traitors who were brought for trial to London. The fate of many Newgate inmates would therefore either be the death penalty or perpetual imprisonment.

Newgate's gaoler was required to be of good character and swear an oath that he would not extort money from those in his care. Since the gaoler's income was derived from various 'customary fees' for goods and services he provided to the inmates, such promises were not always lived up to. One early fourteenth-century incumbent, Edmund de Lorimer, was found guilty of offences such as torturing prisoners to extract money, demanding a discharge fee of up to 1s 4d instead of the customary 4d and overcharging for items supplied to prisoners such as torches.[38] In 1333 another Newgate gaoler, Hugh de Croydon, was accused of placing those held for non-felonious offences in the dungeon amongst serious criminals, and torturing them for money. Financial transgressions were not the only cause for concern. In 1449, another keeper, William Arnold, was himself imprisoned for violating one of the female prisoners.

Following its reconstruction in the 1420s, Newgate provided much improved surroundings for at least some of its inhabitants. There was a central dining hall and a drinking fountain was provided, although decent water only arrived in 1436 when lead pipes were laid to join the St Bartholomew's Hospital supply. Adjoining the hall, there were rooms with chimneys and privies, 'spacious and well-lighted recreation rooms' and a chapel.[39] Elsewhere, however, there were some 'less convenient chambers' and the prison still had secure and windowless basement cells. Those of lesser rank, or from outside the city, were given the inferior rooms, while those involved in serious crimes were kept underground, usually in chains, some in solitary confinement. Descriptions of Newgate invariably describe it as a thoroughly unpleasant place – 'the fetid and corrupt atmosphere that is in the hateful gaol of Neugate'.[40]

LUDGATE

Ludgate prison was established in 1378, partly as a response to the harsh physical conditions that existed at Newgate prison. It was intended to house Londoners found guilty of non-felonious crimes, although it later came to cater primarily for freeman debtors.[41]

Initially, its inmates suffered at the hands of the keeper, John Botlesham, who misappropriated alms intended for the prisoners and clapped in irons those who complained. However, the prison soon gained a reputation for its comfort, so much so that it was positively attracting people, including prostitutes, to take up residence. As a result, the prison was closed down and its inmates moved to the stricter regime at Newgate. Unfortunately, within a fortnight more than sixty of those transferred had died and Ludgate was rapidly reopened.

The prison was enlarged in the fifteenth century and a new water supply installed. It was severely damaged by the great fire of 1666, but was repaired and continued in use until its demolition in 1760. The remaining prisoners were transferred to the City of London Workhouse on Bishopsgate Street, part of which was converted to serve as a prison. In 1794, the prison moved to its final home at the corner of Giltspur Street and Newgate Street.

BRIDEWELL

Bridewell was originally a palace built by Henry VIII on the west bank of the River Fleet, and took its name from the holy waters in the area linked with St Bridget or Bride. In 1553, Edward VI handed over the site to the city authorities as a 'house of occupation' for idlers, vagrants and prostitutes. Bridewell was rather different from other penal establishments in being part of the poor relief system rather than the criminal justice system. Its aims were to reform the idle and disorderly, to make them earn their keep and to deter others from indolence. The costs of running Bridewell were largely met from a tax on local inhabitants rather than fees extracted from the inmates who were mostly penniless.

For the more industrious inmates, productive work was available using materials provided by city merchants. Those who were classed as 'sturdy' (i.e. able-bodied) beggars were required to work and were fed on a 'thin diet onely sufficing to sustaine them in health'.[42] Repeat offenders could be whipped and were given hard labour such as beating hemp.

A remarkable scandal occurred in 1602 when the running of Bridewell was placed in the hands of private 'lessees', who were to be paid £300 a year to undertake the task. Within a few months, chaos reigned at the prison. The contractors, whose sole aim was to maximise their profit, had moved into the best rooms in the building and had released most of the pauper inmates. The diet fed to those who remained had declined to the point where many of them had died. They had left prison staff unpaid and had rented out workshops as homes for their relatives and friends. Finally, in collusion with eight prostitutes resident in the prison, they had turned the premises into an upmarket casino, restaurant and brothel. In the company of their glamorously dressed hostesses, patrons dined on a sumptuous repast of 'crabbes, lobsters, artetichoques, pyes and gallons of wyne at a tyme'. Use of the prison's single chambers for further pleasures could then be had upon a payment of 2–5s. Following an inquiry, the lessees' contract was terminated in October 1602.[43]

One of Bridewell's occasional inmates was Madam Cresswell, a notorious prostitute and brothel-keeper, who is said to have died in the prison in around 1698. Her will offered £10 for someone to preach a funeral sermon that spoke only well of her. The clergyman who eventually took on this challenging task gave a long lecture on public morality then concluded with a few words about the deceased: 'She was born well, she lived well, and she died well; for she was born with the name of Creswell, she lived in Clerkenwell, and she died in Bridewell.'

HOUSES OF CORRECTION

The 1576 Poor Act adopted Bridewell's model and proposed the establishment of a 'house of correction' in each county to deal with the able-bodied poor who refused to work. Every county had at least one bridewell operating by 1630.[44] Houses of correction (also known as bridewells after the original London establishment) were supervised by Justices of the Peace (JPs) and their costs supported from the local poor rates.

The rules of discipline and diet published in 1588 for the house of correction at Bury in Suffolk portray it as a very severe establishment. At admission, every 'strong or sturdy rogue' was given twelve lashes and then manacled. All inmates rose at 4 a.m. in summer (5 a.m. in winter) then, after communal prayers, worked until 7 p.m. except for meal breaks. On 'flesh days', dinner and supper comprised 8oz of rye bread, a pint of porridge, ¼lb of flesh and a pint of beer. On 'fish days', meat was replaced by milk or peas, ⅓lb of cheese or 'one good herring, or two white or red'. White herrings were pickled in brine, while red herrings were smoked – the distinctive smell of the latter was sometimes used by farmers to divert hunting hounds.

Bridewells were often located adjacent to workhouses, or even formed part of the same building. At Yarmouth, the town bridewell stood in the workhouse yard and consisted of four sleeping cells inside which prisoners were attached by a 5ft chain to an iron staple in the floor. Calls of nature were carried out via a wooden tub which was emptied when nearly full.[45]

Despite the original intention for houses of correction to be reforming institutions for the idle and disorderly, by the end of the seventeenth century their Poor Law function had effectively ceased and they had become places of punishment for all manner of petty offenders. Their operation was increasingly carried out on a commercial basis, with the inmates' labour being used to contribute to the cost of their maintenance and to their keeper's income.

The fact that houses of correction had become little different from other 'common' local gaols was recognised in a 1720 Act which empowered JPs to send vagrants and other minor offenders

A village lock-up, dating from the eighteenth century, at Hawarden in Flintshire. The lintel above the doorway proclaims that the structure also served as 'House of Correction' for idlers, rogues and vagabonds.

to a house of correction or to a common gaol as they felt fit. There remained some technical differences between the two institutions – a debtor could only be placed in a common gaol and a vagrant only in a house of correction – until both were re-designated as local prisons in 1865.

LOCAL GAOLS

By 1216, fifty years after the Assize of Clarendon, county gaols existed in all but five English counties.[46] They were often located in existing buildings, particularly castles, in county towns. Where this was not possible, new buildings were constructed either in the county town, as at Warwick, or some other town, such as Buckinghamshire's gaol at Aylesbury. Responsibility for running the county gaol lay with the county sheriff, a servant of the crown.

By the sixteenth century, local gaols also existed in virtually every town. Unlike county gaols, management of local town prisons was in the hands of the mayor and aldermen. Local prisons were set up in a wide variety of locations. As in London, town gates were a popular venue. County gaol sites, too, sometimes included a home for a local prison or house of correction. Local gaols could also be set up in more domestic buildings on a town's main street or on the market-place. Even smaller were the lock-ups erected in many towns and villages, which were mostly used for the short-term confinement of disorderly persons.

Justice at the local level was administered by JPs. Minor offences were dealt with at the Justice's own home or, later, at petty sessions; more serious matters, where a jury was required, went to quarter sessions held four times a year. The most serious cases were held over for the twice-yearly assize courts presided over by visiting judges of the crown. At each session, the assizes would aim to clear or 'deliver' the county gaol of its prisoners.

four

Life in Early Prisons

HOME FROM HOME

Those held in the Tower of London were largely from the upper echelons of society and, for many, their stay there could be far from uncomfortable, even if their ultimate departure was to the scaffold. During Sir Walter Raleigh's thirteen-year stint spent in the Bloody Tower, he was accompanied with his wife and two children. He spent some of the time writing *The History of the World* and even grew some tobacco plants outside his lodgings.

During her internment at the Tower in 1551, Anne Seymour, Duchess of Somerset, enjoyed a midday dinner of mutton stewed with pottage, boiled beef and mutton, roast veal, roast capon and two rabbits. For her supper she again ate mutton with pottage along with sliced beef, roast mutton, two rabbits and a dozen larks, all washed down with either beer or wine at a weekly cost of 77s.[47] Mutton stewed with pottage was evidently a favourite dish of the duchess. Here is a typical recipe from the 1623 edition of Gervase Markham's *Countrey Contentments, or the English Huswife*:

> If you wil make pottage of the best & daintiest kind, you shal take Mutton, Veale, or Kid, & having broke the bones, but not cut the flesh in peeces, and wash it, put it into a pot with faire water, after it is ready to boile, and is throughly skumd, you shal put in a good handful or two of smale oat-meale: & then take whole lettice of the best & most inward leaves, whole spinage, endive, succory [chicory], and whole leaves of colaflorey [cauliflower], or the inward parts of white cabage, with two or three slic't onions; and put all into the pot and boile them well together till the meat be enough, and the herbes so soft as may be, and stirre them oft well together; and then season it with salt and as much verjuice as will onely turne the tast of the pottage; and so serve them up, covering the meat with the whole hearbes, and adorning the dish with sippets. [Verjuice was a sour-tasting condiment made from the compressed juice of green grapes, gooseberries, or crab apples. Sippets were small pieces of toasted or fried bread – the croutons of their day.]

THE COST OF CONFINEMENT

For lesser mortals, though, a spell in prison could turn out to be an expensive business. From 1605, the expenditure began even before the sentence started when a new Act made prisoners liable for the cost of their own transport to the gaol. Newly arrived inmates were then required to pay a number of fees to the gaol keeper, which varied according to their rank and to the level of comfort they wanted to enjoy during their incarceration.

At the Fleet prison, a schedule of 1561 records that the admission fee for giving 'the liberty of the house' (and so avoid being put in leg irons) ranged from £10 for an archbishop, down to 13s 4d for a yeoman. At the Tower of London, the constable of the Tower required a similar payment: £20 for a duke; 20 marks for an earl; £10 for a baron; and 100s for a knight.

The prisoner might also have to stump up for a bond to guarantee his good behaviour and regular outgoings during his stay, a fee to the clerk who drew up the bond, another fee for being entered in the prison register, various tips to the gaoler, chamberlain and porter, and finally a round of drinks for all concerned.

At the end of their stay, the final charge demanded of all prisoners was a discharge fee. At Newgate, the scale of charges began at eightpence, rising to 2s for felons. At the Fleet, generally reckoned to be the most expensive of London's gaols, the cost of discharge ranged from £3 5s down to a minimum of 2s 4d – which even the totally destitute were required to pay or else remain in prison indefinitely.

On top of these 'administrative' fees came various other ongoing charges levied by the keeper. In 1431, for example, Newgate made a charge of fourpence a week towards the running costs of the prison lamps. In 1488, the price for prison-supplied beds at Newgate was set at a penny per week for a bed with sheets, blankets and a coverlet, and a penny per week for a couch. Alternatively, prisoners could bring in their own beds.[48] In the early 1600s, Marshalsea had a 'two-penny ward' – so named because of the daily charge for a bed and a pair of sheets; the charge in the Knight's ward was eightpence a day, and even more in the superior rooms on the Master's side.[49] At the Fleet, the upper crust could enjoy separate rooms with use of a parlour for 4d a night, while the lower ranks could obtain a nightly half-share of a bed in the common hall for 2d.

Although the city authorities made periodic efforts to regulate these charges, they were the source of regular abuse. At Ludgate, one prisoner, who had brought in his own bed, bedding and clothes, was obliged to pay for their use by the gaoler John Bottisham. There were also instances of bedding and lights donated from charitable sources being charged for, although this practice was prohibited in London prisons from 1463.[50]

From 1729, the costs of admission, discharge and so on, could become even more expensive after judges ruled that someone committed to prison for several different offences was liable to pay separate sets of fees for each of them.[51]

GARNISH AND CHUMMAGE

On top of the various fees and charges taken by the gaoler, additional payments in the form of 'garnish' and 'chummage' were exacted from new inmates by the prisoners already in residence.

At Marshalsea, the garnish comprised a flat payment on arrival by new prisoners of 8s for men or 5s 6d for women, regardless of their standing. Payment of the money allowed access to the common room, use of boiling water from the fire, the cooking of food and the reading of newspapers. The poet William Fennor, on entering the Wood Street Counter in 1616, was charged 2s by the chamberlain for being allocated comfortable accommodation. At dinner-time the next day, a garnish of half a gallon of claret was demanded by his fellow prisoners. A further garnish of 6d for two pints of claret was then extracted by the under-keepers to endow him with the liberty of the prison. Finally, a few weeks later, when lack of money necessitated his moving to cheaper quarters, the steward there demanded an additional garnish of 1s 6d. Fennor's refusal to pay resulted in his being given a less than fragrant room situated near a privy.[52] Such fees could sometimes be officially sanctioned by authorities: for example in Richmond in 1671, a table of garnish was approved by local JPs.[53]

In 1814, the arcane principles of the chummage system at Marshalsea prison were revealed to a parliamentary Select Committee. The 'chum-master' issued each new arrival with a 'chum-ticket' which entitled the holder to admission to some room in the prison:

If the prisoner so requiring a ticket is of decent appearance and has the air of good circumstances, one is given him of a room already occupied by a person of his station in life; but if the applicant be poor, he receives his ticket upon a room held by one who is enabled to pay him out … [at] so much per week, which generally amounts to 5s whereby he yields to the existing occupier the whole right to his room, and pays for his lodgings with persons of his own class and situation.

As a result, poorer inmates slept crammed together, on occasion as many as forty-eight in a room measuring 16ft by 13ft. The Select Committee, after battling for several days to comprehend – with limited success – the complexities of chummage, learned that:

The rule of chummage is, that the person who has been longest in prison keeps his room free from having another prisoner chummed on it, till all the rooms held by those of a junior date to himself each have a prisoner chummed upon them … If the prisoner be poor, and wishes to be bought out, he is chummed upon by one who can afford to pay him: if he wish to remain, he is placed in the room of a person who will keep him, and he has accordingly a chum ticket upon the youngest prisoner in one or other of these classes.

A similar system operated at the Fleet prison where the first occupier of any vacant room was called the owner, and a newcomer the chum. Again, ownership of any newly vacant room was offered to all existing owners. The room vacated by the moving owner then came under the ownership of the senior chum in the prison. All quite simple, really …

HOUSING THE POOREST PRISONERS

The prison keeper was under no obligation to supply food or bedding for those who were not able to provide it themselves or pay the required fees. For the totally penniless, the Fleet provided the beggar's ward which might offer a little straw on which to sleep. In 1670, the Keeper of the Poultry Counter recorded that up to fifty prisoners – both men and women – slept, dressed, dined and performed 'all other necessary occasions and offices' in a space less than 20ft square known as 'the Hole'.[54]

At Newgate, the 'Common Felons' side of the prison, 'a most Terrible, Wicked and Dreadful Place', had five wards, three for men and two for women.[55] Male felons who could not pay the 'customary dues' of the prison were placed in the Stone Hold – 'a most terrible, stinking, dark and dismal place, in which no Day-light can come'. The room was 'paved with Stone, on which the Prisoners lie without any Beds, and thereby endure great Misery and Hardship'. The adjacent Lower Ward, for men with unpaid fines, was no better, while above it lay the Middle Ward where those who had been able to pay their admission fees had the comfort of a wooden floor, but still no beds.

Similar conditions existed in prisons across the country. At Penzance's Borough Gaol – locally known as the 'Black Hole' – most of the ceiling was too low for a prisoner to stand upright, and the number of rats living there was such that any resident would never know 'the balm of peaceful sleep'.[56] At the Chester City and County Gaol, felons slept in a 'horrid dungeon' accessed down a flight of eighteen steps:

It has two barrack bedsteads with straw, and is now 12 inches deep in water. Totally dark, and without any communication with the external air, but from two leaden pipes laid in from the gateway about one inch in diameter.[57]

The reception of a debtor at the Fleet prison in around the 1740s. The new arrival is rapidly learning about the prison's fees – both official (such as a payment to have leg irons removed) and unofficial (garnish), while another prisoner relieves him of his hat.

CATERING ARRANGEMENTS

Much of the gaoler's income came from providing the prison inmates with food or from cooking their own food in the prison kitchen. In order to maximise profits, the charges set varied according to the prisoner's rank and where meals were eaten. By 1618, the Fleet's weekly rate, which included wine, ranged from £3 6s 8d for lords, £1 13s 4d for knights, 10s for gentlemen and 5s for commoners. At other London prisons, the usual rate for board and lodging was 3s per week for gentlemen and 2s for yeomen.[58]

In 1616, Elizabethan poet and playwright Thomas Dekker, in custody himself at the King's Bench, described the dinner-time scene at the prison: 'some ambling downe staires for Bread and Beere, meeting another comming up stayres, carrying a platter ... proudly aloft full of powder Beefe and Brewis ... every chamber shewing like a Cookes shop, where provant [food] was stirring'.[59] 'Brewis', according to Samuel Johnson in his great dictionary of 1755, was 'Bread soaked in boiling fat pottage, made of salted meat'.

The menu on offer at the Fleet was recorded in 1592 when the Privy Council sent its details to the keepers of the prisons at Ely, Wisbech Castle and Broughton in Oxfordshire, where recusants were being held. Here are the details despatched to Ely:[60]

Knights' commons
Their diet weeklie at xvjs. [16s]
At dynner: Motton boyled Beef boyled Rabbettes Chickins or capons or such like   } (of these two dishes rosted)
At supper: Motton boyled Motton rosted Rabbettes Chickins or such like.
Their lodgings weekly at vjs. viijd. [6s 8d]
For the fish daies, butter, ling, and other fish such as maie be had after the rates of the flesh daies at the discrecion of the Keeper.
Gentlemen's commons
Their diets weeklie xs. [10s]
At dynner: Motton boyled Beef boyled And one dish rosted of the veal
At supper: Motton boyled Motton rosted Rabbettes &c.
Their lodgings weekly at s. iiijd. [2s 4d]
For the fish daies rateable at the discrecion of the Keeper

The 'Gentlemen's' diet as sent to Wisbech also included 'bread as such as they will eat, small beare [beer] and wine clared, a quart'.

The standard of the cooking at the Fleet and the recusant prisons which adopted its cuisine is unclear. However, cookery books of the period give a picture of how such dishes would be prepared in a domestic kitchen. Thomas Dawson, writing in 1597, offers a simple boiled mutton dish:

Mutton boyled for supper.

First set your mutton on the fire, & trim it cleane, then take out all the broth saving so much as will cover it, then take and put thereto ten or twelve onions pilled [peeled], cut them in quarters, with a handful of parseley chopped fine, putting it to the mutton, and so let them boile, seasoning it with pepper, salt and saffron, with two or three spoonefull of vineger.[61]

Rabbit could be cooked in a variety of ways. Elizabeth Grey's 1653 manual offers the following:

To boil a Rabbet.

Fley and wash a Rabbet, and slit the hinder leggs on both sides of the back-bone, from the forward, and truss them to the body, set the head right up with a sciver right down in the neck, then put it to boyling with as much water as will cover it, when it boyls, scum it, season it with Mace, Ginger, Salt, and Butter, then take a handful of Parsley, and a little Thyme, boil it by it self, then take it up, beat it with a back of a knife, then take up your Rabbet, and put it into a dish, then put your Hearbs to your Broth, and scrape in a Carret root, let your broth boil a little while, put in salt, pour it on your Rabbet, and serve it.[62]

To stew Rabbets.

Half rost it, then take it off the spit, and cut it in little pieces, and put it into a dish with the gravie, and as much liquor as will cover it, then put in a piece of fresh Butter, and some pouder of Ginger; some Pepper and Salt, two or three Pippins minced small, let these stew an houre, then dish them upon sippets.[63]

The general observance of fish days, when the eating of flesh was prohibited, was taken very seriously – defying the ban was punishable by a £3 fine or three months in prison. In 1562, Elizabeth I added Wednesday to the existing fish days of Friday and Saturday, although this was probably not so much a sign of her religious devotion but an attempt to help an ailing fishing industry.

The Fleet's fare on fish days included butter (i.e. the butter-fish or gunnel, a small, eel-like sea fish) and ling (a member of the cod family), which was often dried and salted to preserve it. Fish could be cooked in a number of ways including being boiled or baked, stewed or used as a filling – ling pie was a well-known dish in the early seventeenth century. However, the kitchens at prisons such as the Fleet would probably have limited themselves to boiling or baking.

At Newgate, in 1724, those who could afford it dined together in small groups or 'messes', each member taking it in turns to provide the day's requirements such as a joint of mutton, veal, lamb or beef which was roasted or boiled. A mess of seven persons could, it was said, dine well at a cost of fourpence a head. The food was accompanied by 'Small-Beer very good, for One-penny per Quart Bottle, Strong Drink very good for Three-pence per Winchester Quart [four pints]; Wine Two Shillings per Bottle; Brandy, Six-pence per Quartern [quarter pint] &c.'[64]

Although those who could afford it might prefer to send out for food, rather than eat what the prison kitchen produced, the gaoler sometimes went to some lengths to encourage them otherwise. In 1620, there was a mutiny at the King's Bench prison after the keeper, Sir George Reynell, closed off a window to the street that had previously been used for receiving deliveries of meals from friends or neighbourhood suppliers. The inmates then had to buy their food at inflated prices from the prison kitchen. Sir George's reply was that the closure of the window had been carried out purely for the safe keeping of the prisoners. At the same establishment, another inmate complained that the prison kitchen charged him eightpence for cooking fourpence-worth of fish.[65]

The absence of any form of outside inspection of prisons left opportunity for abuse, although attempts were made to moderate excessive prices. In an effort to prevent the exploitation of prisoners at Newgate, a proclamation of 1370 prohibited any city official – including Newgate officers – from brewing beer, baking bread or selling food. The ban was lifted in 1393 when prison officials were allowed to resume the selling of food to their inmates so long as they charged reasonable prices. In 1434, however, Newgate's gaoler was required to swear that he would not charge extortionate prices for beer or coal. A further revision of the regulations in 1488 outlawed profiteering from prisoners, so that a penny loaf was to be sold for 1d, a gallon of best beer for 2d, and a bushel of coal for 1d.

It was not only the price of the food that could lead to complaint, but also its quality. In 1618, insolvent barrister Geffray Mynshul wrote that an unnamed gaoler had sold the prisoners bullock's liver which he had begged for his dog from a butcher's, and had also charged a halfpenny for a quart of water.[66]

The poorest prisoners' survival at Newgate largely depended on alms. At the front of the prison were iron gratings where the prisoners could call out to passers-by for money for food or to help them pay off their fines or debts. The coins could be collected on long wooden spoons stuck through the holes. Alms were also collected by the prisoners themselves in the streets of the city. In the case of monetary donations, the sealed collecting box was opened under supervision each month and – after the collectors and the gaol keeper had taken their cut – the contents were used to buy food and other goods. Food could also be collected by a 'basket man' who walked the streets calling out 'Bread and meat for the poor prisoners!' Contributions were piled into the basket carried on his back and later shared out. If playwright John Cooke is to be believed, the quality of the food left much to be desired. A character in his 1614 comedy *Greene's Tu Quoque* (roughly translated as 'the same to you') described such offerings as:

> … unsaverie Scraps,
> That come from unknowne hands, perhaps unwasht:
> And would that were the worst; for I have noted,
> That nought goes to the Prisoners, but such food
> As either by the weather has been tainted,
> Or Children, nay sometimes full paunched Dogges,
> Have overlickt …

There were also occasional supplies of food from other sources, for example through charitable donations, bequests or items that had been seized by city officials for contravening some ordinance such as underweight bread or meat offered for sale on a fish day.

From 1572, convicted felons were also eligible to receive 'county bread' or the 'county allowance' – a small allowance of food or money provided out of county funds. The provision varied widely, from as little as the pennyworth of bread a day supplied at the Monmouth County Gaol, to the two pennyworth of bread and two pennyworth of meat at Northumberland County Gaol.[67] Since the price of wheat varied quiet considerably, the amount of food provided rose and fell in step.

DEBTORS

The fees and living expenses that were required from prisoners placed debtors in a particularly hard position. The charges accumulated while they were in prison would usually need to be settled before the debtor could leave. For a debtor without outside friends, this could amount to a life sentence.

Debtors were supposed, in theory, to receive enough money from their creditors to provide them with bread and water. Even if this was forthcoming, which it was often not, the cost had to be repaid. Some prisons provided debtors with a basic subsistence. At Newgate in 1724, this comprised a daily ration of 'one coarse Houshold Wheaten Loaf, almost the Bigness of a common Penny White Loaf', plus a weekly portion of beef.

Debtors could generate a little income by performing work. A 1666 Act for the relief of poor prisoners gave JPs powers to impose a rate with which a stock of material could be bought to provide employment for such people. Another source of assistance came through occasional legacies such as the bequests by Ralph Rokeby of £100 to the prisoners at the Fleet, Newgate, Ludgate, King's Bench, Marshalsea and the two Counters.[68]

Although debtors were often amongst the most wretched of a prison's inmates, some could use imprisonment to exploit their situation. So-called 'politic bankrupts' were those who obtained large amounts of goods or money on credit then feigned bankruptcy. When arrested they lived comfortably in prison and could often force a settlement on their creditors, paying only a proportion of the debt. Such a debtor was described by Thomas Dekker as a 'ten-groats-in-the-pound bankrupt, a voluntary villain, a devouring locust, a destroying caterpillar, a golden thief'.[69] Dekker himself later endured six years in prison for debt. Another group of debtors were those who voluntarily chose to remain in prison for the rest of their lives. As debts were not inheritable, this sacrifice would free their heirs from any further claim.

WOMEN

Special accommodation for female prisoners existed as early as the thirteenth century. In 1237, a proposal was made to establish a women's gaol within York Castle and by 1280 a chamber for female inmates existed at Maidstone.[70] In around 1310, after a lengthy campaign by the Chancellor of Oxford University, a separate women's section was created at the town gaol. Later known as the 'maiden's chamber', it was mostly used to house prostitutes.

By 1724, Newgate had separate areas for female inmates. On the Common Side, women unable to pay their prison fees were placed in the Waterman's Hall, a 'very terrible, dark and stinking Place'.[71] Although supplied with fresh water via a lead cistern, inmates had to sleep on the wooden floor. In another ward, for short-term housing of those awaiting transportation, the women were 'almost poisoned by their own filth'. Throughout the prison, one (male) observer reported that the women were 'exceedingly worse than the worst of the Men, not only in respect to Nastiness and Indecency of living, but more-especially as to their Conversation, which to their great Shame is as prophane and wicked, as Hell itself can possibly be.'[72]

Women prisoners were particularly vulnerable to exploitation by both prison staff and male inmates. During his time in the King's Bench in 1617–8, Geffray Mynshul commented that 'a whore entering into a prison is a hony-pot, about which all the flyes come buzzing, as crowes to a carrion'.[73]

A scene from Hogarth's 1732 sequence *A Harlot's Progress*. Following her descent into prostitution, Moll Hackabout (third from left) has been placed by magistrates in Bridewell prison. The gaoler (left) directs her to beat hemp – used to make hangman's nooses. The gaoler's wife tries to steal Moll's clothes, while Moll's smiling servant (second from right) appears already to have acquired her shoes. Other prisoners include a card-sharp and a pregnant African woman who may have pleaded 'benefit of the belly'. A (presumably idle) man is being held n a pilllory beneath the legend 'Better to Work than Stand thus'.

DISEASE

Prisons were notoriously unhealthy places. The poor conditions and overcrowding that were common amongst the poorer inmates made prisons an ideal breeding ground for infections.

The condition most often associated with prisons is 'gaol fever' or typhus, a highly infectious and life-threatening disease spread by lice or fleas. A 1729 report on the Marshalsea prison found that at the end of winter, up to ten prisoners a day were dying from gaol-fever and malnutrition. A report in the *Gentleman's Magazine* in January 1759 estimated that each year one in four prisoners succumbed to the disease – many times more than were executed.[74] Thirty years later, the prison reformer John Howard also concluded that in the mid-eighteenth century, gaol-fever accounted for more deaths than did the hangman.[75]

Once infected, prisoners could spread disease to the outside world, for example when they appeared in court. At Oxford Castle in July 1577, a bookbinder named Rowland Jencks was tried for sedition and sentenced to lose his ears. After the prisoner was taken away 'there arose such an infectious damp or breath among the people, that many there present … were then smothered, and others so deeply infected that they lived not many hours after.'[76] Amongst the dead were the judge, the high sheriff, the under-sheriff and most of the jury. The death toll eventually reached more than 500. Another gaol-fever outbreak at Taunton Assizes in 1730 resulted in hundreds of deaths again including the sheriff and judge.

five

Prison Reforms

EARLY ATTEMPTS AT REFORM

Early efforts to improve prison conditions came from religious groups such as the Quakers. In the 1650s, their leader George Fox criticised prison hygiene and urged that 'none stay long in prisons, let none be keepers of prisons but such as fear God and hate covetousness, gaming and drunkenness.'[77]

In 1691, after a spell in the Fleet prison for debt, publisher and printer Moses Pitt issued an attack[78] on the prison's warden, the ironically named Richard Manlove. Manlove was accused of abuses such as housing destitute prisoners alongside dead bodies in the prison's dungeons and withholding the corpses of dead prisoners until their families had paid all their outstanding fees.

A decade later, the newly formed Society for the Promotion of Christian Knowledge (SPCK) investigated conditions at prisons such as Newgate and Marshalsea. Their report, authored by Thomas Bray, listed numerous problems: the lewdness of prison officers, especially towards women; officers taking payments to allow male prisoners access to the females; the unlimited use of wine, brandy and other strong liquors; gambling, swearing and blasphemy; the corrupting of newcomers by hardened prisoners; and neglect of all religious observances.[79] The society's proposed reforms included the setting up of an overall management committee for the city's prisons, an improvement in the character of persons appointed as officers, the provision of ministers to every prison, daily prayers, the strict separation of male and female inmates, an end to the 'benefit of belly' for pregnant felons, the provision of work for male inmates, restrictions on the use of strong liquor and – a radical suggestion for its day – the housing of every prisoner in a separate cell. However, apart from the distribution of some religious books to prisons in London and to all the county gaols, little resulted from this initiative.

A number of parliamentary inquiries into the prisons were also instituted. A Select Committee in 1729 accused the Fleet's warden, Thomas Bambridge, of extorting exorbitant fees and keeping debtors locked in heavy irons. A second report laid charges against William Acton, chief officer at the Marshalsea, where up to fifty prisoners slept in a room 16ft square. At night, inmates had no toilet facilities and were forced to use the floor. Debtors who displeased the guards could be locked up for week alongside a vermin-ridden and putrifying corpse. Despite the apparent evidence against Bambridge and Acton, both were acquitted of all criminal charges (although Bambridge was barred from resuming his wardenship of the Fleet).[80]

As well as efforts to reform existing prisons, various schemes for new types of prison were put forward. In 1753, Middlesex JP Henry Fielding and architect Thomas Gibson proposed the building of a combined prison, house of correction and workhouse, which would house 5,000 paupers and 1,000 convicts. Perhaps not surprisingly, this enormously ambitious project was never constructed. On a much more modest scale, in 1758, Robert Dingley, with help from philanthropist Jonas Hanway, set up a successful Magdalen house at Goodman's Fields for 'repenting prostitutes'. Prostitution in the capital at that time employed around 3,000 women with a similar number dying each year from venereal diseases. Whilst in the house, the inmates were expected to work or to sit alone in silent religious reflection – an activity whose benefits Hanway extolled in his 1776 publication *Solitude in Imprisonment*. By 1786, 2,415 women had passed through the house, with only a small number returning to the streets.[81]

One significant influence from outside England was the publication in 1767 of *On Crimes and Punishment* by Italian philosopher Cesare Beccaria. Beccaria argued that punishment should be administered as soon as possible after a crime was committed in order to create a strong association between the two. Punishments should reflect the seriousness of the offence – crimes against property, for example, being punished by fines – and, where possible, be socially useful, such as labouring on public works. He strongly argued against indiscriminate use of capital punishment, suggesting that long-term punishments had a far greater deterrent value and could result in reformation of the offender. Beccaria's ideas were widely debated and undoubtedly paved the way for reforms which, albeit slowly, came in their wake.

JOHN HOWARD

In 1773, at the age of 47, John Howard was appointed high sheriff of Bedfordshire. While attending court sessions he noticed that prisoners found not guilty were still being returned to the county gaol. The reason, he discovered, was that they needed to pay the gaoler for their release, plus any outstanding fees for their board and lodgings. Acquitted prisoners were also retained in case other charges were laid against them before the judge left town.[82] Prisoners who were penniless could then remain in gaol indefinitely even though they were innocent. To try and remedy this situation, Howard requested that JPs appoint a salaried gaoler and abolish prison fees. After being told that this would only be considered if an existing precedent could be found, he visited other prisons in the area, and then further afield, eventually across the whole of Europe. The abuses he uncovered were detailed in his book *The State of the Prisons in England and Wales*, published in 1777.

With regard to prison buildings, Howard noted that they often had barred windows or gratings which opened directly onto the street outside. Inmates could easily communicate with friends outside and obtain beer and spirits, or even a file with which to cut through the bars and escape. Rooms were frequently badly lit and ventilated, and the floor generally damp or even flooded with one or two inches of water. Proper sanitary provision was almost unknown. At Knaresborough in Yorkshire, he found that the prison for town debtors had:

> Only one room, about fourteen feet by twelve. Earth floor; no fireplace; very offensive; a common sewer from the town running through it uncovered. I was informed that an Officer, confined here some years since, for only a few days, took in with him a dog, to defend him from vermin; but the dog was soon destroyed, and the Prisoner's face much disfigured by them.

The town gaol at Plymouth had a room for felons known as the clink which was:

> Seventeen feet by eight, by about five feet and a half high, with a wicket in the door, seven inches by five, to admit light and air. To this, three men who were confined near two months, under sentence of Transportation, came by turns for breath. The door had not been opened for five weeks, when

An engraving of Francis Wheatley's 1787 painting of *John Howard Visiting and Relieving the Miseries of Prison*. Howard (third from right) is shown reproaching an indifferent gaoler over the condition of the prison's hapless inmates.

> I with difficulty entered to see a pale inhabitant. He had been there ten weeks, under sentence of Transportation, and said he had much rather have been hanged than confined in that noisome cell. No yard; no water; no sewer. Fees 15s 10d. No table. Allowance to Debtors, none but on application; Felons twopennyworth of bread a day. No straw.

At the start of Howard's investigations, he travelled in the comfort of a post-chaise carriage. After realising how offensive his clothes became after visiting so many prisons and dungeons, he took to travelling on horseback. To protect himself from the fetid atmosphere and the smallpox and gaol-fever that were rife in many prisons, he carried a phial of vinegar which he sniffed whilst inside.

Although the prison buildings left much to be desired, the inmates were often treated with considerable laxity. No tools or materials were supplied to provide work, and prisoners were allowed to spend their time in 'sloth, profaneness, and debauchery'.[83] Drinking and gaming were the main occupations with the most popular pastimes being cards, dice, skittles, Mississippi, Portobello, billiards, fives and tennis. At the Fleet, there was a wine club on Monday nights and a beer club on Thursdays, each lasting until 1 or 2 a.m. At the Marshalsea, on one Sunday in the summer of 1775, almost 600 pots of beer were brought in from a nearby public-house, the prisoners not liking the prison's own beer.[84]

In a large part due to Howard's revelations, two Acts of Parliament were passed in 1774. The Discharged Prisoners Act required that a prisoner acquitted or discharged by a court be set free immediately, with any outstanding discharge fee being paid out of the rates up to a maximum of 13s 4d. The Health of Prisoners Act directed that prison rooms should be scraped and whitewashed at least once a year, and constantly supplied with fresh air by means of ventilators. Warm and cold baths were to be installed in each prison, and separate rooms were to be provided for sick inmates. Finally, each prison was to appoint an experienced physician who was to make a report to the local Justices each quarter.

As a result of his visits to continental prisons, Howard outlined his ideal institution. It would be on an airy site, near to running water. The gaoler would be a sober man of good character who would live on the premises and receive his income from a salary rather than fees. There would be separate quarters for men, women and juveniles. Debtors and felons would also live apart, with a workshop for those debtors willing to work. Each inmate would have his own sleeping cell. The prison would have its own bath-house and infirmary, and chapel with a separate section for women, out of sight of all the other prisoners. Howard's own designs for a model county gaol were published in *The State of the Prisons* and in the following decade influenced the construction of new buildings such as Bodmin Gaol in Cornwall.

Howard died in 1790 from gaol-fever, contracted on a visit to a prison at Kherson in what is now Ukraine. In 1866, his name was adopted by the newly formed Howard Association, now the Howard League, a charity campaigning for penal reform.

JAMES NEILD

James Neild came from a Quaker family in Cheshire but moved to London in 1760 where he later became a successful jeweller. He became involved in penal reform after visiting the King's Bench prison where a fellow apprentice was being held as a debtor. Shocked at what he saw, he visited a number of other prisons in England and France, becoming increasingly disturbed by the number of people incarcerated for owing small debts. In 1773, he helped found The Society for the Relief and Discharge of Persons Imprisoned for Small Debts and became its treasurer. The group raised funds to secure the release of debtors, especially those who owed less than £10 and who were judged worthy of assistance, such as men with dependant families. By 1800, the society had achieved the release of 16,405 prisoners at a total cost of £41,748 – averaging out to a very small amount.[85] Despite this success, imprisonment for non-payment of debts was not abolished until the passing of the Administration of Justice Act in 1970.

Neild also became increasingly concerned that the reforms initiated by John Howard were often being ignored, frequently because of the apathy of local magistrates. A significant improvement in this state of affairs occurred in the years from 1803 to 1813, when the *Gentleman's Magazine* regularly published reports of Neild's far-flung prison visits, written in the form of letters to his friend John Lettsom. Neild's eye-opening detail of the abuses taking place in some particular prison invariably provoked rapid action from those in charge. Typical was his 1804 description of the gaol and bridewell at Sudbury in Suffolk:

> This miserable prison has for debtors and criminals two rooms on the ground-floor fronting the street, about 13 feet square. A fire-place in each, with iron-bar grated windows, and a small aperture to beg through ... The court-yard being insecure, prisoners have no use of it; and water is not accessible to them. There is no necessary; a bar of wood across one corner of each room with a little straw on the floor is used for this purpose. Gaol very dirty.[86]

ELIZABETH FRY

Perhaps the most influential reformer of the nineteenth century was Elizabeth Gurney, daughter of a large Quaker family in Ipswich. Following her marriage to businessman Joseph Fry in 1800, she eventually settled near London, at East Ham, to bring up her own growing family. In 1813, she heard the report of a visit to Newgate prison by a group of American Quakers who had been shocked to find scenes of 'blaspheming, fighting, dram-drinking, half-naked women'.[87] Her own visits to Newgate, where she witnessed 'riot, licentiousness, and filth' led to her campaigning for the reform of prison conditions and of the inmates themselves. Several years later, following discussions with the prison authorities and the prisoners, a number of changes were introduced, including a scheme of classification and segregation, a prison uniform, paid work, educational and religious classes, and a system of constant supervision by a matron and monitors chosen by the prisoners from their own number.[88] Although some of the changes, such as the banning of alcohol and playing cards, were not totally popular, there was a marked improvement in the prisoners' conduct.

Fry travelled widely, promoting her work, and in 1821 set up a national body – the British Ladies' Society for Promoting the Reformation of Female Prisoners – to co-ordinate the work of the numerous local prison-visiting groups that had sprung up. The society spawned offshoots in a number of other countries including Holland, Italy, Russia and the USA where a group of Quaker women began visiting the Arch Street prison in 1823.

At the heart of Elizabeth Fry's philosophy was that the treatment of prisoners should be based on the principles of justice and humanity. The aim of prison should be reformation – achieved through kindness – rather than degradation, cruelty and neglect. Her particular concern for female prisoners led to significant improvements in their treatment, for example the 1823 Gaols Act, which required the complete segregation of male and female prisoners, led to females being supervised by female officers. Her efforts also resulted in improved conditions for those being transported to Australia aboard convict ships. She arranged for each woman to receive a 'bag of useful items'. These included a Bible, two aprons, a black cotton cap, a large hessian sack (for transporting her clothes) and a sewing kit and material to make a patchwork quilt. The quilt could then be sold or used as proof of her sewing skills for a potential future employer.

Elizabeth Fry on a visit to Newgate. In 1817, Fry and a group of like-minded, mostly Quaker, women formed the Ladies' Association for the Reformation of the Female Prisoners in Newgate which, amongst other activities, provided daily visits and Bible readings for the inmates.

six

Transportation and the Hulks

TRANSPORTATION TO AMERICA

The shipping of felons to Britain's overseas colonies began in 1615, during the reign of James I, and continued, on and off, for the next 250 years. The use of transportation was first introduced as a piece of Poor-Law legislation in the 1597 Vagabonds Act. It provided that 'rogues, vagabonds, and sturdie beggars' could be 'banished out of this realme, and ... conveied unto such parts beyond the seas'.[89] The statute also decreed that such undesirables could be put to service manning galley ships – a type of vessel not much used in England.

Initially, the transportation of convicted lawbreakers was on a voluntary basis, with only a few hundred offenders taking this option up to 1650. The most common destinations were the American settlements of Virginia and Maryland – where the new arrivals were sold as labourers to plantation owners at dockside auctions. Despite attempts in the 1670s by the colonies to halt transportation, the second half of the century saw its use increase with around 5,000 convicts being despatched there.[90] For Britain, transportation had the benefits of both removing serious offenders from its shores and providing a much-needed labour force for its New World territories. By 1775 the total transported had grown to more than 30,000, with two-thirds of all felons convicted at the Old Bailey now being sent to the colonies and sold as servants.[91] This was a policy which one pamphleteer in 1731 applauded as 'Draining the Nation of its offensive Rubbish, without taking away their Lives'.[92]

Among the beneficiaries of the transportation policy were the merchants contracted to ship the convicts to their new homes. It was profitable business as the outgoings were relatively small and the returns high. Contractors were required to pay each prisoner's gaol discharge fees (typically £1) and feed them during the voyage (at a weekly rate of 2s 6d during the eight-week crossing). Other overheads included crew, ship, port and administrative costs (around £2 per head), hire of irons (1s per head) and import duty (£1 per convict), giving a total expenditure of around £5 1s per convict.[93] On the income side, merchants received a fee of £5 per head for transporting the convicts, plus whatever they could get for them at the quayside auction on arrival at their destination port. Typical prices were £15 to £25 for males with useful trade skills, £10 for common thieves and £8 for female convicts. The old and the infirm, however, had to be given away. On a good trip, a merchant could expect to clear an average profit of £9 to £15 per convict. On top of this, the return voyage to Britain, with a cargo of tobacco or grain on board, could generate a further healthy income.

The typical weekly food ration for those being transported comprised 1.2lb of beef and pork, 13.3oz of cheese, 4.7lb of bread, 0.5 quart of peas, 1.7 quarts of oatmeal, 1.3oz of molasses, 0.5 gill of gin and 5.3 gallons of water, providing a total of just 1200 calories a day.[94]

For the American recipients of this human traffic, the deliveries proved increasingly unwelcome – a feeling summed up in a 1751 letter (attributed to Benjamin Franklin) in the *Pennsylvania Gazette*, which proposed that the colonies should repay the kindness of mother England by exporting rattlesnakes to the British Isles and releasing them in St James' Park.[95] Attempts by the colonies to curtail transportation – by charging a duty on each convict landed, or a bond to ensure their good behaviour once in service – all proved unsuccessful and the convict ships continued to arrive until the outbreak of the War of Independence in 1775.

ALTERNATIVES TO TRANSPORTATION

The war with America brought an abrupt halt to the steady stream of convict ships that had been heading to its shores. What did not abate, however, was the flow of convicts sentenced to transportation by the courts, and a crisis in prison overcrowding soon began to loom.

The immediate, and supposedly short-term, solution was to turn two of the hulks of old battleships berthed on the Thames at Woolwich into floating prisons for 100 inmates. At the same time, two pieces of parliamentary legislation were prepared which proposed longer-term remedies for the problem. The first, the Criminal Law Act of 1776, aimed to extend the use of shipboard prisons. It recommended that transportation be replaced by a period of hard labour lasting between three and ten years, with offenders held in houses of correction or 'some proper place of confinement' and fed on a diet of 'bread, and any coarse meat, or other inferior food, and water, or small beer'. Although the Act made no explicit mention of shipboard prisons, the particular form of hard labour that it proposed – 'removing sand, soil, and gravel from, and cleansing the River Thames' – makes it clear that was where its intent lay. Despite some objections, such as the possible nuisance caused to nearby residents, and concerns about the security of the vessels, the bill was passed in May 1776.[96]

The second bill brought before parliament, but which took another three years to receive approval, proposed the erection of a pair of 'Penitentiary Houses' (one for 600 men and one for 300 women) on a site near to London. The houses would impose a strict regime with 'labour of the hardest and most servile kind'.[97]

THE HULKS

In August 1776, the contract for supplying and managing the new prison ships, or hulks as they became known, was awarded to Duncan Campbell – one of the merchants who had previously been engaged in transporting convicts to America. Campbell's initial contract was to provide a ship to house 120 prisoners for each of which he was to receive £32 a year. The first vessel he provided, the *Justitia*, was joined the following year by the *Tayloe*, the two then accommodating 240 prisoners. The *Tayloe* was soon replaced by the much larger *Censor*.

The ships were moored in the middle of the Thames at Woolwich Warren – a mass of foundries, workshops, warehouses and barracks, and a long-established home of naval ship-building and arms manufacture. During the day, prisoners worked at dredging the river or providing labour for building works. At night they were crammed below decks, originally in beds, and then in pairs on low wooden platforms, 6ft by 4ft. During the day, the platforms were stood on their side and used as tables. An experiment in using hammocks for beds was abandoned after it became apparent how difficult these were to use while wearing chains.[98]

John Howard, visiting the *Justitia* in 1776, discovered that the bread provided for the prisoners was mostly crumbs and 'mouldy and green on both sides'. However, the captain assured him that 'they would soon be out of the mouldy batch'.[99] The meat used on the ship mostly came from the heads of butchered cattle, obtained at minimal cost from the slaughtering yards at Tower Hill, 3 miles upstream. A barely edible dish of 'ox cheeks' was served up five days a week but had often gone off. The convicts dined in groups or 'messes' of six and the daily menu for each mess in the early 1780s is shown below.[100] There was also a daily ration of 7lb of bread per mess.

Breakfast	Every day: a pint of barley or rice made into three quarts of soup.
Dinner	Sunday: six pounds of salt pork or seven pounds of beef with five quarts of beer. Monday, Wednesday, Friday: six pounds of bullock's head. Tuesday, Thursday, Saturday: Two pounds of cheese, and five quarts of beer.
Supper	Sunday, Monday, Wednesday, Friday: A pint of pease and barley made into three quarts of soup. Tuesday, Thursday, Saturday: A pint of oatmeal made into burgou.

'Burgou' (also spelled burgoe or burgoo) was a thick oatmeal porridge. Two methods for making burgoo were provided by William Ellis in 1750 which he described as 'best' and 'worse'. Presumably, convicts on the hulks would have been given the second version.

The Cheshire Way of making Burgoo, in the best Manner.—They first boil their Milk, and then thicken it by Degrees with fine Oatmeal, hasty-pudding like, and after boiling it well they eat it with Butter. In Derbyshire they call this thin Pudding.

The Cheshire Way of making Burgoo in a common worse manner.—Here the Farmers make a worse watry Sort of Burgoo with Water. Or Water and Milk mixed, which when boiled they stir their Oatmeal into it by Degres, and eat it hot with some Spoonfuls of Milk. Some few eat Butter with it.[101]

Conditions on the hulks were dire, with ships sometimes housing up to 700 convicts. At night, they were crammed below deck and left in the charge of a single warder. In the first twenty years of their operation, the hulks received around 8,000 prisoners, of which almost a quarter died on board. As well as diseases, such as gaol-fever, tuberculosis, cholera and scurvy, severe depression appears to have been common. During the first two years of the hulks' operation, one physician commented that some of his patients had died 'merely of lowness of spirit, without any fever or other disorder upon them'.[102]

The lack of progress in building a land-based penitentiary led to a steady growth in the number of hulks required to house the growing convict population. By 1788, the fleet included the *Stanislaus* at Woolwich, the *Dunkirk* based at Plymouth, the *Lion* at Gosport, and the *Ceres* and *La Fortunee* at Langstone Harbour. However, the role of the convict hulks as long-term prisons was about to come to an end.

TRANSPORTATION TO AUSTRALIA

Britain's war with America ended in 1783 and resulted in the permanent loss of the American colonies as a destination for Britain's convict ships. Despite there being no immediate alternative yet available, parliament passed an Act[103] reaffirming its belief in the use of transportation. Although Africa was briefly considered as a destination, the place that soon emerged to take on the role was Australia, claimed for Britain by Captain James Cook in 1770. It was decided to found a British prison colony at Botany Bay, the place where Cook had made his first landfall.

The first Australian convict convoy, the so-called First Fleet, comprised the flagship HMS *Sirius*, an armed tender, three store ships and six convict transports.[104] As with the hulks on the Thames, the convicts' accommodation was provided by private contractors. The fleet set sail from Portsmouth on 13 May 1787 carrying 565 male and 192 female convicts, 13 children of convicts, 206 marines with 46 members of their families, 20 officials, 210 seamen of the Royal Navy, and 233 merchant seamen. Commanding the fleet was Captain Arthur Phillip, RN, who was to become the governor not just of the new penal colony, but also of the whole territory of New South Wales where the prison was to be Britain's first permanent settlement.

As well as its human cargo, the First Fleet carried a vast amount of supplies to help the settlers establish the new colony. Two years' supply of food and drink included 448 barrels of flour, 135 tierces of beef, 165 tierces of pork, 50 puncheons of bread, 110 firkins of butter, 116 casks of dried peas, 5 casks of oatmeal, 5 puncheons of rum, 300 gallons of brandy, 3 hogsheads of vinegar and 15 tons of drinking water. For their shelter and comfort on arrival, the ships carried 800 sets of bedding, 40 tents for female convicts, 26 marquees for married officers and a portable canvas house for Governor Phillip. Lighting was provided by 2½ tons of candles, plus 44 tons of tallow with which to make further stocks. Building tools included 700 felling axes, 175 steel hand-saws, 50 pick-axes, 700 shovels, 700 spades, 40 wheel-barrows, 12 brick moulds, 175 hammers, 747,000 nails and 5,448 squares of glass.

To establish agricultural production, 100 bushels of wheat, barley and corn seeds were supplemented at Rio and Cape Town by fig trees, bamboo and banana plants, sugar cane, and coffee and cocoa seeds. Cape Town also contributed to the fleet's livestock with 7 cows, a bull, 3 mares, a stallion, 44 sheep, 19 goats, 32 hogs, 18 turkeys, 29 geese, 200 fowls and chickens, 35 ducks, kittens and puppies, and 5 rabbits. Fishing equipment comprised 14 fishing nets, 8,000 fish hooks, 48 dozen lines, 18 coils of whale line and 6 harpoons. Finally, to nourish the spirit as well as the body, the inventory included a Bible and prayer-book, a box of books and one piano.[105]

The passage took eight months – five times the duration of the crossing to America – and the fleet reached Botany Bay at the end of January 1788. Having surveyed the terrain, Governor Phillip decided that the new colony should be established a few miles to the north of Botany Bay at Port Jackson, now part of Sydney Harbour. Despite an outbreak of dysentery while crossing the Indian Ocean, the fleet suffered only forty-eight deaths on the voyage, a low rate which owed much to the efforts of the principal surgeon, John White, who insisted on fresh fruit and vegetables being obtained at each port en route, together with cleanliness in the cramped quarters below decks and regular exercise.

The colony had a shaky start, having to contend with illnesses such as scurvy, the failure of crops, limited fresh water supplies and trees whose hardness made them impossible to cut down. Discipline, too, was a problem – as well as insubordination from the prisoners, many of those that had been engaged as guards for the voyage refused to help keep order once the crossing had been completed. Finally, the native aborigines proved less than friendly – perhaps having a premonition of the devastation that was to come in 1789, when an outbreak of smallpox killed almost half of their number in the area.[106]

At the end of 1789, a second convict fleet carrying much needed supplies had been delayed, and a serious food shortage was facing the colony. By February 1790:

> There remained therein not more than four months' provisions for all hands, and this at half rations. To prepare for the worst, the allowance issued was diminished from time to time, till in April, that year, it consisted only of 2lbs. of pork, 2lbs. of rice, and 2½lbs. of flour per head, for seven days. More than ever in the general scarcity were robberies prevalent. Capital punishment became more and more frequent, without exercising any appreciable effect … [One] old convict said that he had often dined off pounded grass, or made soup from a native dog. Another old convict declared he had seen six men executed for stealing twenty-one pounds of flour. 'For nine months,' says a third, 'I was on five ounces of flour a day, which when weighed barely came to four. The men were weak,' he goes on, 'dreadfully weak, for want of food. One man, named 'Gibraltar,' was hanged for stealing a loaf out of the governor's kitchen.'[107]

Conditions were also grim on board the transport ships of the Second Fleet, which finally arrived at Port Jackson in June 1790 after losing one of its stores ships to an iceberg. Of the 1,000 or so convicts that set out, more than a quarter perished at sea. A further 150 died not long after coming ashore. The largest transport ship in the fleet, the *Neptune*, accommodated its 421 prisoners on a lower deck measuring no more than 75ft long by 35ft wide, an allowance of just over 6ft square each. Most of the prisoners were chained together in irons. The convicts were grouped into messes of six, with their rations calculated as being two thirds of the standard Royal Navy allowance. Accordingly, each mess should have received a weekly provision of: 16lb of bread, 12lb of flour, 14lb of beef, 8lb of pork, 12 pints of pease, 1½lb of butter and 2lb of rice. Whether they received anything like this appears doubtful. As well as the excessive confinement, malnourishment was a major cause of the fatalities. The contractors, Messrs. Calvert, Camden and King of London, were paid £17 7s 6d per convict embarked, and supplying short rations was an easy option for boosting their profit margin.

Despite all the setbacks, order was gradually achieved and the colony became established, something which probably owed much to the remarkable personal qualities of Arthur Phillip. Life in Australia took its toll on Phillip, however, and ill health forced him to return home in 1792. Despite his departure, the colony continued to develop and, from 1796, the growth of the community outside the prison was helped by a programme of assisted emigration for free settlers who were given a free passage, a grant of land and eighteen months' free rations.

EVOLUTION OF AUSTRALIAN TRANSPORTATION

In the early years of Australian transportation, convicts could either serve out their sentence in the penal colony, join a labour gang on a public works project or be assigned to work for a free settler who might be anything from a government officer to a farmer or even a freed former prisoner. Assigned convicts typically worked as shepherds, cowherds, field labourers, domestic servants or mechanics, with their masters required to provide food, clothing and shelter. However, the conditions experienced by convicts under the assignment system could vary enormously. In 1838, the British parliament received a report on how convicts were treated:

> An assigned convict is entitled to a fixed amount of food and clothing, consisting, in New South Wales, of 12lbs. of wheat, or of an equivalent in flour and maize meal, 7lbs. of mutton or beef, or 4½lbs. of salt pork, 2oz of salt, and 2oz of soap weekly; two frocks or jackets, three shirts, two pair of trousers, three pair of shoes, and a hat or cap, annually. Each man is likewise supplied with one good blanket, and a palliasse or wool mattress, which are considered the property of the master. Any articles, which the master may supply beyond these, are voluntary indulgences.[108]

Some contributors to the report likened the convict's lot to that of a slave, with harsh punishments for any misdemeanour. The law in New South Wales enabled a magistrate to inflict fifty lashes on a convict for 'drunkenness, disobedience of orders, neglect of work, absconding, abusive language to his master or overseer, or any other disorderly or dishonest conduct'. Alternative punishments for these offences included imprisonment, solitary confinement and labour in irons on the roads.

From 1840, a new stage-based probationary system was introduced where prisoners' conditions and privileges and progression through the system were determined by their behaviour. In most cases, transportees began their sentence with an eighteen-month period of detention in a British prison. Stage 1 for 'lifers' was then hard labour on Norfolk Island. Stage 2 for lifers (Stage 1 for non-lifers) was working in labour gang in an unpopulated area on the mainland. Advancement to Stage 3 allowed paid work for private employer, while Stage 4 provided for release on licence. Finally, Stage 5 bestowed a conditional or absolute pardon.

As well as Port Jackson, a number of other prison colonies were subsequently set up, including ones at Hobart in Van Diemen's Land (renamed Tasmania in 1856), Moreton Bay in Queensland, Port Phillip in Victoria, Swan River in Western Australia and on tiny Norfolk Island, 1,000 miles to the east of the mainland. In 1824, a former transport ship, the *Phoenix*, was anchored in Sydney Harbour to hold British convicts in transit to the other land-based penal settlements.

THE END OF TRANSPORTATION

Despite its great size, there were only so many convicts that Australia was prepared to receive. New South Wales closed its doors to the convict ships after 1840, and by 1846 Van Diemen's Land was so overcrowded that transportation there was suspended for two years, finally being halted in 1852. Western Australia continued to accept convicts up until 1867.

As the number of destinations dwindled, the British courts gradually moved away from the use of transportation. In its place, increasing use was made of sentences combining a period of confinement followed by several years of labour at a public-works prison, such as the one at Portland, which opened in 1848.

Transportation finally ended on 9 January 1868, when the last convict ship, the *Hougoumont*, embarked 280 prisoners at Freemantle in Western Australia. Over the preceding eighty years, around 160,000 British convicts had been landed on Australian shores. Despite the hardships they often endured while serving out their sentences, many went on to become permanent settlers in the country.[109]

THE FATE OF THE BRITISH HULKS

The re-establishment of transportation in 1787 did not result in the elimination of the prison hulks, which continued in operation for almost as long as transportation itself. The hulks were initially retained to provide temporary accommodation for transportees awaiting a place on an Australian sailing. Some prisoners, though, such as those who proved unfit to make the voyage, ended up serving the whole of their sentence on the hulks.

In 1802, management of the hulks passed from private contractors to the first Inspector of the Hulks, Aaron Graham. Graham issued new orders for improvements in the domestic routine and hygiene aboard the vessels and in the record-keeping. Officers were no longer to keep pigs or poultry on board for selling meat or eggs to the prisoners. The convicts' daily food allowance was increased, with 'coarse, wholesome meat' now replacing the much-hated 'ox-cheek'. The table below shows the new rations for each mess of six:

	BREAKFAST		DINNER				SUPPER	
	Barley	Oatmeal	Bread	Beef	Cheese	Beer	Barley	Oatmeal
	lbs oz	lbs oz	lbs oz	lbs oz	lbs oz	½ Pints	lbs oz	lbs oz
Sunday	1 4	0 4	7 14	5 14½	- -	18	1 1½	0 6½
Monday	1 4	0 4	7 14	- -	2 10	18	- -	1 8
Tuesday	1 4	0 4	7 14	5 14½	- -	18	1 1½	0 6½
Wednesday	1 4	0 4	7 14	- -	2 10	18	- -	1 8
Thursday	1 4	0 4	7 14	5 14½	- -	18	1 1½	0 6½
Friday	1 4	0 4	7 14	- -	2 10	18	- -	1 8
Saturday	1 4	0 4	7 14	5 14½	- -	18	1 1½	0 6½
Each Mess per Week	8 12	1 12	55 2	23 10	7 14	126	4 6	6 2
	4 6	6 2						
	13 2	7 14					The Bread to be of the Quality served to His Majesty's Troops of the Line.	
Each Man per Week	2 3	1 5	9 3	3 15	1 5	21		
Each Man per Day	0 5	0 3	1 5	0 9	0 3	3		

A Select Committee in 1810–11 noted that the cost of feeding each convict amounted to 13¼d a day, compared to the 9d a day expended at gaols such as Southwell and Gloucester. It was proposed that savings should be made by renegotiating the contracts for supplying the hulks' food. The committee also looked at the widely varying daily allowances that the convicts received from their employers while working ashore. At the Woolwich Ordnance department, the men received beer and biscuit ranging in value from 2*d* to 4½*d*; at Portsmouth Dockyard, the daily allowance was small beer and biscuit to the value of 2¼*d*, with smokers receiving ½*d* worth of tobacco on top; at the Portsmouth Ordnance Department, the allowance amounted to 1*d* per day, while at the Sheerness Dockyard, no allowances were given at all. The committee proposed that some parity be established.

The committee's report portrayed the prisoners' quarters as dens of 'gambling, swearing, and every kind of vicious conversation'. The counterfeiting of coins also went on. It appeared that night-time visual supervision of the men below decks was non-existent. In fact, it seemed 'doubtful whether, in some of the Hulks at least, an officer could go down among the prisoners at night without the risk of personal injury'.[110] After consultation with the Navy Board, a new plan was devised for subdividing the convicts' quarters into a number of separate cells off a central corridor, although it took until 1817 for all the vessels to be fitted out in this way.

A regular concern about the hulks was the occurrence of sodomy and rape, which were said to be commonplace. George Lee, a convict on the *Portland* in Langstone Harbour in 1803 claimed that 'the horrible crime of sodomy rages … shamefully throughout'. According to Jeremy Bentham, new inmates on the Woolwich hulks were routinely raped as a matter of course: 'an initiation of this sort stands in the place of garnish and is exacted with equal rigour.'[111] The 1810 Select Committee, in a circumspectly worded appraisal of such claims, were happy, however, to accept that 'the Captains of the different Hulks all concur in disbelieving the existence among them of the more atrocious vice, which rumour has sometimes imputed to them'. Such activities, they believed, would be viewed as abhorrent by the other convicts and dealt with accordingly.[112]

Aaron Graham's successor, John Capper, held the post of what became the Superintendent of the Hulks from 1815 to 1847. Capper's main contribution in the early years of his tenure was the introduction of a scheme whereby convicts were classified as 'Very Good', 'Good', 'Indifferent', 'Suspicious', 'Bad' or 'Very Bad'. Prisoners of each class were housed in separate areas of the ship so that, for example, docile inmates would not be bullied by aggressive ones. The classification was subsequently extended to separate youthful offenders from adults, with a separate hulk, the *Bellerophon*, allocated for boy convicts in 1824.

Further parliamentary appraisals of the hulks took place in 1828, 1831 and 1835. Despite repeated concerns about the convicts' work being too lenient and the discipline too lax, little changed. The 1831 review by the Committee on Secondary Punishments heard from a former convict identified as 'A.B.' who, from the age of 17, had spent four years on the hulk *Retribution* at Sheerness. A.B. recounted that the convicts worked, slept and ate in irons weighing up to 4lb. The work they were given – pulling down buildings and unloading ships – often resulted in serious injury. Anyone judged to be shirking had his pay stopped and was placed in double-irons. The captain used only a fraction of the money officially allocated for buying the prisoners' rations, but always kept a small quantity of top quality bread and meat to hand so that he could demonstrate to any visitors how well the men dined. Unfortunately, A.B. lost any sympathy he had gained when he revealed what went on below decks. New arrivals were routinely robbed of any valuables. Singing, dancing, fighting and gambling regularly took place. Newspapers, 'improper' books and quantities of spirits (smuggled inside a bladder) found their way on board. Some inmates operated small businesses selling tea, bread, tobacco and groceries to the other prisoners. A convict could receive visitors during the daytime, on which occasions he was excused from work. All in all, it was – as A.B. happily admitted – 'a jolly life'. Shocked at such revelations, the committee recommended a clampdown on such indulgences and an increase in the convicts' daily hours of work.[113]

The convict ship *Discovery* was moored at Woolwich and Deptford between 1824 and 1830. She could house up to 200 convicts.

A lull in parliamentary concern about the hulks ended abruptly on 28 January 1847, when Thomas Dunscombe, MP, addressed the Commons on the appalling conditions that he claimed existed on the Woolwich hulks. Based on information he had been sent by William Brown, a convict nurse on the hulk *Warrior*, Dunscombe recited a catalogue of cases of inmates who had been mistreated or neglected by the ship's surgeon Peter Bossey. One, a lunatic named George Monk, suffering from a broken leg, had been 'allowed to lie in bed in his own water and filth until such time as a large piece fell out, putrid with his urine, from the bottom of his back bone'. At times, Monk had also been handcuffed to his bed or strait-jacketed. Another man, Peter Bailey, near to death, had requested the attendance of a Wesleyan Methodist minister but had been refused by Bossey, who had laughed at him and told him that he would die in the bed where he lay. Bailey died a few days later. A prisoner named Henry Driver, labelled as a 'schemer' by Bossey, died a few days after arriving at the *Warrior*. While the body was still warm, its entrails had been removed and thrown in the river.

An investigation by prison inspector Captain William John Williams found that most of William Brown's specific claims were untrue or much exaggerated, but that the hulks suffered from lax management. A lack of regular inspection had resulted in two of the vessels, the *Justitia* and the hospital ship *Unité*, being filthy and infested with vermin. There had been an excessive use of corporal punishment, particularly on mentally disturbed prisoners, with the birch and cat o' nine tails. An inadequate diet, much of which was regularly thrown overboard by the prisoners, had led to a high rate of scurvy. Amongst Williams' recommendations were an improvement to the diet – cocoa should be served instead of gruel at least once a day, white bread instead of brown two or three times a week, and 6oz of pork instead of cheese. Each prisoner should also receive an extra daily allowance of 12oz of potatoes.[114]

From 1849, overall management of the remaining hulks moved to a new body, the Directors of Convict Prisons. However, the increasing use of land-based prisons saw the hulk fleet continue to shrink until, by 1857, only two vessels remained – the *Defence*, whose inmates were mostly invalids, and the hospital ship *Unité*. On 14 July 1857, a fire broke out in the *Defence*'s coal store. Within a few weeks, both vessels had been abandoned and most of their inmates transferred to an old war prison at Lewes in Sussex. So ended the eighty-year-long 'temporary' measure for holding convicts in floating prisons on the Thames.

Left: A convict ward set for dinner aboard the hulk *Defence* in the 1850s.

Below: The death of a convict on the hulk *Justitia* – attributed to the illustrator George Cruickshank. After severe criticism of conditions aboard the *Justitia* in 1847, and a cholera outbreak the following year, the vessel was condemned and replaced by the newly refitted *Defence*.

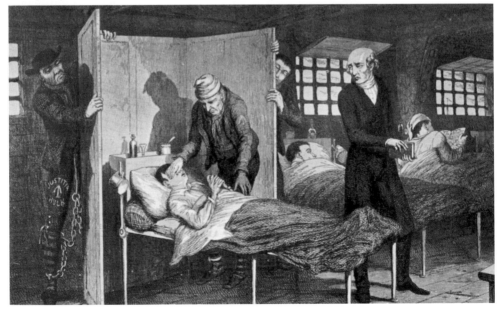

seven

Prisoners of War

The endless succession of wars in which England was involved up until the twentieth century regularly resulted in the capture of prisoners – men who then had to be housed somewhere. Because such prisoners only needed to be accommodated until an exchange was arranged or until the conflict ended, the facilities they needed were fairly basic – food, somewhere to sleep and medical care. At times, however, the sheer numbers of war prisoners caused problems. In 1763, following the Seven Years War, around 40,000 Frenchmen were being held in improvised prisons, while half a century later, at the end of the Napoleonic Wars, more than 120,000 were held captive. Over a similar period, the number of civilian prisoners rose from a mere 4,000 to around 16,000.[115] Conflicts with America, Spain and Holland during the 1770s and 1780s also swelled the volume of war prisoners being held.

Over the years, the accommodation provided for prisoners of war took several different forms. A floating hulk, the *Cornwall*, was used for French prisoners of war from 1755, with up to sixty others later established at Portland and Plymouth. On the *Brunswick*, moored off Chatham, 460 prisoners were crowded at night into a deck measuring 125ft by 40ft, with a ceiling only 4ft 10in high.[116]

Existing buildings were also pressed into service such as the castles at Edinburgh and Portchester. In 1756, Sissinghurst Castle was leased to the government for use as a prison. Over the following seven years, 3,000 French prisoners were held there in cold and overcrowded conditions that were terrible for prisoners and guards alike. Much of the house and furniture were destroyed by the inmates and used for firewood. In 1779, a new prison was opened at Stapleton in Bristol to hold naval prisoners of war who were being landed at Bristol – by 1782 it housed almost 800 Spaniards and Dutchmen. In 1783, a former orphans' home at Shrewsbury was converted to house up to 600 Dutch prisoners.[117] A camp for French and Dutch soldiers and sailors was built in 1796 at Norman Cross, near Peterborough. From 1796 to 1816, it held about 10,000 prisoners, of whom at least 1,700 died.

THE KING'S HOUSE, WINCHESTER

Between 1778 and 1780, the King's House at Winchester was home to over 6,000 French and 1,500 Spanish prisoners. The house, designed by Sir Christopher Wren, was originally intended to be a palatial residence for Charles II, but the scheme had never been completed due to lack of money.

Following the outbreak of a 'distemper' amongst French prisoners in April 1779, and another amongst the Spanish in April 1780, a parliamentary committee investigated the conditions at Winchester and its medical facilities. A list of complaints from the Spanish inmates had blamed the outbreak on the prison's poor quality bread which was described as 'not even fit for dogs'. The committee, on the other hand, concluded that the disease, 'a contagious malignant fever of the gaol kind', had probably been brought ashore by the sailors themselves and its spread owed much to their own 'indolence and want of cleanliness'.[118] Increased space for the prison hospital, improvements in the prison's ventilation and hygiene, with regular bathing of the inmates, airing of their hammocks and bedding, and a twice-weekly fumigation of the rooms with sulphur, had now dealt with the problem. A change in the sick dietary was also instituted. The standard and sick diets at Winchester are shown below:

Days	Beer	Bread	Beef	Butter	Cheese	Peas★	Salt
	Quarts	Pounds	Pounds	Ounces	Ounces	Pints	Ounces
Sunday	1	1½	¾	—	—	½	⅓
Monday	1	1½	¾	—	—	—	⅓
Tuesday	1	1½	¾	—	—	½	⅓
Wednesday	1	1½	¾	—	—	—	⅓
Thursday	1	1½	¾	—	—	½	⅓
Friday	1	1½	¾	—	—	—	⅓
Saturday	1	1½	¾	4 *or* 6		½	⅓
Total	7	10½	4½	4	6	2	2⅓

★Or a pound of good cabbage.

Scheme of diet for the Prisoners in the Hospital.	
Low Diet	Water Gruel, Panada, Rice Gruel, Milk Pottage or Broth, 8oz of Bread (and if Butter is ordered, 2oz.) —For Drink, Toast and Water, Ptisan, or White Decoction.
Half Diet	For Breakfast, Milk Pottage. For Dinner, 8oz of Mutton, some light Bread Pudding, or in lieu of it some Greens, a Pint of Broth, a Pound of Bread, and Three Pints of Small Beer.
Full Diet	Breakfast as above.—For Dinner, One Pound of Meat, One Pint of Broth, One Pound of Bread, and Two Quarts of Small Beer. Supper in the Two last-mentioned Diets to be of the Broth left at Dinner, or, if thought necessary, to be of Milk Pottage.
Rice Milk, Orange Whey, Orange and Lemon Water, Tamarind Whey, Vinegar Whey, Balm and Sage Tea, to be discretionally used by the Surgeon. Besides the Cordial Medicines of the Dispensary, Wine is always allowed for such sick Prisoners as the Surgeon judges it to be proper for.	

Panada, included in the hospital's low diet, was made from bread boiled to a pulp in water and sometimes flavoured with sugar, nutmeg, currants or other ingredients. The following recipe for panada 'for a sick or weak stomach' was provided by Richard Bradley in the 1762 edition of *The Country Housewife*:

> **Panada for a sick or weak stomach.**
>
> Put the Crumb of a Penny white Loaf grated into a Quart of cold Water; set both on the Fire together with a Blade of Mace: When it is boiled smooth, take it off the Fire, and put in a Bit of Lemon-peel, the Juice of a Lemon, a Glass of Sack, and Sugar to your Taste. This is very nourishing, and never offends the Stomach. Some season with Butter and Sugar, adding Currants, which on some Occasions are proper; but the first way is the most grateful and innocent.[119]

Ptisan (many alternative spellings include tisane, thisan, petisane etc.) was a medicinal drink of which barley water was the most common form. Here is Hannah Glasse's recipe from 1758:

> **To make Barley Water.**
>
> Put a Quarter of a Pound of Pearl Barley into two Quarts of Water, let it boil, skim it very clean, boil half away, and drain it off. Sweeten to your Palate, but not too sweet, and put in two Spoonfuls of white Wine. Drink it Luke-warm.[120]

DARTMOOR

Overcrowding at the Stapleton and Norman Cross prisons and aboard the hulks at Plymouth resulted in the building of a large new prison at Princetown on Dartmoor. The site chosen was near to granite quarries which supplied stone for construction of the prison. Within a few months of its opening in May 1809, it housed 5,000 French prisoners. A subsequent extension was used to hold captives from the Anglo-American war of 1812–5.

The prison's distinctive layout, reflecting the popular radial designs of the day, comprised five large rectangular blocks arranged around a semi-circle, like the spokes of a wheel. Each block, two storeys high, could house 1,500 men, sleeping in two tiers of hammocks. At the central hub, an open space was used as a daily market place where local people could sell vegetables and other wares. Other buildings included a large hospital and an officers' block. The site was surrounded by two walls with a road in between where guards patrolled.

At its height, the prison held over 8,000 inmates whose diet was rather better than that received by many of the prisoners in England's civilian gaols. The daily ration for Dartmoor's healthy prisoners is shown below:[121]

Sunday **Monday** **Tuesday** **Thursday** **Saturday**	One pound and a half of bread. Half a pound of fresh beef. Half a pound of cabbage or turnips fit for the copper. One ounce of Scotch barley. One-third of an ounce of salt. One-quarter of an ounce of onions.
Wednesday	One pound and a half of bread. One pound of good sound herrings (red herrings and white pickled herrings to be issued alternately). One pound of good sound potatoes.
Friday	One pound and a half of bread. One pound of good sound dry cod fish. One pound of good sound potatoes.

The food was provided by private contractors and its quality was specified in some detail:

Bread—To be made of whole meal, the produce of good marketable British or foreign wheat, and well dressed through a thirteen shilling seam-cloth. The said bread to be well baked into loaves of four pounds and a half, or three pounds Avoirdupois; to be weighed at the end of six hours after the same shall have been baked; to be made with salt and not with sea-water, and to be equal in quality in all respects to the bread supplied by the Victualling Board to the Ordinary of His Majesty's Navy.

Beef—To be good and wholesome fresh beef, not bull beef, and delivered in clean quarters, a fore and hind quarter alternately, when the number of prisoners is sufficient for the expenditure of that quantity; but if it be not so, then in parts of such quarters, a fore and hind quarter alternately.

Cod fish—To be the produce of the British fisheries, or the fishery at Newfoundland. To be delivered in whole fish. Cabbages or turnips to be issued as the agent of the said Commissioners shall from time to time direct.

Three different levels of diet were provided for prisoners of war who were sick, with plenty of greens – and beer – for the less seriously ill:

Patients on Low Diet	A pint of tea in the morning for breakfast, and a like quantity in the evening, 8oz bread, 2oz butter, or in lieu of butter, 1 pint milk, ½ pint broth, or such an additional quantity thereof as the surgeon shall judge proper. For drink, barley-water, toast and water, water-gruel, lemon-water, vinegar-whey, balm or sage-tea. In febrile cases the barley-water may be acidulated with lemon juice.
Patients on Half Diet	Tea morning and evening as above, 16oz bread, 8oz beef or mutton, 8oz greens, or good sound potatoes, 1 pint broth, and 3 pints small beer. For common drink, barley-water.
Patients on Full Diet	Tea morning and evening as above, 16oz bread, 16oz beef or mutton, 1 pint broth, 16oz greens or good sound potatoes, and 2 quarts small beer. For common drink, barley-water.

In 'particular cases of debility, or where the appetite may be capricious':

The surgeon may substitute fish, fowl, veal, lamb, or eggs, provided the expense incurred for the same do not exceed the price of the beef or mutton allowed. One dram and a half of good souchong tea, seven drams of good muscovado sugar, and one sixth part of a pint of genuine milk, to be allowed to every pint of tea. The broth to be made by boiling together the meat allowed in the half and full diet, with the addition of twelve drains of good sound barley, twelve drains of good onions, or one ounce of leeks, and three drains of parsley for every pound of meat.

Again, the quality of the items was carefully stipulated:

> **Beer**—Every seven barrels to be brewed from eight bushels of strong amber malt, and six or seven pounds of good hops, such as are used by the common brewers.
> **Bread**—To be the best wheaten bread.
> **Butter**—To be good salt butter.
> **Mutton**—To be good wether mutton.
> **Beef**—To be good ox beef.
> **Greens**—To be stripped of the outside leaves, and fit for the copper.
> **Potatoes**—To be good sound potatoes.

Despite the relatively good fare provided to the Dartmoor inmates, food was still the cause of problems, particularly amongst a group of French prisoners known as the 'Romans'. These were men who, largely because of the gambling that was rife in the prison, had literally lost their shirts – together with their bedding and any other possessions. Such men formed a commune in the large lofts beneath the prison roofs which had been intended to provide exercise space during bad weather. The Romans rarely tasted the prison's official dietary:

> From morning till night groups of Romans were to be seen raking the garbage heaps for scraps of offal, potato peelings, rotten turnips, and fish heads, for though they drew their ration of soup at mid-day, they were always famishing, partly because the ration itself was insufficient, partly because they exchanged their rations with the infamous provision-buyers for tobacco with which they gambled. In the alleys between the tiers of hammocks on the floors below you might always see some of them lurking, if a man were peeling a potato a dozen of these wretches would be round him in a moment to beg for the peel; they would form a ring round every mess bucket, like hungry dogs, watching the eaters in the hope that one would throw away a morsel of gristle, and fighting over every bone. [122]

After the prison's own bakehouse was burned down in October 1812, the prisoners refused to accept the bread sent in from Plymouth by the contractor, claiming that it was damp and sour. After satisfying himself that the bread was of good quality, the prison's chief officer Captain Cotgrave announced that any man who refused the bread would forfeit the ration for that day. According to one account, the starving Romans:

> Fell upon the offal heaps as usual, and when the two-horse waggon came in to remove the filth they resented the removal of their larder. In the course of the dispute, partly to revenge themselves upon the driver, partly to appease their famishing bloodthirst, these wretches fell upon the horses with knives, stabbed them to death, and fastened their teeth in the bleeding carcases. This horror was too much for the stomachs of the other prisoners, who helped to drive them off. [123]

A rather more salubrious part of the premises, known as the Petty Officers' prison, housed French naval and merchant service officers. Many were fairly well-to-do men who were able to buy provisions from the daily market and also hire prisoners from other sections to perform menial tasks such as cleaning for them. Even here, though, life was not uneventful:

> One day at dinner a man pulled out of the soup bucket of his mess a dead rat which he held up by the tail, whereupon heads and tails and feet were dredged up from every bucket in such

numbers that they would have furnished limbs for fully a hundred animals. We may judge whether the regulation diet of the prisoners was sufficient, from the fact that out of all these Frenchmen of the middle classes only a handful of the most squeamish went without their soup that day. For a time the life of the cooks hung by a thread, and it was only upon the intervention of the Commissaire that the head cook was allowed to speak in his own defence. The coppers, as it seemed, had been filled with water overnight as usual, but through forgetfulness the covers had not been closed, and the coppers had thus been converted into rat traps. It had not occurred to the cooks to dredge them for dead bodies, and the meat and vegetables had been thrown in atop and the fires lighted.[124]

Naturally enough, some foreign prisoners attempted to recreate their home cuisine. Some of the more enterprising French inmates 'opened booths for the sale of strange and wonderful dishes compounded of the Government rations with ingredients purchased in the market. The favourite was a ragout, called "ratatouille," made of Government beef, potatoes and peas.'[125] When American prisoners came to Dartmoor, some shaved a thin layer from the crust of their bread which was then scorched over coals to make a form of coffee.

CONVICT PRISON PRINCETOWN 9999.

An aerial view of Dartmoor prison. After 1815, Dartmoor was unoccupied until 1850 when it was re-opened as a public works prison. Within a few years it was mainly being used as an invalid prison and by 1858 housed up to 1,200 convicts capable of performing light labour.

eight

The Evolution of Prisons 1780s – 1860s

PENITENTIARY HOUSES

As an alternative to transportation, the 1779 Transportation Act had sanctioned the building of two large 'penitentiary houses', one for men and one for women, near to the capital. The Act went into considerable detail about the operation of the proposed houses. As well as the prisoners' own quarters, the buildings were to include stores, workshops, an infirmary, a chapel, burying-ground and 'dark but airy dungeons'. New arrivals would be washed, issued with a distinctive prison uniform and given a medical examination. For up to ten hours a day, Sundays excepted, prisoners would be put to 'Labour of the hardest and most servile Kind, in which Drudgery is chiefly required … such as treading in a Wheel, or drawing in a Capstern, for turning a Mill or other Machine or Engine, sawing Stone, polishing Marble, beating Hemp, rasping Logwood, chopping Rags, making Cordage'. Work suggested for the less able included picking oakum, weaving sacks, spinning yarn and knitting nets. A small part of any profit from such work could be used by the prisoner or their family. The inmates were to sleep in individual cells, each measuring at least 7ft by 10ft by 9ft high, and heated by flues from the prison fires. Association between the prisoners would be confined to work hours, meal times, exercise periods and during twice-daily chapel services. The prison diet would consist of 'Bread, and any coarse Meat, or other inferior Food, and Water, or small Beer'. However, each prison was also to have a kitchen garden. Finally, prisoners were to be divided into three categories known as First, Second, or Third Class, through which they would automatically progress during each third of their sentence. First Class prisoners would receive the most severe treatment and Third Class the most lenient.

Implementation of the proposals was placed in the hands of a supervisory committee whose initial membership included John Howard. However, despite their efforts to get the project off the ground, the scheme ground to a halt.

LOCAL PRISONS

The 1780s and 1790s did, however, see a burst of activity in the modernisation of local prisons, with more than sixty rebuilt during this period, many the work of architect William Blackburn, a disciple of John Howard.[126] Although a wide variety of designs were constructed, the buildings typically included separate sections for different classes of prisoner, individual sleeping cells, work-rooms, exercise yards, a chapel, laundry and infirmary. Cells opened onto a linking corridor or walkway placed either on the inside or the outside of the building.

The simplest type of plan, used at county gaols such as Exeter and Winchester, was a single block with the keeper's quarters placed at the centre. Courtyard designs, such as those in new county gaols at Hertford and Moulsham, were based on the layout of monastic cloisters and placed wings around the sides of a quadrangle. What were to prove more significant were Blackburn's polygonal and radial designs. An example of the first of these was the new gaol erected at Northleach in the late 1780s. The cell block formed five of the sides of an octagon, providing good visibility of all the cells from a central point. The radial design, where a number of wings emanated from a central hub, was used at the new county gaol in Ipswich. The radial principle was widely adopted in Victorian workhouses and prisons, although Blackburn's designs lacked the internal open galleries that characterised many later prison buildings.[127]

BENTHAM'S PANOPTICON

While the national penitentiary scheme was languishing, some alternative proposals were put forward by philosopher and social reformer Jeremy Bentham. One idea was for a set of colour-coded institutions – a white-walled building for debtors and those awaiting trial, a grey one for short-term prisoners and a black one for those serving life sentences. Outside the latter two would stand the figures of 'a monkey, a fox and a tiger, representing mischief, cunning, and rapacity, the source of all crimes'; inside, two skeletons would flank an iron door.[128]

A later scheme, the 'panopticon' or inspection house, was based on a design for a workshop by Bentham's brother Samuel. It consisted of a circular or polygonal building with cells on each storey and, at the centre, an inspection 'lodge' from where prisoners could be supervised. The establishment would be managed by a contractor who would provide profitable work from which the inmates would receive some income. The contractor would be penalised for any prisoners who died or escaped while in his custody. Bentham's plans included a glass roof and mirrors to aid observation of the inmates, a complex system of pipes for ventilation and heating and a network of 'conversation tubes' allowing staff or visitors to speak to prisoners from the central lodge.

Bentham's vigorous and persistent lobbying of ministers eventually resulted in some modest backing for a panopticon prison and in 1799 he acquired a site for its construction on the north bank of the Thames at Millbank. However, like the original penitentiary houses project, the scheme never gained sufficient momentum and was effectively abandoned by the government in 1803. Panopticon-style buildings were later erected in other countries, including the Koepelgevangenis at Haarlem in Holland, the Presidio Modelo in Cuba and the Stateville Correctional Center in the USA.

MILLBANK

In 1810, more than thirty years after its conception, the plan to build a new, large, national penitentiary was revived. A parliamentary Select Committee was set up and took evidence from a number of leading figures. Sir George Onesiphorus Paul, another devotee of John Howard, who had transformed the county prisons in Gloucestershire, described his use of a 'stage' system in which the first third of a prisoner's sentence was spent in solitude. The Rev. John Becher gave details of the 'association' system used at the Southwell House of Correction where groups of inmates were encouraged to work by receiving a share of the profits from their labour. The committee also heard the views of Jeremy Bentham who was still eager to promote the virtues of his panopticon, but he was effectively sidelined from the project.

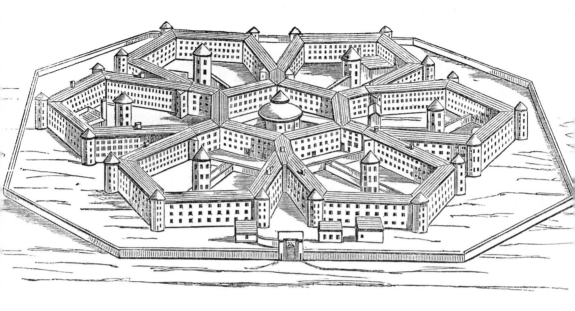

A bird's-eye view of the Millbank prison. Occupants of the present-day site include the Tate Gallery and the headquarters of the Prison Service.

The committee decided to recommend construction of a single, large prison for up to 600 convicts – a figure later increased to 1,000. A competition for its design took place, the winning plan being submitted by William Williams. The construction work, initially expected to cost in the order of £300,000, began in 1812 at Bentham's own Millbank site. For the land and for all his trouble, Bentham received compensation to the tune of £23,000. Problems with the marshy ground delayed the opening of the prison until 1816 and building was not finally completed until 1821, by which time the cost had risen to the then huge sum of £450,000.[129]

Millbank's novel design revolved around a central hexagon which housed the governor, matron, steward, surgeon, chaplain, master manufacturer and the bakery. Each of the hexagon's six sides then formed the inner edge of a three-storey pentagonal cell block. The area within each cell block was divided into five airing yards with a tall watch-tower at the centre. Each of the cell blocks was, in effect, a miniature panopticon.

Despite an optimistic start, including a visit by the Duchess of York in 1817, Millbank was beset by problems. The sheer size of the building, its circular layout and the labyrinth of winding staircases, dark passages, and innumerable doors and gates proved totally confusing. One old warder, even after several years at the prison, still carried a piece of chalk to help him mark his way around.[130] There were also regular disturbances and even riots. One particularly embarrassing incident took place in April 1818 during a Sunday morning service in the chapel at which the Chancellor of the Exchequer was present. Discontent about recent problems with the prison's bread came to head with male inmates banging the flaps on their seats and throwing loaves around. Some of the women began chants of 'Give us our daily bread' and 'Better bread!' while others began screaming or fainting, and eventually were all escorted from the room. Further unrest was only quelled with the help of the Bow Street Runners.[131]

The regime at Millbank combined those in use in the gaols at Gloucester and Southwell. Those prisoners serving the first half of their sentence (known as First Class inmates) worked and slept in the seclusion of their individual cells. Those in the second half of their sentence (the Second Class) performed their labour in groups. Complete isolation of the First Class inmates proved to be impossible, however – staff were unable to prevent them communicating when they were attending chapel, taking exercise or working a shift on the prison's corn mills or water pumps. It was soon concluded that any beneficial effects of the First Class were rapidly undone in the Second so, from 1832, inmates spent the whole of their sentence in solitude. Even that proved ineffective. Each cell had two doors, an inner one of bars and an outer one of wood. Because of the building's poor ventilation, the outer doors were left open during the day – allowing prisoners in adjacent cells to talk to one another.

New arrivals at the prison were given a haircut, bath and medical examination. Their own clothes were either sold or, if 'foul or unfit to be preserved', burned. The prison uniform, slightly different for the two classes, was decreed to be made of cheap and coarse materials, and distinctively marked so as to identify escapees. The wearing of a black armband (or ribbon for women) was permitted following the death of a near relation.

The prisoners' daily routine comprised ten sections, each signalled by the ringing of a bell:

Bell	Time	Activity
1	5.30 (or daybreak in winter)	Rise, dress, comb hair, visit washroom under supervision of Turnkey.
2	6.00	Begin work.
3	8.30	Prisoners appointed Wardsmen/Wardswomen collect porridge or gruel from kitchens for distribution to other inmates.
4	9.00	Eat breakfast.
5	9.30	Resume work.
6	12.30	Wardsmen/Wardswomen collect dinners.
7	13.00	Eat dinner and take air or exercise.
8	14.00	Resume work.
9	18.00 (or sunset in winter)	Finish work.
10	18.00 (or 19.00 in winter)	Return to cell for night. Gruel or porridge delivered to cell.

Establishing what was eventually to become normal prison practice, all food for Millbank's inmates was supplied by the institution. The prison's 1817 dietary (below) also includes one of the first instances of porridge making its appearance as the standard prisoner's breakfast fare:

DAILY, 1lb of Bread, made of whole Meal; and to serve the day.		
BREAKFAST		1 pint of hot gruel or porridge.
DINNER	Sundays Tuesdays Thursdays Saturdays	6oz of clods, stickings, or other coarse pieces of Beef (without bone, and after boiling) with ½ a pint of the Broth made there from 1lb of sound Potatoes, well boiled.
	Mondays Wednesdays Fridays	1 quart of Broth, thickened with Scotch barley, rice, potatoes, or pease, with the addition of cabbages, turnips, or other cheap vegetables. 1lb of sound Potatoes, well boiled.
SUPPER		1 pint of hot gruel or porridge.

N.B.—Prisoners may reserve such part of the provision previously delivered out for their Supper.
Salt and Pepper as the Committee shall direct.
The only Liquor allowed to prisoners in health (except broth, gruel or porridge) shall be Water.
Prisoners confined to Bread and Water diet, for punishment, shall be allowed an addition of ½lb of Bread, instead of other provisions.
Prisoners, employed in works of extraordinary labour, or under circumstances which may render it necessary, may be allowed an addition to the quantity of their provisions.

The only variation in the dietary came on Christmas Day, when the meat was roasted (rather than boiled) and an additional 8oz of baked pudding was served. Prisoners who were 'deficient in cleanliness' were liable to have their meat and vegetables withheld. More serious offences could be punished by a diet of bread and water and/or confinement in a dark cell for up to a month.

In 1822, Millbank's Medical Superintendent, Dr Copland Hutchinson, concluded that the Millbank dietary was more liberal than that found in most other prisons. He persuaded the prison's Committee of Management to adopt the new dietary shown below. The most significant change was in the midday dinner provision – the daily pound of potatoes and four-times-a-week ration of meat had gone and in its place was an unchanging portion of soup.

MORNING	Males	12oz of Bread, and 1 pint of Gruel
	Females	9oz of Bread, and ¾ pint of Gruel
NOON	Males	12oz of Bread, and 1 pint of Soup
	Females	9oz of Bread, and ¾ pint of Soup
EVENING	Males	1 pint of Soup
	Females	¾ pint of Soup

The Soup to be made with Ox heads, in lieu of other meat, in the proportion of one Ox head for about 100 Male prisoners, and the same for about 120 Female prisoners; and to be thickened with Vegetables and Pease, or Barley alternately, either weekly or daily, as may be found most convenient.

Within a few months, the health of the prisoners was in serious decline. They became pale, languid, thin, feeble and unable to perform their usual labour. There were also numerous cases of diarrhoea and dysentery. More than half the inmates were affected, females more than males, and those in the Second Class more than those in the First. One group of prisoners who were almost entirely unscathed were those who worked in the prison kitchens. Eventually, two outside physicians were called in and diagnosed the mysterious illness as a combination of infectious dysentery and 'sea-scurvy'. Scurvy, whose symptoms included spongy and bleeding gums, results from a vitamin C deficiency but was then attributed to factors such as insufficient food, cold, damp, fatigue and sea air. An immediate change in the Millbank diet was ordered, with a daily allowance of 4oz of meat and 8oz of rice replacing the dinner-time soup, and white bread being provided instead of brown. Each prisoner was also given an orange at each meal. In the longer term, it was recommended that the amount of meat in the diet should be increased, that only good quality white bread be used, and that at least one meal a day should be given in solid form. The potato ration was not restored, however.

Although the change in the Millbank diet appeared to produce a rapid improvement in the prisoners' health, there was then a widespread relapse. It was decided that the building itself was contributing to the problems and would have to be evacuated while the necessary changes were made. Four naval vessels at Woolwich were pressed into service as prison hulks, the *Ethalion* and *Dromedary* (housing 467 male convicts) and the *Narcissus* and *Heroine* (167 females). The transfer of Millbank's residents began in August 1823 and the prison was closed for a year, during which time all the rooms were fumigated with chlorine and extensive improvements made to the ventilation and drainage. For the Millbank prisoners now on the hulks, conditions were often no less unpleasant than those they had left behind. The continuing level of sickness among the women in particular led to many of them being given free pardons, while some of the men were transferred to the fleet of regular hulks.

Despite the efforts to improve the running of Millbank, it continued to suffer from problems and a frequent turnover of governors. More seriously, it became increasingly clear that keeping prisoners separated over long periods was not without its consequences. In 1841, a disturbing increase in the numbers of inmates diagnosed as insane led to the initial period of separation being reduced to three months. Finally, in 1843, the Home Secretary, Sir James Graham, admitted that, as a penitentiary, Millbank had been an entire failure and it would become a short-term holding prison for those awaiting transportation.

THE SEPARATE AND SILENT SYSTEMS

During the 1830s, considerable debate took place about the relative merits of two systems of discipline, both of which had come into use at different prisons in America. The 'silent' system, developed at Auburn prison in New York State, allowed prisoners to associate during their daytime activities but not speak. The alternative 'separate' system, deployed at prisons such as Cherry Hill in Philadelphia, kept prisoners in isolation – work, exercise and mealtimes all took place in solitude. Opponents of the silent system criticised the corporal punishment that was invariably required to suppress communication and saw the separate system as one that fostered penitence and reformation. Opponents of the separate system saw it as depriving prisoners of natural human contact and, in purely practical terms, being more expensive to implement in terms of the accommodation and staff required.

Use of the separate system in England gained momentum following the 1835 Prisons Act, which increased central involvement in all the country's prisons. Each prison's rules were now required to be submitted for the Home Secretary's approval, and inspectors were appointed to visit every prison at least once a year. The inspectors appointed for the 'Home District' were the Reverend Whitworth Russell (a former chaplain at Millbank) and William Crawford – both staunch supporters of the separate system. In the scheme they favoured, inmates would sleep, work and eat in a spacious and self-contained cell, with no contact allowed with other prisoners. The daily routine would include time for reflection, religious devotions, exercise and receiving regular visits from prison officers, particularly the chaplain.

Crawford and Russell produced a number of designs for model prisons in which their scheme could be implemented, with some of their plans being taken up by local prisons interested in introducing the separate system. This trend was given added impetus in the 1839 Prisons Act under which all new prison plans required approval from the central government in the shape of Joshua Jebb, the Home Office's advisor and subsequently Surveyor General of Prisons. The Act effectively gave official endorsement to the separate system which, it insisted, was quite different from solitary confinement.

Crawford and Russell's greatest success, however, came in 1838 when their proposal to erect a large model prison in London gained support from the Home Secretary, Lord Russell, who also just happened to be Whitworth Russell's uncle.

PENTONVILLE

The site chosen for the new 'Model Prison, on the separate system' was at Pentonville in north London. Construction began in April 1840, and the first inmates arrived in December 1842.

In addition to its role as a model prison, Pentonville's function within the penal system was to provide an initial term, normally eighteen months, of probationary discipline and labour for selected convicts prior to their transportation to Van Diemen's Land. Those behaving well would receive a 'ticket-of-leave', effectively freedom in their new country. Those performing indifferently would be given a probationary pass, a status which imposed some restrictions of their movement and earnings. For those whose conduct at Pentonville was deemed unsatisfactory, their destination would be a convict labour settlement.

The architect of Pentonville was Joshua Jebb, but its design was clearly based on the ideas of Crawford and Russell. The main prison building comprised a central administration block from which four wings radiated like the spokes of a half-cartwheel. Each wing contained 130 cells arranged in three galleries, one above the other, with each floor containing forty or so individual cells. From the central hall it was possible for staff to have a view of every cell door. Inside each cell was an alarm handle which rang a bell and raised a semaphore indicator outside the cell's sound-proof door.

The regime imposed at Pentonville was a rigorous form of the separate system. Prisoners slept, worked and ate in their cells, only going outside for exercise or to attend chapel, at which times they wore turned-down caps (later masks) to conceal their faces. The circular exercise yards were divided into individual segments at the centre of which was an observation post. The chapel, too, was constructed with partitions between each seat to prevent communication.

An important aim of Pentonville was to equip each inmate with a trade by which they could earn their living in Australia. Instructors were employed for a variety of trades including carpentry, shoemaking, tailoring, rug and mat weaving, linen and cotton weaving, and basket making. Prisoners were also provided with twice-weekly classes which included reading, writing, arithmetic, history, geography, grammar and scripture. A Bible, prayer book and hymn book were given to every inmate able to use them.

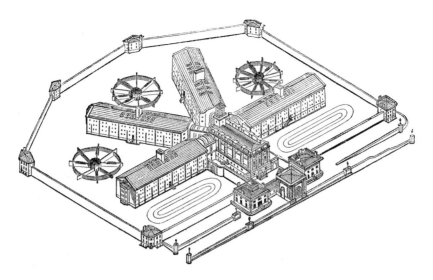

A bird's-eye view of Pentonville prison showing the prison buildings, segmented circular exercise yards and perimeter wall.

Pentonville cells, 13ft by 7ft by 9ft high, were fitted with a hammock, table and stool, and a copper wash-basin which drained into an earthenware lavatory. Each cell had a non-opening window high up in its wall, with ventilation and heating provided through a system of flues and gratings in the walls.

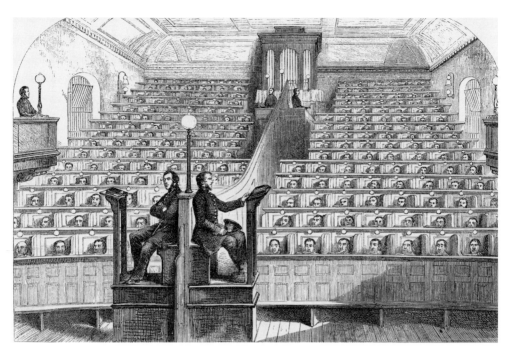

The individual high-sided pews in Pentonville's prison chapel were intended to prevent inmates communicating during services. However, the governor's report for 1852 noted seventy attempts to do so, plus a further six of 'dancing in chapel, mimicking chaplain, and other misconduct during divine service'.

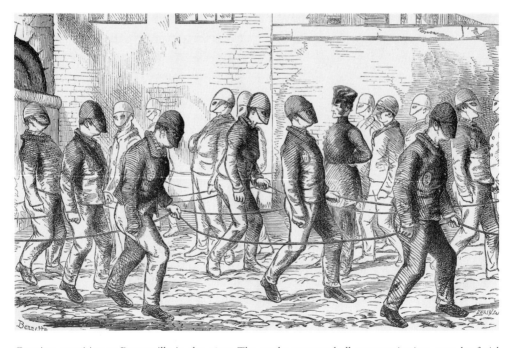

Convicts exercising at Pentonville in the 1850s. The masks prevented all communication, even by facial expression, and also prevented prisoners from recognising one another.

As at Millbank, the daily routine, from rising at 05.30 until lights out at 21.00, was timetabled with military precision. Parties of sixteen prisoners, in single file at 5-yard intervals, were marched from their cells for sessions of exercise, worship or labour – pumping water from the prison's own 370ft deep artesian well. The warders' activities were regulated by special clocks around the prison, with levers requiring to be pressed at preset times. Moving inmates from their cells to the chapel, for example, was to occupy exactly six and a half minutes.

The formulation of the dietary at Pentonville received special attention, with the prison's medical officer, Dr Owen Rees, examining those in use at other prisons, on board the hulks and in hospitals and workhouses. He also weighed prisoners regularly to assess the adequacy of the food. His initial dietary, comprising bread, cocoa, gruel, five meat and potato dinners a week, and two cheese dinners, resulted in 62 per cent of the prisoners losing weight. Increasing the daily bread allowance from 16oz to 20oz reduced weight losses but still resulted in health problems such as 'debility'. Restoring the bread to 16oz but serving meat and potato dinners every day still resulted in a modest but widespread weight loss. Upping the daily bread allowance to 20oz and the potato ration from ½lb to 1lb, at last gave an acceptable level of weight maintenance.[132] The final dietary is shown below:

Breakfast: ¾oz of flaked cocoa or cocoa nibs, made with 2oz of milk and 6 drams of molasses, into ¾ pint of liquid cocoa.

Dinner: 4oz of cooked meat, weighed when cooked, without bone, and ½ pint of soup, and 1lb potatoes, weighed when boiled.

Supper: 1 pint of gruel, sweetened with 6 drams molasses.
Bread, 2oz per diem. A liberal allowance of salt.

Soup made with liquor of meat of the same day, strengthened by three ox-heads to 100 pints. Barley, peppers, and carrots added, and a seasoning of onions. Gruel, 1½oz oatmeal to 1 pint.

In November 1843, *The Times* reported that after barely six months at Pentonville, two inmates had been 'driven mad by the severity and the seclusion of its discipline', requiring their removal to the Bethlehem Hospital. It condemned the prison's 'maniac-making system' which, it noted, subjected prisoners to solitude for a period six times as long as that which the Millbank authorities had now agreed was the safe maximum for such confinement.[133] For the first few years of its life, the level of such problems was insufficient to cause the authorities serious concern. However, in 1848, the Pentonville Commissioners noted 'the great number of cases of death and of insanity, as compared with that of former years'.[134]

Ironically, it was not only the convicts who appeared to suffer ill effects from the new prison buildings. In 1847, Whitworth Russell committed suicide at Millbank. William Crawford died in the same year after collapsing during a meeting at Pentonville.[135]

CHANGES TO LOCAL PRISONS

A fresh impetus to the reform of local prisons came with the Gaol Fees Abolition Act of 1815, which decreed that 'all Fees and Gratuities paid or payable by any Prisoner, on the Entrance, Commitment or Discharge, to or from Prison, shall absolutely cease, and the same are hereby

In 1834, the Middlesex House of Correction at Coldbath Fields adopted the silent system where prisoners could work in association, but not communicate. Here, in the oakum room, the closely supervised inmates were required to pick apart 3½ pounds of old rope per day – a hook attached to the knee could assist in the task.

abolished and determined'.[136] Responsibility for paying gaolers' salaries now rested with local JPs with the money being provided from town or county rates.

Sir Robert Peel's Gaol Act of 1823[137] took the view that prisons should be 'an object of terror' but that those in prison should not become 'worse members of society, or more hardened offenders'. The Act consolidated and reiterated a number of previous measures relating to hygiene and diet, the prevention of gambling and sale of alcohol, and the payment of prison staff through salaries rather than prisoners' fees. The Act required separate accommodation to be provided for different categories of prisoner, such as debtors, felons and those awaiting trial. Males and females were to be housed separately and women were to be supervised only by female warders. Each prisoner was to have a hammock or bed provided, either in a cell of their own or sharing with at least two others. Those on hard labour were to work up to ten hours a day. Prisoners were to be provided with instruction in reading and writing. The Act also clarified the distinction between common gaols and houses of correction, with the latter to be used for all 'idle and disorderly Persons, Rogues and Vagabonds, incorrigible Rogues and other Vagrants'. Prison keepers were to make quarterly reports to local JPs and, along with the chaplain and surgeon, keep regular journals. The Act's main deficiency was that it applied only to the larger locally administered prisons, less than half of those in operation, and thus ignored those most in need of reform.[138]

The passing of a statute and its demands actually being put into practice were still two rather different matters, however. In 1841, the governor of the St Alban's county gaol was found still to be charging sick inmates for 'extras' prescribed by the prison surgeon – meat and vegetables at 8*d* per plate, beer at 4*d* per quart and tea or broth at 3*d* per basin. The governor professed complete ignorance of the 1823 Act, claiming that he had never been made aware of its contents.[139]

In 1842, London's three debtors' prisons, the Fleet, the Marshalsea and the Queen's (formerly King's) Bench, which were all excluded from the 1823 Act, were 'consolidated'. The former two were wound down and closed with their prisoners transferring to what became known as the Queen's prison and which then operated in line with the Act.

Further moves towards more standardised operation came in the wake of the 1835 Prisons Act which set up the Inspectors of Prisons. In 1843, under the direction of Home Secretary, Sir James Graham, the inspectors examined the whole system of prison 'discipline', including such matters as the employment, diet and health of prisoners, arrangements for their religious instruction and moral improvement, the use of punishments such as the tread-wheel, and the temperature of the cells. As a result of their investigations, a set of regulations was devised to try and bring some consistency to the operation of the 220 or so prisons then operating in England and Wales.

Despite the problems experienced at Pentonville, it marked the start of a boom in prison construction. In the six years following its building, fifty-four new prisons were erected, providing 11,000 separate cells.[140] Pentonville's open gallery radial design became a model for many new local prison buildings and between 1842 and 1877 around twenty gaols or houses of correction were erected on similar lines.[141] These included new county prisons at Reading, Clerkenwell, Wakefield, Aylesbury, Winchester, Exeter, Wandsworth, Lewes, Warwick, Coldbath Fields (Middlesex), Salford and Lincoln, together with borough prisons at Leeds, Birmingham, Manchester, Liverpool, Hull and Portsmouth. Most were located on green-field sites at the edge of town, although some, such as Reading and Clerkenwell, reconstructed existing buildings. The new City of London House of Correction, opened in 1852, was located to the north of London at Holloway since no suitable site could be found within the city itself.

Even at prisons where wholesale rebuilding was not possible, such as those occupying castles or confined town sites, there was a move to adopt Pentonville's principles by converting buildings to provide separate cells, or by constructing new separate-cell blocks, as happened at prisons such as Stafford, Gloucester, Oxford, Bodmin, Maidstone and Newgate.

Despite the adoption of the separate system at Pentonville, some local prisons such as Wakefield, Derby and Coldbath Fields opted to use the silent system. Journalist Henry Mayhew, visiting Coldbath Fields in the late 1850s, reported that the system required a higher proportion of officers to supervise the prisoners than at Pentonville, and that the relative number of punishments inflicted was also higher. Mayhew was particularly critical of the 'stark waste of intellect' resulting from the silent system, where the prisoners could not even be read aloud to during the enforced 'utter mental idleness'. Despite the strict regime, the Coldbath Fields governor admitted that some prisoners did manage to communicate using 'significant signs'.[142] Touching one's nose to indicate a wish for tobacco may be the origin of 'snout' – a slang word for the substance, particularly associated with prisons.

PUBLIC WORKS PRISONS

By the 1840s, the decline in the number of available destinations for transporting convicts led to the development of alternative forms of sentence at home. In 1848, a 'public works' prison housing 840 prisoners was opened at Portland in Dorset where the inmates were employed in the local quarries and naval dockyard. A similar but much larger establishment was constructed at Portsmouth in 1852. On Dartmoor, part of the old prisoner-of-war prison – largely empty since 1815 – was put to use as a public-works project, with over 1,000 prisoners working on the land, renovating the building and adapting it to house invalid prisoners.

From 1848, convicts sentenced to between seven and ten years transportation could instead receive twelve months of separate confinement at Pentonville (or Millbank for women), followed by up to three years hard labour at Portland, Dartmoor or on the hulks, with good conduct earning a shorter stay. They would then be transported to Van Diemen's Land or Western Australia, there receiving a pardon so long as they did not return to Britain.

Van Diemen's Land closed its doors to convicts in 1852, leaving just Western Australia available for transportation, and then only of men. The following year, the Penal Servitude Act replaced transportation sentences of less than fourteen years by a shorter sentence of imprisonment in England. This again comprised an initial period of separate confinement, now reduced to nine months, at Pentonville, Millbank or the new women's convict prison at Brixton opened in 1853. This was followed by a period of labour on public works, then release on licence – the beginnings of the parole system. This was a development which aroused some concern amongst the public.

The general use of transportation ceased in 1857, replaced in all cases by sentences of penal servitude. The same year also saw the demise of the last remaining hulks. To cope with the

A view of the West Riding County Gaol at Wakefield, erected in 1843–7, and one of the many prison designs of the period influenced by Pentonville's radial layout.

The galleried interior of one of Wakefield's cell wings.

PRISON QUARRIES, PORTLAND. (Copyright.)

From 1848, up to a thousand convicts extracted and dressed stone at the public-works quarries at Portland. Between 1849 and 1872, 6 million tons of the stone were used to create a breakwater for Portland harbour.

increasing numbers now needing prison accommodation, a further public-works prison was opened on St Mary's Island at Chatham.

YOUNG OFFENDERS

Prior to the 1850s, children who broke the law were subject to exactly the same penalties as adults, including execution, transportation and flogging. Some typical examples of Old Bailey sentencing were proffered by a schoolmaster who had spent eight months in Newgate. One boy, aged no more than 13 and not a known offender, was to be transported for life for stealing his companion's hat while at a puppet show. The unfortunate child said that he had knocked the hat off in fun, and that someone else must have picked it up. Other boys of a similar age were sentenced to death for petty offences:

> I have had five in one session in this awful situation; one for stealing a comb almost valueless, two for a child's sixpenny story-book, another for a man's stock, and the fifth for pawning his mother's shawl.[143]

An early attempt to deal with young offenders came in 1838 when a former military hospital at Parkhurst on the Isle of Wight was converted for use as a juvenile penitentiary. It aimed to provide under-18s who had been sentenced to transportation with a preparatory period of discipline, education and training in a useful trade. Each boy's progress at Parkhurst would determine whether he would be transported as a free emigrant, with a conditional pardon or to be detained on arrival. The Parkhurst regime was extremely strict and included a prison uniform, leg irons, silence on all occasions of instruction and duty, constant surveillance by officers and 'a diet reduced to its minimum'.[144] The original dietary, with breakfasts and suppers largely consisting of oatmeal, led to numerous health problems such as skin eruptions. A revised dietary, issued in 1843, included bread and cocoa for breakfast, bread and gruel for supper, and dinners of bread and potatoes accompanied by either mutton or beef and vegetable soup.[145] The conduct of Parkhurst boys after arrival in Australia did not live up to expectations and in 1863 Parkhurst was turned over for use as a women's convict prison.

A completely new approach to the treatment of young offenders came in the Reformatory School Act of 1854, which enabled courts to place under-16s for a period of two to five years in reformatory schools that had been certified by the Inspectors of Prisons.

The 1857 Industrial Schools Act provided for children aged 7 to 15 and convicted of vagrancy to be placed in a broadly similar type of establishment known as an industrial school. From 1861, unruly children from workhouses or pauper schools could also be sent to industrial schools, so long as they had not been previously convicted of a felony.

Most reformatories and industrial schools were privately run, often by religious groups, although a few, such as the Feltham Industrial School, were operated by public authorities. Boys at Feltham were taught trades such as carpentry, bricklaying, tailoring and shoemaking – all the boys' clothes and boots were made at the school.[146] They also worked on the school's own farm

Tothill Fields prison, the Middlesex House of Correction for women and juveniles in the late 1850s. Henry Mayhew, observing the boys exercising, could 'tell by their shuffling noise and limping gate, how little used many of them had been to such a luxury as shoe leather'. The majority of the boys were imprisoned for pickpocketing or other petty thieving.

which was cultivated entirely by manual labour. The school was run very much along military lines and had a rigged ship fitted out for performing drill and naval exercises.

The schools were not always successful and some closed within a few years. A reformatory opened in 1856 by the monks of St Bernard's Abbey at Whitwick in Leicestershire took up to 250 delinquent Roman Catholic boys and was run with the help of lay assistants. However, the staff were unable to control their charges. There were several riots, and in 1878 sixty boys escaped after attacking the master in charge with knives stolen from the dining room. The establishment closed in 1881 after its certification was withdrawn.

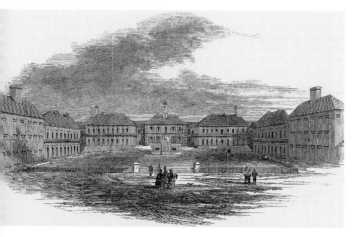

A general view of Parkhurst juvenile prison in 1847 with some of the longer established inmates engaged in 'spade husbandry'. For their first few months, new arrivals spent nineteen hours a day alone in cells measuring 11ft by 7ft, leaving only for exercise, cleaning, chapel and school. Misbehaviour could result in a spell inside a 'dark cell'.

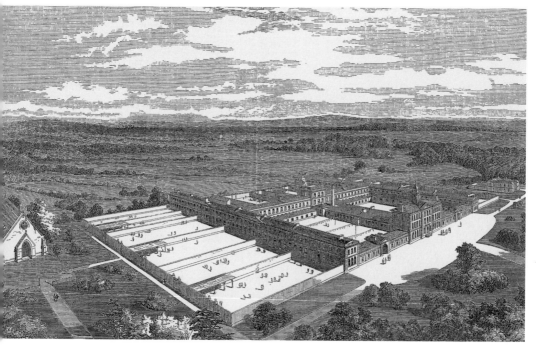

The Middlesex Industrial School was established in 1854 by a private Act of Parliament and was the first institution of its type. Its new premises, erected on a 100-acre site at Feltham in Middlesex, could hold up to 700 boys aged seven to thirteen.

nine

Changes in Prison Food 1800 – 1860s

By the start of the nineteenth century, the majority of prisoners were being provided with at least some food by their prison. However, up to the formation of the national prison system in 1877, the food that a particular prisoner might receive often depended on an elaborate and often almost impenetrable combination of factors. These included the nature of the institution and its management, the prisoner's offence, the stage of his progress through the legal process, his state of health, whether he was performing certain types of labour within the prison, and the governor's interpretation of phrases such as 'coarse but wholesome food' which appeared in national prison legislation. Even in the same prison, inmates in apparently similar situations could receive very different rations – something that often led to great discontent.

COMPLEXITIES AT COLDBATH FIELDS

A good example of these dietary intricacies was provided in 1800 by a Royal Commission investigating the recently rebuilt Coldbath Fields prison at Clerkenwell. The prison's dietary then comprised:

> on One Day about Eight Ounces of meat, which, by boiling, is reduced to about Six Ounces; and the Day following, the Prisoners have the Broth produced by that Meat; and so alternately from Day to Day, One Pound of Bread Daily. Besides this Allowance, there are about Fifty Prisoners who have Water Gruel, by Order of the Doctor.[147]

However, the majority of Coldbath prisoners did not actually receive this supposedly standard allowance. More than half the inmates were being held under the 1779 Transportation Act which demanded that they be 'fed and sustained with Bread, and any coarse Meat, or other inferior Food, and Water, or small Beer', at public expense and were not to have 'any other Food [or] Drink'. Those at the prison in its role as a house of correction, and given hard labour, were required 'to be sustained with Bread, and any coarse, but wholesome Food and Water'; those not doing hard labour were to be maintained by the county with up to half of any of their earnings taken as a contribution towards their food. Inmates awaiting trial and those held as 'idle apprentices' received only the basic bread ration of 1lb per day, although one apprentice who had been further convicted on a charge of aggravated assault was then eligible to the full meat allowance. Two convicted women in the 'disorderly' section received the full allowance while a third, yet to be tried, was given just bread. Women working in the prison laundry received a double allowance of bread and a pint of porter (dark beer) each day.

The best-fed inmates at Coldbath Fields turned out to be a group of sailors imprisoned after joining a mutiny at the Nore (an anchorage on the Thames estuary) in 1797. The mutineers had a daily ration of 1½lb of bread, 6oz of meat, rice soup on alternate days, a 'warm breakfast' and a pint of porter with permission to buy a further pint if they had money. This generous treatment was at the direction of the prison surgeon who saw it as a protection against the scurvy to which seamen were well known to be disposed.

Not surprisingly, many Coldbath Fields prisoners complained about their food. A common grievance was of portions being underweight. Enquiries by the commissioners revealed that loaves were sometimes underweight, but also often overweight. The inconsistency appeared to be due to loaves sticking together during baking and then being unevenly separated. An unpleasant taste in the bread was also reported by some prisoners. The baker said this arose from the present necessity of using a proportion of imported wheat which sometimes acquired a disagreeable flavour when it became too warm during its sea voyage. Another prisoner stated that he had occasionally been served with tainted meat during hot weather. The prison's butcher explained that this was probably because he was obliged to slaughter meat on Friday but not send it to the prison until the following Monday. The timing of the prison meals caused objection from some prisoners. Being served their bread at 8 a.m. and their meat or soup at noon, they were effectively forced to fast for up to eighteen hours. The commissioners suggested that 'as the lower classes accustom themselves to eat frequently', a later hour for serving the dinner meal would benefit the health of those serving long sentences. One 'very healthy looking' young inmate protested about a lack of food. This, it transpired, was because he had opted to have his food supplied by his mother who brought him provisions twice a week. However, he always ended up eating his three days' supply on the day that it was delivered and then had to rely on the daily 1lb ration of the 'prison loaf' until his mother's next appearance.

PROBLEMS BREWING

Compared to Coldbath Fields, the dietary for crown prisoners at Lancaster County Gaol in 1812 was relatively straightforward. It consisted of 1lb of bread and a penny's worth of butter per day, supplemented by a weekly ration of 2½lb of oatmeal and 10lb of potatoes. On Sundays there was an extra ration of ½lb of boiled beef and a quart of broth. Debtors received a county allowance of a shilling's worth of bread, although when bread prices were high this was supplemented by potatoes. As was the usual practice at this time, those who were able could buy extras to add to the prison issue. The purchase of tea and coffee, however, was denied to female inmates – a matter that caused some complaint. The women, it appeared, were so partial to a daily brew that they had been selling their bread allowance in order to buy supplies and had consequently fallen into a bad state of health.[148]

For prisoners at the Fleet, the quality of their beer was a regular concern. One inmate, Philip Maine, described it as 'flat, thick, and weak, and bad in general'. Another prisoner, James Newham, was deputed by the other Fleet prisoners to complain about 'the unwholesomeness of the beer' which he said produced 'a violent fermentation in my bowels and other injurious effects'. The suppliers, a local brewery company Messrs Barclay, Perkins & Co., were baffled by the complaints and implied that the fault lay with the prison's keeper of the cellar-head who supervised the storage of the beer.

NEWGATE

By 1818, Newgate had decided that prisoners cooking their own food resulted in too much filth and had ended the practice, although inmates could still use the prison's own potato steamer.[149] The prison dietary allowance, formerly a daily pound of bread plus a twice-weekly pound of beef, was revised, with the food now being prepared by an employed cook in the prison kitchen. The new dietary comprised a pint of gruel for breakfast and a dinner which alternated between 6oz (cooked weight) of beef and a quart of soup prepared from the previous day's meat liquor with barley and vegetables added. Members of a Parliamentary Select Committee tasted the bread, soup and gruel and pronounced them good. The bread, baked at the Giltspur Street Compter, was held to be particularly good and wholesome. Nonetheless, complaints from prisoners about the bread led the Select Committee to interview the baker, George Anderson.[150] One particularly leaden batch had, claimed Anderson, been due to substandard yeast supplied by a brewer. Other problems were blamed on defective flour, some of which had been 'damaged' while being ground in the prison's own mill. He also revealed that the bread had formerly been baked in large tin pans, sixteen loaves to a pan, but since his oven's brick bottom had been replaced by proper baker's tiles he could now place the bread there directly.

LOCAL VARIATIONS

One of the most progressive local prison dietaries recorded by the 1818 Select Committee was that in use at the Maidstone House of Correction. It had resulted from experiments in adjusting the diet and ventilation in the prison following an outbreak of typhus fever there. It included variations for prisoners with and without hard labour, the former receiving a weekly serving of suet pudding – an early appearance of what was later to become a staple of prison menus:

Prisoners engaged in labour	Sunday and Wednesday: 1lb bread, ½lb beef, 1lb potatoes. Monday: 1lb bread, 1 pint ox-head soup, 1lb potatoes. Tuesday and Thursday: 1lb bread, ½lb oatmeal, 2lbs potatoes. Friday: 1lb bread, 1 pint of soup. Saturday: 1lb bread, 1lb of suet pudding.
For prisoners not engaged in labour	Sunday: 1lb bread, ½lb beef, 1 pound of potatoes. Wednesday: 1 pint of soup. Other days: 1½lbs of bread per day.

After 1835, the new prison inspectorate discovered that diets varied widely, even for similar types of establishment. At Grantham's House of Correction in 1836, the weekly rations comprised just 48½oz of bread and 16oz of meat, while at Haverfordwest the inmates received a massive 288oz of bread, 24½oz of cheese, 21 pints of gruel and 21 pints of milk pottage.[151]

Even plainer than Grantham's was the dietary at Derby County Gaol. Here, the inmates' breakfast and supper each day consisted of a quart of gruel, made with a meagre 2oz of oatmeal, plus a portion of bread. Dinner, every day, comprised 1lb of boiled potatoes and a portion of bread. The total bread allowance each day was 24oz of 'good wheaten bread' and there was a daily ration of ¼oz salt. Those imprisoned for more than three months received an additional 2oz of onions a day (or, when onions could not be procured, a red herring was substituted every second day). The prison's surgeon justified the absence of meat from the diet by his view that 'the agricultural labourer in Derbyshire has cheese and a little bacon, but butcher's meat seldom forms a portion of his food'.[152]

At York County Gaol prisoners received a weekly ration of 10lb of bread plus an allowance of a shilling to spend as each inmate wished. The inspectors' criticism of this 'improper and inconvenient' practice resulted, by the time of their next report in 1839, in the introduction of a new dietary (below). Seventeen of the week's twenty-one meals comprised oatmeal pottage and bread, with meat featuring in the remaining four:

	Breakfast and Supper	Dinner
Sunday, Tuesday	1 quart oatmeal pottage, ½lb bread	1 quart stew of heads and shins, &c., with ½lb potatoes, ½lb bread.
Monday, Wednesday, Saturday	Same	1 quart oatmeal pottage, ½lb bread; or occasionally, ½lb boiled rice, made from 4oz in a raw state, seasoned with a small quantity of allspice, and ½lb bread.
Thursday	Same	5oz beef without bone, after boiling, 1lb potatoes, ½lb bread.
Friday	Same	1 quart broth from the beef of yesterday, &c.; ½lb bread, with leeks or onions, and ¼oz oatmeal for each prisoner.
	1oz salt per week for each prisoner.	

Across the Pennines, at Lancaster County Gaol, prisoners on hard labour received the same breakfast and supper as at York, but enjoyed a somewhat more varied dinner menu with around five times the allowance of beef, and potatoes served almost every day.

Sunday	1 quart stew made from cows' shins, one shin to every 14 prisoners.
Monday	½lb beef, boiled, and potatoes.
Tuesday	1 quart rice soup, and potatoes.
Wednesday	½lb beef, boiled, and potatoes.
Thursday	1 quart peas soup, and potatoes.
Friday	½lb beef, made into scouce [scouse].
Saturday	Potatoes and cheese.
	3½oz salt per week for each prisoner.

Of the 153 dietaries examined by the prison inspectors in 1836, just over half served meat, usually in the form of beef, with occasional instances of mutton or bacon. Ox heads were often used in soup recipes. Cheese was included in twenty-eight dietaries, mostly in agricultural areas in northern England and the south Midlands. Beer appeared on the regular menu at only five prisons, although at some of the others it could be bought or was provided as a perk to wardsmen. Tea and coffee featured rarely, usually at prisons where they were given to very short term prisoners. Inmates at the Gloucester County Gaol and Penitentiary were unique in receiving a daily pint-and-a-half of mint infused in (presumably hot) water.[153]

At the other end of the country, the Exeter Gaol and House of Correction prescribed three dietaries in their 1841 regulations. Dietary No 1, the most generous, was given to prisoners awaiting trial, to those who were condemned, sentenced to transportation or hard labour, or to females nursing their children. The smaller rations of Dietary No 2 were given to those serving a sentence without hard labour. Dietary No 3, the lowest scale, was reserved for vagrants. The allowances for each of the Exeter dietaries are shown below:

Dietary	Males	Females
No. 1	22oz bread and 1½lb potatoes daily; 1lb bacon per week	16oz bread and 1lb potatoes daily; 1lb bacon per week
No. 2	16oz bread and 1½lb potatoes daily; 1lb bacon per week	Same as No.1
No. 3 (1st imprisonment)	22oz bread and 1½lb potatoes daily	16oz bread and 1lb potatoes daily
No. 3 (2nd and subsequent imprisonments)	22oz bread daily	16oz bread daily

Most prisons by now had separate arrangements for debtors, who either maintained themselves or, if they could not afford to do so, lived on the daily 'county allowance' – typically 1lb of bread and 1½lb of potatoes. This was sometimes supplemented by charitably funded contribution – at Lancaster it included a weekly provision of four red herrings and 1lb of rice. Lancaster's debtor inmates, as elsewhere, were noted as being a particular nuisance. Despite rules to the contrary, they invariably demanded garnish from new arrivals. They were also each allowed to introduce up to a quart of beer a day into the prison, which was often 'sold' at twice its value on an internal black market conducted in one of the prison rooms which acted as an informal tavern. It was observed that the allowance of those not requiring or unable to pay for beer was always taken up by those involved in this enterprise.[154]

More shady dealings were revealed by the prison inspectors' 1837 report on London's Giltspur Street. Here, it was discovered that wardsmen – convicted prisoners appointed in each ward to help maintain order and cleanliness – were making an income by illicitly selling goods such as coffee, sugar, butter, raw bacon, eggs, flour and beer. One wardsman's account book recorded that he had sold one prisoner 12½ pints of beer in a single day.

EARLY RECIPES

As well as the dietaries, official reports sometimes included recipes, or at least ingredient lists, for dishes on prison menus. At Maidstone in 1818, soup and suet pudding were on offer:

> Receipt for soup for eighty persons:— 2 bullock's heads, 14 bushels of potatoes, 6lbs of whole rice, 1½ gallons of pea-flour, onions, leeks, pepper, and salt.
>
> Suet-pudding for eighty persons:—8 gallons of flour, 8lbs of suet.

At Wakefield House of Correction in 1842, the gruel was enlivened by a pinch of spice while the dinner menu included scouse and onion porridge.[155]

> **Gruel** — four ounces of oatmeal to each quart, seasoned with ground ginger or allspice.
>
> **Scouse** — one pint and a half made from four ounces of beef, cut off from the bone, one pound and a half of potatoes, and a proportionate quantity of pepper, salt, onions and vegetables.
>
> **Broth** — to be made from the bones of the preceding day's beef, together with one ox-head, to every fifty prisoners, thickened with one ounce of oatmeal to each pint, and a proportionate amount of salt, herbs, and pepper.
>
> **Soup** — stewed from the preceding day's bones, broken small, along with four ounces of peas, pearl or Scotch barley, to each pint, seasoned with herbs, salt and pepper.
>
> **Onion porridge** — two ounces of oatmeal and a proportionate quantity of onions to each pint and a half.

DIETARY STANDARDISATION

The prison inspectors' investigations of the nation's local prisons soon made it apparent that reforms were urgently needed. In 1842, under the direction of Home Secretary Sir James Graham, a comprehensive review was launched. One particular focus for the inspectors' inquiry was the subject of prison dietaries and how these varied in relation to the prisoners' age, sex, length of sentence, imposition of hard labour and so on.

Their report, in 1843, proposed a scheme in which prisoners were allocated to one of ten dietary classes according to the length of their sentence, whether it included hard labour, etc. The guiding principle behind the dietaries was that the quantity of food provided should be 'sufficient, and not more than sufficient, to maintain health and strength, at the least possible cost'. The inspectors were clear, however, that 'diet ought not to be made an instrument of punishment'.[156] Within these constraints, it was recommended that prisoners should always receive three meals a day, of which at least two should be hot, that a considerable portion of the food should be solid, and there should be occasional variety. For prisoners employed at hard labour, 'animal food' (i.e. meat) was required to form part of the diet. The proposed minimum rations for each dietary class are listed in the tables below:

CLASS 1 — Prisoners confined for any term not exceeding three days.		
	Males	Females
Breakfast/Supper	1 pint oatmeal gruel.	1 pint oatmeal gruel.
Dinner	1lb bread.	1lb bread.

CLASS 2 — Convicted prisoners for any term exceeding three days, and not exceeding fourteen days.

	Males	Females
Breakfast/Supper	1 pint oatmeal gruel, 6oz bread.	1 pint oatmeal gruel, 6oz bread.
Dinner	12oz bread.	6oz bread.

Prisoners of this Class employed at hard labour to have, in addition, one pint of soup per week.

CLASS 3 — Prisoners employed at hard labour for terms between fourteen days and six weeks.

	Males	Females
Breakfast/Supper	1 pint oatmeal gruel, 8oz bread.	1 pint oatmeal gruel, 6oz bread.
Dinner—		
Sun, Thu.	1 pint soup, 8oz bread.	1 pint soup, 6oz bread.
Tue, Sat.	3oz cooked meat without bone, 8oz bread, ½lb potatoes.	3oz cooked meat without bone, 6oz bread, ½lb potatoes.
Mon, Wed, Fri.	8oz bread, 1lb potatoes, or 1 pint gruel when potatoes cannot be obtained.	6oz bread, 1lb potatoes, or 1 pint gruel when potatoes cannot be obtained.

CLASS 4 — Prisoners employed at hard labour for terms between six weeks and three months.

	Males	Females
Breakfast/Supper	1 pint oatmeal gruel, 8oz bread.	1 pint oatmeal gruel, 6oz bread.
Dinner—		
Sun, Tue, Thu, Sat.	3oz cooked meat without bone, ½lb potatoes, 8oz bread.	3oz cooked meat without bone, ½lb potatoes, 6oz bread.
Mon, Wed, Fri.	1 pint soup, 8oz bread.	1 pint soup, 6oz bread.

CLASS 5 — Prisoners employed at hard labour for terms exceeding three months.		
	Males	Females
Breakfast— Sun, Tue, Thu, Sat.	1 pint oatmeal gruel, 6oz bread.	1 pint oatmeal gruel, 6oz bread.
Dinner	4oz cooked meat without bone, 1lb potatoes, 6oz bread.	3oz cooked meat without bone, ½lb potatoes, 6oz bread.
Breakfast— Mon, Wed, Fri.	1 pint cocoa, made of ¾oz flaked cocoa or cocoa nibs, sweetened with ¾oz molasses or sugar. 6oz bread.	1 pint cocoa, made of ¾oz flaked cocoa or cocoa nibs, sweetened with ¾oz molasses or sugar. 6oz bread.
Dinner	1 pint soup, 1lb potatoes, 6oz bread.	1 pint soup, ½lb potatoes, 6oz bread.
Supper, all days.	1 pint oatmeal gruel, 6oz bread.	1 pint oatmeal gruel, 6oz bread.

CLASS 6 — Convicted Prisoners not employed at hard labour for periods exceeding 14 days.		
	Males	Females
Breakfast/Supper	1 pint oatmeal gruel, 8oz bread.	1 pint oatmeal gruel, 6oz bread.
Dinner— Sun, Tue, Thu, Sat.	3oz cooked meat without bone, ½lb potatoes, 8oz bread.	3oz cooked meat without bone, ½lb potatoes, 6oz bread.
Mon, Wed, Fri.	1 pint soup, 8oz bread.	1 pint soup, 6oz bread.

CLASS 7 — Prisoners sentenced by Court to solitary confinement — As Class 6.
CLASS 8 — Prisoners for examination, before Trial, Misdemeanants of 1st Division — As Class 4.
CLASS 9 — Destitute Debtors — As Class 4.

CLASS 10

Prisoners under punishment for Prison Offences, for terms up to three days: 1lb of bread per diem. Prisoners in close confinement for Prison Offences under the 42nd section of the Gaol Act:

	Males	Females
Breakfast/Supper	1 pint of oatmeal gruel, 8oz of bread.	1 pint of oatmeal gruel, 6oz of bread.
Dinner	8oz of bread.	6oz of bread.

A suggested recipe was also provided for the prisoners' soup:

The soup to contain, per pint, 3oz of cooked meat without bone, 3oz of potatoes, 1 ounce of barley, rice, or oatmeal and 1 ounce of onions or leeks, with pepper and salt. The gruel, when made in quantities exceeding fifty pints, to contain 1½ ounce of oatmeal per pint, and 2oz per pint when made in less quantities. The gruel, on alternate days, to be sweetened with ¾ ounce of molasses or sugar, and seasoned with salt.

One somewhat unexpected item that appeared in the new scheme was the cocoa provided to Class 5 prisoners – those serving long sentences with hard labour. Its introduction, without apparent comment, in three of the weekly breakfasts was perhaps intended to add both variety to the menu and also extra nutrient through its fat content.

Although the new dietaries were not imposed on prisons, magistrates were strongly encouraged by Sir James Graham to adopt them in their local establishments.

THE NUTRITIONAL VALUE OF VICTORIAN PRISON DIETS

In the 1850s, the science of nutrition was still in its infancy. Diets were largely judged in terms of the weights of the solid food they provided, even though the widely differing water content of, say, potatoes (around 75 per cent) and bread (35 per cent) made such comparisons misleading. The body's use of different types of food was also little comprehended. However, the study of prison diets was to lead to some of the most significant advances in nutritional understanding.

The problem of scurvy, which frequently afflicted long-term prisoners as well as seafarers, was still not understood. Although the remedial effects of lime and lemon juice had been known since the sixteenth century, exactly why these were effective was still a mystery. It was also not widely appreciated that protection against scurvy was provided by the inclusion of other fruit or vegetables in the diet, as the disastrous effect of removing potatoes from the Millbank dietary had shown in 1822. That eating raw potatoes could protect against scurvy just as well as citrus fruits had been recognised by the 1780s[157] but was apparently little known outside nautical circles. In 1842, physician William Dalton recalled a sea voyage he had taken in the 1820s where the sailors had been provided with 'scurvy grass' – raw potatoes, peeled and sliced like cucumber, and served with vinegar. Not a single case of scurvy was reported on the expedition which lasted almost three years.[158] The fact that cooked potatoes could be equally effective was reported in 1843 by William Baly, medical officer at Millbank, who noted that scurvy only occurred amongst military prisoners and never amongst the convict population. The only significant difference between the two groups was that the military prisoners did not receive cooked potatoes in their diet – once this was changed, no further cases of scurvy developed. Baly also analysed data from local prisons and found that an absence of potatoes or other vegetables from the diet was linked with the appearance of scurvy.[159]

Even when the value of other vegetables in preventing scurvy came to be realised, their addition to the diet was not always appreciated by the prisoners. An attempt to introduce onions and lettuces onto the menu at Portland had to be abandoned after some of the men threw them from their cells into the corridor in disgust.[160]

One area where prison studies significantly contributed to nutritional knowledge was in the roles played by carbohydrates and proteins in the diet. In 1842, Baron Justus von Liebig – a German-born chemist of some repute – published his influential work *Animal Chemistry*. The book claimed that protein was the only true nutrient and the primary source of the body's energy, while fats and carbohydrates had a fairly minor role, for example in maintaining the body's temperature. Disciples of Liebig's theory interpreted any dietary-related disorder as being caused by a lack of protein. An outbreak of scurvy at a prison in Perth in 1846 was thus diagnosed – despite William Baly's results – as resulting from a protein deficiency.[161]

A challenge to Liebig's views eventually came from Edward Smith, a London hospital physician who was not afraid of getting his hands dirty in his quest for scientific data. His early researches, carried out on himself and convicts at Coldbath Fields prison, measured the carbon dioxide produced during exercise and rest. Later, for a period of more than two years – even during his seaside holidays – Smith collected and measured his own daily faeces and urine production, the latter being analysed with particular respect to its content of nitrogen-containing urea. Another study involved a three-week long investigation of the waste products of four Coldbath Fields convicts who worked the tread-wheel three days a week. From his experiments, Smith concluded that exercise led to increased production of carbon dioxide, but not to any change in the excretion of urea. Contrary to Liebig's theory, Smith found that urea production was related to the amount of protein in the diet. Thus, it was carbohydrates rather than proteins that that were the body's primary source of muscular energy.[162]

Smith also questioned the whole rationale for standard dietaries, as the labour given to convicts in different establishments was so varied. His analysis of the 1843 recommended dietaries led him to conclude that the food was seriously inadequate, with a carbon content for Class 1 prisoners amounting to as little as one third of what was nutritionally required to perform tread-wheel labour. Even the diet given to Class 5 prisoners provided only three fifths of the daily requirements for the tread-wheel.[163] In Class 2, the concession to those performing hard labour of a single pint of soup per week he described as 'manifestly ridiculous'.[164]

A contrary view – that prisoners were generally overfed – was voiced by William Guy, Medical Superintendent at Millbank from 1859. In a comparison of the food served in workhouses and prisons, Guy noted that even Millbank's Penal Class dietary (280oz of solid food and 10½ pints of liquid per week) compared favourably with the most generous workhouse dietary (187½oz solids and 12 pints liquid) provided to able-bodied male paupers.[165] A Royal Commission on Penal Servitude in 1863 noted that paupers in some workhouses received only 4oz of meat per week, while a convict on public works received 39oz as well as a daily ration of 27oz of bread and 16oz of vegetables.

Vegetarians and vegans may appreciate one further contribution from the prison system to nutritional knowledge. Based on reports from the Devizes House of Correction and Stafford Gaol, where prisoners had been given only bread, potatoes and gruel for up to eighteen months with no ill effects, William Guy concluded that neither meat, nor any other animal-derived nutrient, was essential to a healthy diet.[166]

The exercise yard and tread-wheel at the Coldbath Fields House of Correction. The tread-wheel was invented in 1819 by engineer William Cubitt. Odd and even-numbered slots alternated fifteen minutes of wheel exercise with fifteen minutes of rest or reading. In the course of a day, the distance climbed by a prisoner could be equivalent to the height of Mount Kilimanjaro. From 1843, use of the tread-wheel was restricted to males over the age of 14, with a maximum ascent of 12,000 feet.

ten

The Victorian Prison Kitchen

In 1862, the Victorian journalist and social researcher Henry Mayhew, in collaboration with John Binny, published *The Criminal Prisons of London*, an extensive survey of the capital's prisons based on first-hand visits to each establishment compiled over the previous six years or so. Unlike official reports, Mayhew's descriptions convey the colours, smells and sounds of prison life. His visit to the kitchens at Coldbath Fields prison was typical:

> The kitchen, where the daily food of the 1,300 inhabitants of Coldbath Fields prison is cooked, is as large and lofty as a barn, so that despite the heat required for the culinary purposes, the air is cool, and even the panes in the sky-lights let into the slanting wood roof, are free from condensed vapour. Everything is cooked by steam, and the whole place seems to be conducted on the gigantic scale of an American boarding-house; for there is but one pot to be seen, and that holds at least ten gallons. The different articles of food are being prepared for the prisoners' dinners in the immense square iron tanks — for they are more like cisterns than boilers — ranged against the wall. In one, with the bright copper-lid, which is so heavy that it has to be raised by means of an equipoise, are 100 gallons of cocoa, the red-brown scum on the top heaving and sinking with the heat; in another are suspended hampers of potatoes; whilst other compartments contain 150 gallons of what, from the 'eyes' of grease glittering on the surface, you guess to be soup, or which, from its viscid, pasty appearance, you know to be the prison gruel.
>
> It takes two cooks three hours and a half merely to weigh out the rations required for this enormous establishment. One of these stands beside a mass — high as a truss of hay — of slices of boiled meat, and, with extraordinary rapidity, places pieces of the pale lean and the yellow fat in the scales, until the six-ounce weight moves. The other is occupied with the potatoes, dividing the hamper filled with the steaming, brown-skinned vegetables into portions of eight ounces each. The sight of such immense quantities of provisions, and the peculiar smell given off from the cooling of boiled meats, has rather a sickening effect upon anyone, like ourselves, not hungry at the time. All the soup is made out of bullocks' heads; and in the larder, hanging to hooks against the slate-covered wall, we beheld several of these suspended by the lips, and looking fearfully horrible, with the white bones showing through the crimson flesh, so that the sight called up in our mind our youthful fancies of what we had imagined to be the character of Bluebeard's closet. A curious use is made of the jaw-bones of these bullocks' heads. After the flesh and all its 'goodness' has been boiled from it, the 'maxilla inferior,' as doctors call it, is used to form ornamental borders to the gravel walks in the grounds, in the same way as oyster-shells are sometimes turned to account in the nine-feet-by-six gardens in the suburbs.

At Holloway prison, the kitchen was located in the basement of 'D' wing:

There are six large boilers in the kitchen with copper lids—each of them having a steam pipe communicating with a large boiler in an adjoining recess. One boiler contained a large quantity of broth, with huge pieces of beef. The cook uplifted several of them on a large fork: they appeared to be of excellent quality. They were carried away by one of the prisoners in attendance, to be cut up into small portions to be put into the dining tins, and distributed to the various prisoners in the different cells. Another boiler contained a large quantity of potatoes which had just been cooked. They were York Regents of an excellent quality. A different boiler contained an enormous quantity of gruel, made of the best Scotch oatmeal, to be served out for supper in the evening. It was filled to the brim, with a white creamy paste mantling on the surface.

THE BAKERY

The staple of all prison diets was bread. Although some prisons, such as Holloway, bought in their bread, many larger prisons had their own bakery. The portions of bread specified by the dietary could be produced either by cutting up large loaves or by baking individual loaves of the required weight. At Pentonville, Mayhew descended a spiral staircase into the basement:

The kitchens at Holloway, showing some of its six steam-heated boilers. Off the kitchen were a cutting-up room, where cooked food was placed in metal pannikins before distribution, and a scullery, where the used tins were washed in two large sinks.

and knew, by the peculiar smell of bread pervading the place, that we had entered the bakery. There was but little distinctive about this part of the prison; for we found the same heap of dusty white-looking sacks, and the same lot of men, with the flour, like hair-powder, clinging to their eyebrows and whiskers (four of these were prisoners, and the other a free man – 'the master baker' placed over them), as usually characterises such a place. Here we learnt that the bread of the prison was unfermented, owing to the impossibility of working 'the sponge' there during the night; and of course we were invited to taste a bit. It was really what would have been considered 'cake' in some continental states; indeed, a German servant, to whom we gave a piece of the prison loaf, assured us that the 'König von Preussen' himself hardly ate better stuff … 'Yonder are some of the ten-ounce loaves, that are just going to be served out for breakfast,' added the cook; and, as he said the words, he pointed to a slab of miniature half-quarterns, that looked not unlike a block of small paving-stones cemented together.

At Brixton Female Prison, the working of the fermenting dough or 'sponge' presented an almost lyrical scene:

The bakery was a pleasant and large light building, adjoining the kitchen, and here we found more females, in light blue gowns, at work on the large dresser, with an immense heap of dough that lay before them like a huge drab-coloured feather-bed, and with the master baker in his flannel jacket standing beside the oven watching the work. Some of the female prisoners were working the dough, that yielded to their pressure like an air-cushion; and some were cutting off pieces and weighing them in the scales before them, and then tossing them over to others, who moulded them into the form of dumplings, or small loaves.

At Wandsworth prison, mechanisation had been introduced to the bakery which was equipped with two nine-bushel ovens made by the firm of Thomas Powell of Lisle Street, Leicester Square, London. The baker, Mr Claridge, described the bread-making process:

I have four men assisting me in the bakehouse. We commence to work at six o'clock in the morning, when we put in the sponge with one of Stevens' patent dough-making machines. At seven o'clock the assistant bakers (prisoners) leave the bakehouse to attend chapel. On their return they clean and prepare the bread. After breakfast, the bread prepared on the previous day is put into a basket ready for delivery to the storekeeper at ten o'clock, and carefully weighed.

The dough after lying an hour is thrown out by the machine and weighed off to be made into the several loaves. The loaves are baked three-quarters of an hour. We generally have about four batches. The ovens hold about 1200 of the six ounce, and about 1000 of the eight ounce loaves. We finish work about half-past five, when the prisoners who officiate as assistant bakers are taken back to their different cells.

The bread remains in the bakehouse for the night, and is delivered to the storekeeper in the morning, as before stated. The bread is brown, of a coarse but wholesome quality. In addition to this we prepare some of finer flour for the infirmary.

PRISON COOKS

At Holloway, where bread was bought in, the cook outlined the kitchen's working day:

The fire is generally lit about three o'clock in the morning by one of the night watchmen, when the steam is got up to prepare the gruel or cocoa, served up for breakfast on alternate days.

'I begin my duties,' said the cook, 'at seven o'clock in the morning, when the gruel and cocoa is served up with bread to the different corridors; sometimes cocoa and bread, at other times gruel and bread. The butcher in general arrives about ten o'clock, when we prepare for dinner, consisting of meat and potatoes, or soup and potatoes, which are served up at one o'clock to all the branches of the prison.

'The gruel for supper is prepared at an early period of the day, generally at dinner-time, and stands in the copper for several hours. By this means it becomes thicker, and its qualities are improved, and besides it economizes our fuel. The bread is cut and weighed out, to be served up with the gruel for the prisoners' supper, which ends the ordinary operations of the day.'

Keeping track of all the different dietaries and the daily numbers required of each one, not to mention all the 'extras' required by sick prisoners, was not a trivial task. The cook at Pentonville had devised his own method, as Mayhew observed:

'Yes, sir, that's my slate,' added the man, as he saw us looking up at a long black board that was nailed against the wall in the serving-room, and inscribed with the letters and figures of the several wards of the prison, together with various hieroglyphics that needed the cook himself to interpret. 'On that board I chalk up,' he proceded, 'the number of prisoners in each ward, so as to know what rations I have to serve. The letter K there, underneath the figures, signifies that one man out of that particular ward is at work in the kitchen, and B, that one prisoner is employed in the bakehouse. That mark up there stands for an extra loaf to be sent up to the ward it's placed under, and these dots here for two extra meats; whilst yonder sign is to tell me that there is one man out of that part of the building gone into the infirmary. Yes, sir, we let the infirmary prisoners have just whatever the medical officer pleases to order – jelly, or fish, or indeed chicken if required.'

PRISON DINING

At Coldbath Fields, dinner was eaten communally at 2 p.m. each day in large sheds where a little light reading was provided to occupy the inmates after they had eaten:

Big tubs, filled with thick gruel, had been carried into the dining-sheds, and a pint measure of the limpid paste had been poured into the tin mugs, and this, together with a spoon and the 6 ounces of bread, were ranged down the narrow strips of tables that extend in three rows the whole length of the place. As the clock struck two, the file of prisoners in the yard received an order to 'Halt,' and, after a moment's rest, the word of command was given to take their places at the table. Then the chain moved to the door; and, as each human link entered, he took off his old stocking-like cap, and passing down between the forms reached his seat. The men sat still for a second or two, with the smoking gruel before them, until the order was given to 'Draw up tables!' and instantly the long light 'dressers' were, with a sudden rattle, pulled close to the men. Then the warder, taking off his cap, cried out, 'Pay attention to grace!' and every head was bent down as one of the prisoners repeated these words:— 'Sanctify, we beseech thee, O Lord, these thy good things to our use, and us to thy service, through the grace of Jesus Christ.' A shout of 'Amen!' followed, and directly afterwards the tinkling of the spoons against the tin cans was heard, accompanied by the peculiar sound resembling 'sniffing,' that is made by persons eating half-liquid messes with a spoon. Two prisoners, carrying boxes of salt, passed along in front of the tables, from man to man, while each in his turn dipped his spoon in and helped himself. The 'good things,' as the water-gruel and bit of bread are ironically termed in the grace, were soon despatched, and then the men, reaching each little sack of books which had been suspended above their heads from the ceiling, like so many fly-catchers, passed the remainder of their dinner-hour reading.

In the convict prisons, the separate system required that food be distributed from a central kitchen to each individual cell, a task carried out by prisoners under the direction of a warder. Mayhew observed the operation in progress at Brixton:

At a few minutes before one o'clock the 'breads' are counted out into large wicker baskets, while the tin cans being filled with soup and meat on one side, and potatoes on the other, are ranged in large potboy-like trays, which are inscribed with the letters of the several wards to which they appertain.

At one o'clock a bell is heard to ring, and then the matrons of the old prison enter in rotation, each accompanied with four prisoners, one of whom seizes one tray, while two more of the gang go off with another that is heavier laden, and the last hurries off with the basket of bread, with an officer at her heels.

After this, large trucks are brought in, and when stowed with the trays and breadbaskets for the 'wings,' they are wheeled off by the attendant prisoners, one woman dragging in front, and the others pushing behind.

We followed the two trucks that went to the east wing of the prison, and here we found a small crowd of women waiting, with the matrons at the door, ready to receive the trays as the vehicles were unladen. 'That's ours!' cried one of the female officer in attendance; and immediately the prisoners beside her seized the tray with the basket of bread, and went off with it, as if they were so many pot-girls carrying round the beer.

Then a large bell clattered through the building, and one of the warders screamed at the top of her voice, 'O Lord, bless this our food to our use, and us to thy service, through Jesus Christ our Lord. Amen!'

No sooner was the grace ended, than the officers of the several wards went along the galleries, opening each cell-door by the way, with three or four prisoners in their wake, carrying the trays. The cell being opened, the matron handed in the bread from the basket which one of the prisoners carried, and then a can of soup from the tray, the door being closed again immediately afterwards, so that the arcade rang with the unlocking and slamming of the doors in the several galleries. When the dinners were all served, the cell-doors were double locked, and then another bell rang for silence.

A curious part of the process consisted in the distribution of the knives before dinner, and collection of them afterwards. For the latter purpose, one of the best-conducted prisoners goes round with a box, a matron following in her steps, and then the knives, ready cleaned, are put out under the door. These are all counted, and locked up in store for the next day. But if one of the number be short, the prisoners are not let out of their cells till the missing knife be found, each convict and cell being separately searched, with a view to its discovery.

At Millbank, the prison's labyrinthine layout made the distribution process more complex. Three separate kitchens were located around the central hexagon, each serving two of the outer pentagons:

'They are now preparing for breakfast,' said our guide. 'There, you see, are the cans for the cocoa,' pointing to a goodly muster of bright tin vessels, in size and shape like watering-pots, and each marked with the letters of the wards from A to H. On the table were rows of breads, like penny loaves, arranged in rank and file, as it were.

At Holloway, as at a number of other London prisons, the kitchen was located in the basement. At mealtimes, trays of cooked food were lifted to the upper floors by means of a hand-cranked hoist.

'This is the female compartment. Here, you see,' said the officer, pointing to the farther side of a wooden partition that stood at the end of the kitchen, 'is the place where the women enter from pentagon 3, whilst this side is for the men coming from pentagon 4.' Presently the door was opened and files of male prisoners were seen, with warders, without.

'Now, they're coming down to have breakfast served,' said the cook. 'F ward!' cries an officer, and immediately two prisoners enter and run away with a tin can each, while another holds a conical basket and counts bread into it — saying, 6, 12, 18, and so on.

When the males had been all served, and the kitchen was quiet again, the cook said to us, 'Now you'll see the females, sir. Are all the cooks out?' he cried in a loud voice; and when he was assured that the prisoners serving in the kitchen had retired, the principal matron came in at the door on the other side of the partition. Presently she cried out, 'Now, Miss Gardiner, if you please!' Whereupon the matron so named entered, costumed in a gray straw-bonnet and fawn-coloured merino dress, with a jacket of the same material over it, and attended by some two or three female prisoners habited in their loose, dark-brown gowns, check aprons, and close white cap.

The matron then proceeded to serve and count the bread into a basket, and afterwards handed the basket to one of the females near her. 'I wish you people would move quick out of the way there,' says the principal female officer to some of the women who betray a disposition to stare.

Convicts delivering food cans and bread to the cells at an unnamed London prison in around 1900.

While this is going on, another convict enters and goes off with the tin can full of cocoa. Then comes another matron with other prisoners, and so on, till all are served, when the cook says, 'Good morning, Miss Cromwell,' and away the principal matron trips, leaving the kitchen all quiet again — so quiet, indeed, that we hear the sand crunching under the feet.

Almost without exception, the food sampled by Mayhew in London's prison kitchens received his approbation. At Horsemonger Lane, the soup was of 'excellent quality', while that at Holloway was 'very wholesome and palatable'. At Wandsworth, the meat and potatoes were 'of good quality and carefully prepared; superior to what is generally sold in many respectable eating houses in the metropolis'. At Pentonville, the cocoa – 'made with three-quarters of an ounce of the solid flake, and flavoured with two ounces of pure milk and six drachms of molasses' – reached positively gourmet standards. The cocoa beans were freshly ground on the premises by a steam-engine and then brewed with water not from 'the slushy Thames', but which had been raised from the prison's own artesian well several hundred feet below the surface. Whatever the reasons for Mayhew's particularly rosy view of prison cuisine, his reports provide a unique inside view of London's Victorian prisons and their kitchens.

eleven

Towards a National Prison System 1863 – 1878

For many convicts during the 1850s, the hardships of penal servitude became less severe. The initial period of confinement at Pentonville came down to nine months and the wearing of masks by prisoners outside their cells was dropped. The compartmentalised chapel seats became open benches, and segregated exercise yards were replaced by circular tracks. Such relaxations did not, however, meet with universal approval. Much of the criticism was aimed at Joshua Jebb who, in 1850, had become chairman of the Directors of Convict Prisons. An opportunity for Jebb's critics came early in 1863 after London had been subjected to an outbreak of 'garrotting' or violent mugging, which many people blamed on convicts let out of prison under licence. In February 1863, a House of Lords Select Committee was set up under Lord Carnarvon to examine 'the present state of discipline in gaols and houses of correction'.

HARD LABOUR, HARD FARE AND A HARD BED

The Carnarvon Committee's report noted the 'many and wide differences, as regards construction, labour, diet and general discipline' in the country's prisons, which resulted in an 'inequality, uncertainty and inefficiency of punishment'.[167] To rectify this situation, the committee recommended that all prisons should adopt the separate system of confinement. The primary aims of the prison, it believed, were punishment and deterrence, achieved through a regime characterised by 'hard labour, hard fare, and a hard bed'. The interpretation of 'hard labour', it was observed, varied widely and the report proposed that it should be precisely defined using measurable tasks. As well as the tread-wheel, these included shot drill (where a heavy metal ball was raised and lowered in various sequences) and crank turning (where a handle whose stiffness could be adjusted was turned a specified number of times). Prison diets were viewed by the committee as forming part of an inmate's punishment and should be set accordingly. There should be no incentive for workhouse inmates, for example, to commit crimes in order to enjoy a better standard of food in prison. As regards a 'hard bed', the Carnarvon Report recommended that prisoners should spend at least part of their sentence sleeping on planks, with no more than eight hours spent in bed per night. Despite the more severe conditions favoured by the report, it also proposed a system of 'marks' where a prisoner's good conduct and hard work could be rewarded by promotion to a grade demanding less labour and better food.

The Carnarvon Committee's recommendations resulted in the 1865 Prisons Act,[168] which made adoption of the separate system compulsory in all local prisons. It defined two classes of hard labour. The first required male convicts during the first three months of their sentence to work for up to ten hours a day at the tread-wheel, shot drill, crank, capstan or stone-breaking.

The second, less onerous, class of labour was left for local Justices to approve. Exercise, diet and the use of plank beds were also left to local discretion, but all dietaries had to be submitted for central approval. To create consistency of operation, the 1865 Act included a list of 104 regulations for the running of prisons. Finally, the long-standing legal distinction between local gaols and houses of correction was abolished. It was decreed that any prison that was unwilling or unable to adopt the requirements of the Act would have to close or amalgamate with a neighbouring institution. This was a course taken by a number of prisons, especially smaller establishments or those with old buildings where the cost of meeting the new regulations proved prohibitive. Of the 187 prisons operating in 1850, only 126 remained open in 1867.[169]

In parallel with the Carnarvon Committee, a Royal Commission, chaired by Earl Grey, reviewed sentencing policies. The resulting 1864 Penal Servitude Act specified that five years should be the minimum length of a sentence of penal servitude, or seven years for re-offenders. Responding to concerns over the garrotting outbreak, it also introduced stricter supervision of convicts released under licence. The changes necessitated a gradual increase in the provision of public-works prisons, with new ones opening at Borstal in 1874 and Chattenden in 1877.

THE 1864 DIETARIES REPORT

After hearing lengthy – and sometimes contradictory – scientific evidence from Edward Smith and William Guy on matters such as the relationship between adequacy of diet and resulting

A prisoner doing a shift of crank-turning at the Surrey House of Correction, Wandsworth, in around 1860.

changes in body weight, the Carnarvon Committee had felt unable to propose a specific new dietary. Instead, a three-man committee of prison medical officers, chaired by William Guy, was set up to examine Sir James Graham's 1843 dietaries and devise new ones for use in local prisons.

In their report, published in May 1864, the committee concluded that the existing dietaries were 'strangely anomalous and eminently unsatisfactory' – for example, the amounts of bread and potatoes given to female prisoners appeared to bear no consistent relationship to the corresponding allowances received by male inmates.[170] The committee also noted the very wide range of tasks that were provided as 'hard labour'. This had led to significant inequalities in the discrepancies in the dietaries allocated to inmates at different prisons, with some establishments even giving the same dietary to those serving sentences with or without hard labour. The report side-stepped the disagreements between William Guy and Edward Smith on what constituted a sufficient diet by deciding that the available scientific evidence was of 'limited and uncertain practical value'. At the end of the day, it was 'experience' and 'prevailing opinions' that guided the committee's conclusions.[171]

The committee recommended that the diet provided for prisoners should be related to the labour that they actually performed. The basic dietary would therefore provide for those not undertaking hard labour, with various additions allowed where labour was imposed. As before, the report proposed a graded series of dietaries for different lengths of sentence, with prisoners on longer terms eventually being allowed items such as meat and cheese. However, based on advice from various prison authorities, it was now recommended that prisoners sentenced to longer terms of imprisonment should progressively pass through the diets of all the sentences shorter than their own. Women were, as standard, to receive three quarters of the rations provided to male prisoners. The new dietary scheme is summarised in the table below:

1864 Dietaries for County and Borough Gaols for Prisoners without Hard Labour											
Meals	Articles of Food	Class 1		Class 2		Class 3		Class 4		Class 5	
		One week or less.		After 1 week, to 1st month inclusive.		After 1 month, to 3rd month inclusive.		After 3 months, to 6th month inclusive.		After 6 months	
		M	F	M	F	M	F	M	F	M	F
		oz	oz	oz	oz	oz	oz	oz	oz	oz	oz
Breakfast	Bread	6	5	6	5	8	6	8	6	8	6
	Gruel	–	–	1pt	1pt	1pt	1pt	★1pt	★1pt	★1pt	★1pt
Supper	Bread	6	5	6	5	6	6	8	6	8	6
	Gruel	–	–	–	–	1pt	1pt	1pt	1pt	★1pt	★1pt
Dinner Sunday	Bread	8	6	8	6	10	8	10	8	12	10
	Cheese	–	–	1	1	2	2	3	2	3	2

Mon, Wed, Fri.	Bread	6	5	6	5	4	4	4	4	4	4
	Potatoes	–	–	–	–	12	8	16	12	16	12
	Suet Pudding	–	–	–	–	8	6	12	8	12	8
	Indian Meal Pudding	6	4	8	6	–	–	–	–	–	–
Tue, Thu, Sat.	Bread	6	5	6	5	8	6	8	6	8	8
	Potatoes	8	6	12	8	8	6	8	6	16	12
	Soup	–	–	–	–	¾pt	¾pt	1pt	1pt	1pt	1pt

★ To contain 1oz of molasses on Sundays.

Additions for prisoners on Hard Labour

Male prisoners at Hard Labour, and women employed in the laundry or other laborious occupations, to have the following additions and substitutions:

In Class 2: 1oz extra of cheese on Sundays, and 1 pint of gruel for supper daily

In Classes 2–5: 1oz extra of cheese on Sundays, and 1 pint of gruel for supper daily

In lieu of the pudding on Mondays and Fridays – Men: 3oz of beef in Class 3; 4oz in Class 3; and 4oz in Class 5. Women 2oz in Class 3; 3oz in Class 3; and 3oz in Class 5.

The soup to contain in each pint, 2oz of split peas, instead of 1oz of barley.

Prisoners awaiting trial and destitute debtors were to be given the Class 3 diet for their first month, the Class 4 for their second month, then the Class 5 for any further time of imprisonment. Debtors and bankrupts committed for fraud or other serious offence, and also deserters, were placed on the Class 3 diet for the duration of their stay.

A new dish on the menu was Indian meal pudding. Indian meal (milled maize corn, or cornmeal) was not a traditional foodstuff in England though supplies from North America were sometimes used as pig-feed. It was, however, eaten by the poor in many countries, for example in Italy as the dish polenta. Supplies had also been shipped to Ireland to feed the starving poor during the famine between 1845 and 1850. For those in Classes 3–5, Indian meal pudding was replaced after a month by suet pudding, an item which had occasionally featured on prison menus since at least 1818 when it was part of the dietary at the Maidstone House of Correction. It was now commended as 'easily made and measured' and 'palatable without being luxurious'.[172]

At first glance, the basic dietary appears to lack any meat. However, the ingredients list that accompanied it includes some in the soup served for dinner three times a week:

Ingredients of Soup

In every pint: the meat and liquor from 6oz of the necks, legs, and shins of beef, weighed with the bone, previous to cooking; 1oz of onions or leeks; 1oz of Scotch barley; 2oz of carrots, parsnips, turnips or other cheap vegetable, with pepper and salt.

On Tuesdays and Saturdays, the meat liquor of the previous day is to be added.

Ingredients of Suet Pudding		
1½oz of suet; 6½oz of flour, and about 8oz of water to make 1lb.		
Ingredients of Indian Meal Pudding		
To consist of ½ pint of skimmed milk, to every 6oz of meal.		
Ingredients of Gruel		
To every pint, 2oz of coarse Scotch oatmeal, with salt. The gruel for breakfast on Sunday in Class 4, and for breakfast and supper in Class 5, to contain 1oz of molasses.		

As with the 1843 dietary proposals, the new scheme was presented only as a recommendation for local prisons to follow, should they decide to do so in consultation with local magistrates.

At the same time as local prison dietaries were being reviewed, another committee was reassessing those in use at the convict prisons. For male convicts in separate confinement, the following dietary was proposed for those engaged in 'industrial employment':

BREAKFAST (All days)		Bread. ¾ pint cocoa (containing ½oz cocoa, 2oz milk, ½oz molasses).
DINNER	Sunday	Bread. 4oz cheese.
	Monday	Bread. 1lb potatoes. 4oz hot mutton (with its own liquor, flavoured with ½oz onions, and thickened with bread left on previous day).
	Tuesday	Bread. 1lb potatoes. 4oz hot beef.
	Wednesday	Same as Monday.
	Thursday	Bread. 1lb potatoes. 1lb suet pudding (containing 1½oz suet, 8oz flour, 6½oz water).
	Friday	Same as Tuesday.
	Saturday	Bread. 1lb potatoes. 1 pint soup (containing 8oz shins of beef, 1oz pearl barley, 3oz fresh vegetables including onions).
SUPPER	(All days)	Bread. 1 pint gruel (containing 2oz oatmeal, 2oz milk, ½oz molasses).
		Bread, per week: 148oz (20oz per weekday, 28oz Sunday)

Males not at industrial employment received the same dietary but with the bread allowance reduced by 4oz a day. Women convicts had a single 'ordinary' dietary – a slightly reduced version of the men's rations – with those engaged in washing or other heavy work receiving the men's meat allowance plus a lunch of bread and cheese between breakfast and dinner. Finally, for anyone breaking prison rules, a punishment dietary consisted of bread (1lb per day) and water. For punishments above three days, a 'penal class' diet of bread, porridge and potatoes was served every fourth day. Cocoa, which the committee reviewing local prison dietaries had decided was an unnecessary luxury, was retained at convict prisons.

NATIONALISATION

Although the 1865 Prison Act brought local prisons under some degree of central control, they were still funded by local rates, with local JPs playing a part in their administration. The final step in creating an integrated national prison system came with the 1877 Prison Act which placed control of all prisons in the hands of a new body known as the Prison Commissioners. At the same time, the Exchequer took over all the costs of running the prison system.

The nationalisation of the prisons aimed to make the operation of the penal system both uniform and economical. To this end, the Commissioners, chaired by Sir Edmund Du Cane, set about rationalising the country's stock of 113 prisons. In the summer of 1878, forty-five were shut down – mostly small town gaols, although eleven county prisons were closed. The remainder provided space for 24,812 inmates – about 4,000 more than the expected requirements.[173]

Unlike its predecessor in 1865, the new Act did not include detailed prison regulations. Instead, a new set of rules devised by the Prison Commissioners was introduced in April 1878. One innovation was a system of four stages through which convicted prisoners could progress during their sentence. In Stage 1, prisoners slept on a plank bed with no mattress. They were employed for ten hours a day in First Class hard labour, of which six to eight hours were to be on a crank- or tread-wheel. No money could be earned. In Stage 2, a mattress was provided for the plank bed on five nights a week. After completing a month of First Class hard labour, Stage 2 prisoners were moved to Second Class hard labour – light industrial work, for which a small payment could be earned. Stage 2 also offered inmates school instruction and a period of exercise on Sunday. Stage 3 reduced the bare plank bed to one night a week, allowed library books to be kept in cells and gave a higher rate of earning. Finally, at Stage 4, prisoners had a mattress every night and a further increase in earnings. More significantly, they could be given jobs of trust within the prison, have a visitor every three months and write and receive a letter.

Progress through the stages was achieved by the accumulation of marks, of which six to eight could be earned each day. Attaining a total of 224 marks (i.e. twenty-eight times eight) in a stage earned advancement to the following one, although idleness or misconduct could be punished by loss of earnings, stage privileges or even temporary demotion to an earlier stage.

Second Class labour covered a variety of tasks and could result in the learning of a trade that would make an inmate employable after release. At Manchester in 1886, the work for men included brush making and calico weaving, while women were occupied at knitting, sewing, cotton picking and making mail bags.[174] At Wakefield, the men's employment included mat-making, stocking weaving and hammock making. Many of the goods produced by prisoners were supplied to government departments such as the War Office, Admiralty and Post Office.

THE NATIONAL PRISON DIETARY

Following the creation of a national prison system in 1877, a review of prison diets was undertaken with the aim of finally establishing a scheme that could be used by all the country's prisons. A committee was set up to consider the matter and made its report in February 1878.

In its report, the committee noted that the dietaries in use at local prisons were now more varied than ever, with eighty-one differing widely from current official recommendations, compared to eighteen in 1864.[175] Many prisons were still using dietaries similar to those issued following the 1843 review. The committee endorsed the existing view that those serving short terms should receive a more severe diet than those on longer sentences. It also broadly agreed with the principle that longer-term inmates should progress through the various diets given to those with shorter sentences. However, it recognised that the number of potential dietary combinations of male and female prisoners, with and without labour, and at different stages of their sentence, could be excessive – with some prison kitchens having to deal with up to eighteen different diets on the same day. To address this, the committee proposed that the number of basic dietary classes be reduced to four. It was also recommended that female prisoners should generally receive the same amounts as males not performing hard labour. For longer-term prisoners, a revised system of progression was devised, with each prisoner receiving just the last two dietaries applicable to their length of sentence. The revised scheme is shown below:

	Dietary			
Sentence Length	Class 1	Class 2	Class 3	Class 4
Up to 7 days	Whole term			
From 7 days to 1 month	First 7 days	Remainder		
From 1 month to 4 months		First month	Remainder	
More than 4 months			First 4 months	Remainder

From 1878, Stage 4 prisoners could periodically send and receive a letter. A group of inmates engrossed in their writing are seen here at Wandsworth prison in 1896.

By the end of the nineteenth century, unproductive labour such as the tread-wheel had been replaced by more useful occupations which could result in a prisoner learning a trade. This 1898 scene shows the mechanical shop at Wormwood Scrubs where small metal containers are being made under the careful watch of prison officers.

Prisoners at Portland were not solely occupied in the quarries, as shown by this view of the fitter's shop.

The governor and staff at Shepton Mallet prison in Somerset, early 1900s. In 1878, a national scale was created for prison staff's pay. Governors of prisons with 1,000 inmates or more started at £710 a year, with free accommodation and medical care. At a smaller prison like Shepton Mallet, the governor received a rather more modest £200. A warder's salary was £70, plus uniform and accommodation.

In terms of the food provided in each class, the committee was decidedly of the view that 'the shorter the term of imprisonment, the more strongly should the penal element be manifested'; that 'a spare diet is all that is necessary for a prisoner undergoing a sentence of a few days or weeks'; and that 'to give such a prisoner a diet necessary for the maintenance of health during the longer terms would be to forgo an opportunity for the infliction of salutary punishment'.[176] For longer terms, however, it was accepted that a more substantial and varied diet was appropriate. The details of the new dietary recommendations are shown below:

	CLASS 1			CLASS 2			
Meals			Men, Women, and Boys under 16, with or without Hard Labour.			Men with Hard Labour.	Men not on Hard Labour, Women, Boys under 16.
Breakfast	Daily	Bread	8oz	Daily	Bread	6oz	5oz
					Gruel	1 pint	1 pint

Dinner	Daily	Stirabout	1½ pints	Sun, Wed.	Bread	6oz	5oz
					Suet Pud.	8oz	6oz
				Mon, Fri.	Bread	6oz	5oz
					Potatoes	8oz	8oz
				Tue, Thu, Sat.	Bread	6oz	5oz
					Soup	½ pint	½ pint
Supper	Daily	Bread	8oz	Daily	Bread	6oz	5oz
					Gruel	1 pint	1 pint

Meals			CLASS 3				CLASS 4	
			Men with Hard Labour.	Men not on Hard Labour, Women, Boys under 16.	Destitute Debtors, Prisoners awaiting trial, etc.		Men with Hard Labour.	Men not on Hard Labour, Women, Boys under 16.
Breakfast	Daily	Bread	8oz	6oz	6oz	Daily	Bread	8oz	6oz
		Gruel	1 pint	1 pint	1 pint; or		Porridge	1 pint	
		Cocoa			½ pint		Gruel		1 pint
Dinner	Sun, Wed.	Bread	4oz	4oz	4oz	Sun, Wed.	Bread	6oz	4oz
		Potatoes	8oz	6oz	6oz		Potatoes	8oz	8oz
		Suet Pud.	8oz	6oz	6oz		Suet Pud.	12oz	10oz
	Mon, Fri.	Bread	8oz	6oz	6oz	Mon, Fri.	Bread	8oz	6oz
		Potatoes	8oz	8oz	8oz		Potatoes	12oz	10oz
		Ckd. Beef	3oz	3oz	3oz		Ckd. Beef	4oz	3oz
	Tue, Thu, Sat.	Bread	8oz	6oz	6oz	Tue, Thu, Sat.	Bread	8oz	6oz
		Potatoes	8oz	6oz	6oz		Potatoes	8oz	8oz
		Soup	¾ pint	¾ pint	¾ pint		Soup	1 pint	1 pint
Supper	Daily	Bread	6oz	6oz	6oz	Daily	Bread	8oz	6oz
		Gruel	1 pint	1 pint	1 pint; or		Porridge	1 pint	
		Cocoa			½ pint		Gruel		1 pint

On Mondays, beans and fat bacon may be substituted for beef. After nine months, 1 pint of cocoa, with 2oz extra of bread, may be given at breakfast three days a week in lieu of 1 pint of porridge or gruel.

Economy, as always, was kept in mind and the authors of the 1878 report were keen to extol the virtues of pulses – peas and beans. For Class 3 and 4 inmates, replacing Monday's cooked beef by 'beans and bacon' (9oz haricot beans, 1oz fat bacon, 12oz potatoes, 8oz bread) would, it was claimed, be more nutritious and also reduce the cost from 4¾d to 2¼d a portion.

A notable absence from the new dietary was Indian meal pudding, introduced for Class 1 and 2 prisoners in the 1864 review. Indian meal continued in use, for Class 1 prisoners, in the guise of 'stirabout', a thick porridge containing equal parts of Indian meal and oatmeal. Despite appearances, 'stir' – one of the English slang terms for prison – is not a shortened form of stirabout, but is said to derive from the Romany word *'sturiben'*, meaning 'to confine'.[177]

The new diets were endorsed by an 1878 Royal Commission who found that the quantities were 'fairly proportioned to the amount of labour required of the prisoners, whether in separate confinement or at public works'. The meals themselves also received a seal of approval: 'though they are coarse in quality, they are good and of their kind nutritious, and sufficient in quantity to maintain ordinary convicts in good health and vigour.'[178] This was not a view that everyone felt inclined to agree with.

Located in the town's market place, Buckingham's borough prison was erected in 1748 in the style of a castle, the traditional setting for a prison. By the 1870s, its inmates rarely numbered more than three and it became one of many small local prisons to close following the nationalisation of the prison system in 1877. The building, now a museum, has also served as a police station, fire station, ammunition store, public conveniences and an antiques shop.

twelve

From Worms to Beans

STIRRINGS OF DISCONTENT

Despite the periodic reforms of prison food, culminating in the creation of a standard national dietary in 1878, complaints about what ended up on prisoners' plates were never far away.

The quantity of food provided was regularly a source of grievance. One former inmate of Dartmoor in the 1870s claimed that prisoners were so hungry that they resorted to eating dead rats and mice, grass, candles, dogs and earth worms. If caught, they would be starved even further by a spell on bread and water.[179] Elsewhere, items such as beetles, slugs, snails, toilet paper and even a poultice were devoured by prisoners to stave off the pangs of hunger.[180]

In 1887, socialist politician John Burns spent six weeks in prison, for most of which time he received the Class 2 daily allowance of 12oz of bread and a pint of gruel. He recalled:

The bakery at Wormwood Scrubs in 1898 where prisoners, under the direction of the prison baker, roll out and cut up the dough into weighed individual portions.

I had the bread at 5.30 p.m. and nothing till 7.45 next morning. I am not ashamed to say that at 1 or 2 o'clock in the morning I have wetted my hands with my spittle and gone down on my hands and knees in the hope of picking up a stray crumb.[181]

Bread, the staple of all prison diets, could be very variable in its quality. Lord William Nevill, an inmate of Wormwood Scrubs and Parkhurst between 1898 and 1901, found that the bread 'at times was very good, but often it was quite the reverse. It seemed either to be made of bad flour, or to be half baked, and there is nothing more unwholesome than sour, sodden bread.'[182] At Strangeways in 1906, suffragette Hannah Mitchell found that 'the gruel was not too bad, but the bread was quite uneatable. If it had been of sawdust flavoured with road sweepings it could not have tasted worse.'[183] Equally unappetising was the bread at Portland, which was said to be half baked 'in order to keep it wet and damp to keep it up to weight; [it] was what you call soaked, you could squeeze it up like a lump of putty'.[184]

By the 1890s, the adulteration of foods such as flour and bread had become a criminal offence, although Oscar Wilde in his 1897 *Ballad of Reading Gaol* suggested it was still taking place:

> The brackish water that we drink
> Creeps with a loathsome slime,
> And the bitter bread they weigh in scales
> Is full of chalk and lime,
> And Sleep will not lie down, but walks
> Wild-eyed, and cries to Time.

Wilde was also highly critical of the food given to children placed in prison while awaiting trial or sentence – a matter he had gained first-hand experience of while at Reading. In a letter to the *Daily Chronicle* in May 1897, he wrote that:

> The food that is given to [a child] consists of a piece of usually badly baked prison bread and a tin of water for breakfast at half-past seven. At twelve o'clock it gets dinner, composed of a tin of coarse Indian meal stirabout, and at half-past five it gets a piece of dry bread and a tin of water for its supper. This diet in the case of a strong grown man is always productive of illness of some kind, chiefly, of course, diarrhoea, with its attendant weakness … A child who has been crying all day long, and perhaps half the night, in a lonely, dimly lit cell, and is preyed upon by terror, simply cannot eat food of this coarse, horrible kind.

Wilde's comments were provoked by the revelation that a kindly warder at Reading who had taken pity on a child and given it some sweet biscuits had been dismissed from his post.

Suet pudding had become a regular item on the prison dinner menu in 1864, when it had been praised as 'palatable without being luxurious'. This was not a view that was always shared by the diners. Manchester councillor Frederick Brocklehurst, after a month-long stay at Strangeways prison in 1896, recorded that it was 'of the solidity of putty, and about the colour of burnt umber' and 'clung tenaciously to the stomach'.[185] Another consumer's appraisal came from George Foote, imprisoned for blasphemy at Holloway in 1883:

> On Sundays and Wednesdays … I was served with six ounces of suet pudding baked in a separate tin. I never saw such pudding, and I never smelt such suet. Brown meal was used for the dough, and the suet lay on the top in yellow greasy streaks. I can liken the compound to nothing but a linseed poultice.[186]

Some prisons grew their own vegetables, both as a form of employment for the inmates and also as a means of keeping costs down. At Holloway, a team of up to twenty raised a large quantity of potatoes, leeks, cabbage and other vegetables for use by the prison. However, many establishments bought in their potatoes – at least when supplies were cheap and plentiful. Nevill complained that when prices were higher, the quantity and quality of those purchased was reduced and 'the unfortunate prisoners had to eat rotten potatoes, or else go without half their dinner, for weeks at a stretch'.[187] At one prison in 1880, the potatoes 'usually consisted of two, or occasionally three, shabby-looking tubers, the dirt still adhering to them, and soft and spongy to the taste'.[188] A prisoner at another establishment recalled that on cutting into the potatoes, 'half the interior was often found to be a mass of foul, black, spongy disease'.[189]

Following its inclusion in the local prison dietary in 1878, stirabout soon became the most detested item on the prison menu. Brocklehurst described it as having 'the consistency of "stickphast" paste'.[190] Class 1 female prisoners were spared its pleasures after 1895 when an amendment to the dietary instead allowed them bread and a pint of gruel at each meal.

Even traditional porridge and gruel, particularly in those dietaries where it was served unsweetened, were not liked much better. The poet and writer Thomas Cooper, describing a stay in Stafford Gaol, recalled that 'at eight, they brought us a brown porringer, full of "skilly" – for it was such bad unpalatable oatmeal gruel, that it deserved the name'.[191]

Some of the worst food served to inmates involved meat that was either substandard or in advanced stages of decay. Nevill related how the mutton served for one dinner was 'perfectly rotten' – one man had thrown his dinner through the ventilator because the smell of it made him horribly ill. On another occasion, the pork used in the dinner soup was 'absolutely putrid':

> It came out that when the meat was issued to the master-cook on the Saturday, he pointed out that it was tainted, and that, as the weather was very hot, it would be quite bad by the following day. The steward, however, told him that the meat must be used. On Sunday, of course, it was quite unfit for human consumption. If a butcher had exposed it for sale he would have been heavily fined. Yet, as the master-cook had nothing else to make the soup of, he had to use the decayed pork. He tried to smother it by putting in an extra quantity of vinegar, but the mess was so disgusting that no one could swallow it.[192]

At Warwick Gaol in 1839, the chartist William Lovett was served with 'a pint of what was called beef soup'. In a subsequent official complaint, it was said that it contained 'no other appearance of meat than some slimy, stringy particles, which, hanging about the wooden spoon, so offended your petitioners' stomachs that they were compelled to forgo eating it'.[193]

Prison regulations did, of course, include a provision for a prisoner to complain about the diet given to him, although at least one version of the regulations at Millbank included the interesting restriction that this must be done before the food was tasted. A prisoner could also request that the portions be weighed in his presence.[194] Repeated complaints of a frivolous or groundless nature could, however, result in punishment.

One item of the prison diet that received relatively little complaint was cocoa. It was introduced for some longer-term inmates in Sir James Graham's 1843 dietaries but was cut and then restored in successive reviews. In his evidence to the Carnarvon Committee in 1863, William Guy, the Medical Superintendent at Millbank, was asked whether cocoa was a rather unnecessary luxury. He replied that although not an essential item, it was 'a very good article of

Manchester's Strangeways prison was completed in 1868. This view of the prison kitchens, probably dating from the early 1900s, shows how central the use of steam was to cooking operations.

diet, and contains a good deal of that oily element which … should always exist in food'.[195] This richness of oil sometimes appeared as an oily slick on the surface although this did not deter Jabez Balfour when served with his 'very fat – but most excellent – Navy cocoa'.[196]

By far and away the best food provided in prison was that served to inmates who were sick, and prisoners could go to remarkable lengths to gain medical exemption from their normal 'hard labour and hard fare'. According to one estimate, 150 of Dartmoor's 1,000 inmates applied to see the doctor each day, 100 of whom had nothing wrong with them. Methods of faking illness included eating soap, soda, poisonous insects and ground glass. Self-mutilation could be performed with a needle or piece of glass or, in extreme cases, placing a hand or arm under the wheels of a moving quarry wagon. Medical officers were, of course, wise to prisoners' ploys and discouraged them by various means, for example, by prescribing suspected malingerers with a dose of some suitably unpleasant mixture. For a man feigning fits or paralysis, a douche of cold water could rapidly expose the deception.[197]

Regardless of the quality of prison food, physically consuming it could sometimes present problems. One Holloway inmate received a tin of porridge but was unable to eat it because no spoon was provided. At Pentonville, shallow wooden spoons were supplied but had to serve for dealing with every type of food – even tough meat, which had to be cut up using hands and teeth.[198]

DARK PLACES

In January 1894, the prison administration was thrown into crisis by a series of three articles which appeared in the *Daily Chronicle* under the title 'Our Dark Places'. The unnamed author, referred to as 'Our Special Commissioner', appears to have been the Reverend William Morrison, an assistant prison chaplain at Wandsworth.[199] The articles condemned the chairman of the Prison Commission, Sir Edmund Du Cane, for his dictatorial style and for ignoring all foreign innovations in penal administration. The separate system was described as torture, especially for less hardened prisoners; staff were underpaid, overworked and badly selected; the local prison system had suffered a 'complete and utter breakdown', yet 'the great machine rolls obscurely on, cumbrous, pitiless, obsolete, unchanged'.[200] It was also claimed that there was a high rate of insanity amongst prisoners – a rate of 40 per 10,000 as compared with 3 per 10,000 amongst the general population.

In response to the heated debate sparked by the articles, a Departmental Committee was set up to examine prison administration and the treatment and classification of inmates, particularly juveniles and first offenders. It was chaired by Herbert Gladstone MP, son of former Prime Minister William Gladstone. The committee's report, published in 1895, acknowledged that 'a sweeping indictment had been laid against the whole of the prison administration' and that 'many grave evils were alleged to exist.'[201] Starting from the principle that 'prison treatment should have as its primary and concurrent objects, deterrence and reformation', it agreed with much of the criticism, concluding that 'the main fault of our prison system is that it treats prisoners too much as irreclaimable criminals, instead of as reclaimable men and women'.[202] The Prison Commissioners were described as 'too unbending' and ran 'in grooves too narrow for the application of higher forms of discipline and treatment'.[203]

Amongst the report's recommendations were: the amalgamation of convict and local prisons; improvements in prison staffing; a reduction in the period of separation for convicts; the replacement of unproductive labour, such as the crank- and tread-wheel, by productive activity, for example gardening and farming; the provision of more books for prisoners; special treatment for drunkards, the 'weak-minded', first offenders, habitual criminals and juveniles; and the setting up of an experimental reformatory for offenders aged 16 to 21. The committee broadly supported the continued use of the separate system, but proposed that in local prisons association should be permitted during industrial labour as it was healthier, simplified the provision of labour and training, and could be used as a privilege that could be withdrawn.

The 1898 Prison Act implemented many of the Gladstone Committee's recommendations. Classification of prisoners was improved, with first offenders being placed in a special 'Star Class' and housed separately from 'habitual criminals'. The administration of convict and local prisons was to be merged, although convict prisons remained as a special category of prison until 1948. Formulating detailed regulations for the running of prisons was placed in the hands of the Secretary of State, with the first set being issued in 1899.

THE END OF THE PENAL DIET

In the wake of the Gladstone Report, the nineteenth century's final review of prison food began, in the usual manner, with the setting up, in 1898, of a Departmental Committee. In a carefully worded brief, the Home Secretary, Sir Matthew White Ridley, reminded the committee of several important guidelines: that 'the food given to prisoners should be sufficient and not more than sufficient to maintain health and strength'; that 'the ordinary prison diet is not to be regarded as an instrument of punishment'; and that 'prison diets may not bear too favourable a comparison with the diets of free labourers in the outside world or the inmates of workhouses'.[204]

Information was gathered from a wide range of sources including Members of Parliament, prison officials, prisoners' aid societies and local Justices. The committee also made a number of unannounced visits to Dartmoor, Portland, Parkhurst, all the London prisons and several provincial ones, where kitchens and food were inspected, prisoners talked to and notes made of what was left unconsumed.

The most widely voiced topic of complaint was the existing Class 1 male dietary, which comprised 8oz of bread for breakfast and supper, and 1½ pints of stirabout for dinner. The committee's report, published in 1899, concluded that Indian meal 'as an article of diet is neither recognised nor used by the general population, and it is universally objected to by the inmates of prisons'.[205] This was a view confirmed on visits to several prisons where stirabout was virtually the only foodstuff left uneaten by prisoners, a finding which echoed the views of the Gladstone inquiry.[206]

The committee recommended a considerable simplification of the dietary system. It endorsed the existing practice of varying diets with length of sentence, but felt that the number of classes should be reduced to three. The report also disagreed with the 1878 review's belief that there should be a penal element in the food served those serving short terms. Their proposed new Class A diet, provided in the first week of sentences lasting up to fourteen days, would provide 'the plainest food, unattractive, but good and wholesome'. The Class B dietary, for those serving up to three months, and Class C, for longer sentences, would each offer an increased amount and variety of food. The system of dietary progression was almost entirely removed.

On the question of a separate dietary for those serving sentences with hard labour, the report noted that 60 per cent of such prisoners were exempted from onerous tasks such as the tread-wheel on grounds of age, infirmity or physical defect. Accordingly, it recommended that no distinction be made between hard-labour and non-hard-labour diets. With regard to age and sex, it proposed a new three-way categorisation, namely: males over 16, females over 16, and juveniles under 16 of either sex.

The new Class A diet offered a breakfast and supper of bread and gruel, with extra milk for juveniles. The despised stirabout was abolished and replaced on different days of the week by potatoes, suet pudding or porridge. Nutritionally, the Class A diet was superior to both the old Class 1 and 2 dietaries.

The new Class B diet, effectively a replacement for the former Class 2 and Class 3 dietaries, was an enhanced version of the latter. It offered three meat dinners a week instead of the previous two, and larger portions. Bacon and beans became a standard dish, and other portion sizes were increased. For men, supper time now included larger helpings of bread, and porridge instead of gruel. In nutritive terms, it was calculated that the Class B diet provided 128oz of carbohydrates and 33oz of 'nitrogenous matters' per week, compared with the 116oz and 23oz in the old Class 3 dietary, an increase which took it above the minimum daily needs of a working adult male.[207] A slightly modified version of the Class B diet was recommended as one appropriate for debtors and prisoners awaiting trial, with tea being given instead of gruel at breakfast, and cocoa instead of porridge or gruel at supper.

The Class C diet, a replacement for the existing Class 4, was a more generous version of Class B. For women with sentences over three months, tea was substituted for the usual breakfast gruel, which it was believed would make their lives 'more contented'. For all inmates, supper was to be oatmeal-free with a pint of cocoa provided instead. The new dietaries for men (M), women (W), and juveniles (J), are presented in the accompanying tables. Broadly speaking, women and juveniles received the same food apart from some slight differences in the breakfast and supper menus:

	CLASS A				CLASS B				CLASS C		
		M	W	J		M	W	J		M	W	J
Breakfast	Daily				Daily				Daily			
	Bread	8oz	6oz	6oz	Bread	8oz	6oz	6oz	Bread	8oz	6oz	6oz
	Gruel	1pt	1pt	1pt	Gruel	1pt	1pt	1pt	Porridge	1pt		1pt
	Milk			½pt	Milk			½pt	Tea		1pt	
									Milk			½pt
Supper	Daily				Daily				Daily			
	Bread	8oz	6oz	6oz	Bread	8oz	6oz	6oz	Bread	8oz	6oz	6oz
	Gruel	1pt	1pt	1pt	Porridge	1pt			Cocoa	1pt	1pt	1pt
	Milk			½pt	Gruel		1pt					
					Cocoa			1pt				

	CLASS A			CLASS B			CLASS C		
		M	W and J		M	W and J		M	W and J
Dinner	Sun			Sun			Sun		
	Bread	8oz	6oz	Bread	6oz	6oz	Bread	6oz	6oz
	Porridge	1pt	1pt	Potatoes	8oz	8oz	Potatoes	12oz	8oz
				Meat	4oz	3oz	Meat	5oz	4oz
	Mon			Mon			Mon		
	Bread	8oz	6oz	Bread	6oz	6oz	Bread	6oz	6oz
	Potatoes	8oz	8oz	Potatoes	8oz	8oz	Potatoes	12oz	8oz
				Beans	10oz	8oz	Beans	12oz	10oz
				Bacon	2oz	1oz	Bacon	2oz	2oz
	Tue, Fri			Tue, Fri			Tue, Fri		
	Bread	8oz	6oz	Bread	6oz	6oz	Bread	6oz	6oz
	Porridge	1pt	1pt	Potatoes	8oz	8oz	Potatoes	12oz	8oz
				Soup	1pt	1pt	Soup	1pt	1pt
	Wed, Sat			Wed, Sat			Wed, Sat		
	Bread	8oz	6oz	Bread	6oz	6oz	Bread	6oz	6oz
	Suet Pud.	8oz	6oz	Potatoes	8oz	8oz	Potatoes	12oz	8oz
				Suet Pud.	10oz	8oz	Suet Pud.	12oz	10oz
	Thu			Thu			Thu		
	Bread	8oz	6oz	Bread	6oz	6oz	Bread	6oz	6oz
	Potatoes	8oz	8oz	Potatoes	8oz	8oz	Potatoes	12oz	8oz
				Beef	4oz	3oz	Beef	5oz	4oz

The Sunday meat ration – served cold – was to be 'Cooked meat, preserved by heat', also known as Colonial beef because it originated in Australia or other British colonies. It was manufactured by encasing raw meat in a tin, then heating it gradually in a boiling solution of calcium chloride. Air and steam were allowed to escape by a small vent hole which was then sealed up to make it airtight. Thursday's dinner-time beef could also be replaced by Colonial beef, mutton or – occasionally – fish, either 8oz of fresh fish or 12oz of salted fish. Potatoes could be substituted by other fresh vegetables or 'sparingly' by rice.

For 'ill-conducted or idle' prisoners, the punishment diet broadly continued existing practice, with a daily allowance of 1lb of bread, with water, for up to three days. Beyond this, the Class B diet was alternated with bread and water for three days at time. For those on hard labour, the punishment diet – for up to twenty-one days – comprised 8oz of bread at each meal, with an additional 8oz of potatoes and a pint of porridge at dinner time.

BEANS AND CUSTARD

As well as the food in local prisons, the 1898 review also examined convict dietaries, which had been largely unchanged since 1864, but were said by many of those giving evidence to be deficient in three main respects: the breakfast and supper were insufficient; a greater variety of food was desirable; and the amount of fat in the dietary was deficient. To address these complaints, the committee recommended a new convict dietary based on its proposed Class C local dietary, but with some alterations. The weekly bread allowance for male convicts on hard labour was increased from its former 1680oz per week to 1960oz per week, while that for those on light labour rose from 1450oz to 1680oz. The new hard labour diet included porridge instead of gruel for breakfast, plus a daily supplement of ½oz of butter in the autumn and winter, or ¼ pint of milk in the spring and summer. All convicts received an increase in their weekly allowance of potatoes and meat, and a more varied dinner menu, which now included bacon and beans.

Finally, a new hospital dietary for sick prisoners was introduced which, for the first time, was to be used at both convict and local prisons. The scheme, based on the existing convict hospital dietary, contained three variations ('Ordinary', 'Pudding' and 'Low') covering different grades of illness:

	Ordinary Diet	Pudding Diet	Low Diet
Breakfast	8oz bread 1 pint tea	6oz white bread 1 pint milk	6oz bread 1 pint tea
Dinner	5oz (cooked) meat 8oz potatoes 4oz vegetables 6oz bread ½oz salt	Rice pudding (1½oz rice, 1 egg, 10oz milk), or Batter pudding (3oz flour, 1 egg, 10oz milk), or (1 egg, 10oz milk)	Cornflour (1oz cornflour, 1 pint milk, 1oz sugar)
Supper	8oz bread 1 pint tea	6oz white bread 1 pint milk	6oz bread 1 pint tea

The cooked meat in the hospital dietary was specified as fresh beef or mutton which was to be roasted, baked, stewed or boiled; when boiled, it was to be served in its own liquor, thickened with ⅙oz of flour and flavoured with ½oz of onions with pepper and salt. The meat could also be substituted by fowl, rabbit or fish. Sago or tapioca could be served instead of rice. The Low Diet's cornflour dish is what we would now generally call a custard sauce.

On the topic of food preparation, the committee recorded their experience of some prison kitchens being 'slovenly and ill-provided', with appliances for the preparation of food being 'scanty or defective'. The replacement of tin utensils by enamel-ware was also recommended.

thirteen

The Prison Cookbook

The idea of a cookery book for prison staff had its roots in the report of the committee inquiring into prison dietaries, published in 1878. In addition to its dietary proposals, the report complained that much food was wasted by unskilful cooking. This was particularly said to be true of meat, which prison kitchens often cooked at too high a temperature, turning it into 'a condensed shrunken mass of little or no nutritive value'. The use of a thermometer had been suggested as a remedy for this problem.

To try and improve culinary skills, the committee recommended 'the advisability of forwarding instructions on this important subject to each prison, or of passing the prison cooks through a short course of tuition'.[208] In the meantime, it offered a brief list of 'ingredients and instructions' for various dishes in the revised dietary:

Bread	To be made with whole meal, which is to consist of all the products of grinding the wheaten grain, with the exception of the coarser bran.
Soup	In every pint 4oz clod (or shoulder), cheek, neck, leg, or shin of beef; 4oz split peas; 2oz fresh vegetables; ½oz onions; pepper and salt.
Suet Pudding	1½oz mutton suet, 8oz flour, and about 6½oz water to make 1 pound.
Gruel	2oz coarse Scotch oatmeal to the pint, with salt.
Porridge	3oz coarse Scotch oatmeal to the pint, with salt.
Stirabout	Equal parts of Indian meal and oatmeal, with salt. The Indian meal requires more cooking than the oatmeal. To make 1½ pint stirabout, boil 2½ pints water, to which a ¼oz of salt should be added; stir in 3oz of Indian meal, and afterwards 3oz of oatmeal; keep constantly stirring.
Cocoa	To every pint, ¾oz flaked or Admiralty cocoa. Sweetening: For flaked cocoa, ¾oz molasses or sugar to the pint. For Admiralty cocoa, ½oz molasses or sugar to the pint.
Meat liquor, or broth	The liquor in which the meat is cooked on Mondays and Fridays is to be thickened with ¼oz flour, and flavoured with ¼oz onions to each ration, with pepper and salt to taste.

THE MANUAL OF COOKING AND BAKING

The call for a prison recipe book was reiterated by the Departmental Committee conducting the 1898 dietary review. The report also expressed disapproval of the existing method of issuing cooking instructions on loose sheets. Instead, it proposed that a 'manual of cooking' similar to that issued for military cooks should be placed in the hands of cooks in the prison service. The result was the *Manual of Cooking & Baking for the Use of Prison Officers* – published in 1902 and printed at Parkhurst prison.

The *Manual*, reproduced in its entirety as part of this book, was much more than a list of recipes. It encouraged its readers to understand the scientific principles that underpinned successful food preparation, and to adopt a methodical approach, without which the results would often be 'unsatisfactory and disappointing'. It thus contained chapters on: the chemistry of food; basic kitchen practice; guidance on the inspection, selection and storage of ingredients; the basics of cooking; prison diets; hospital diets; and – being a prison cookbook – an extensive section on the principles and practice of bread-making. Despite its 'scientific' approach, a modern reader will often be surprised by some of the directions, particularly for the cooking times of various items, for example porridge ('for at least half an hour'), cabbage ('40 to 45 minutes'), carrots ('one hour when old') and cornflour sauce ('fifteen minutes'). Tea was to be brewed for 'about 10 minutes'. On the subject of hospital food, the *Manual* had a fairly liberal interpretation of the official dietary and included recipes for dishes such as veal broth, chicken balls, fishcakes and stewed figs.

Coincidentally, the *Manual* appeared the year after a similar though unconnected work was published for use by workhouses.[209] Comparison of the two shows how much attitudes towards the workhouse had changed, with inmates there now receiving dishes such as meat pasties, sea pie or hotch-potch stew, with roley-poley pudding, golden pudding or seed cake to follow.

A similar broadening of the prison diet took several decades to materialise. A second edition of the prisons' *Manual* appeared in 1935 when, thanks to the work of the 1925 Departmental Committee on Diets, items such as Irish stew, hot pot, shepherd's pie and treacle pudding had joined the menu.

THE GUIDE FOR COOK AND BAKER OFFICERS

A more comprehensive overhaul of the *Manual* resulted in the 1949 *Guide for Cook and Baker Officers*, itself updated in 1958. By this time, the contents of the *Guide* looked little different from a typical domestic cookery book of the day, except that the quantities specified in its recipes were to serve 100. The making of cocoa, for example, required 4lb 11oz of cocoa, 7 pints milk and 12 gallons water – the cocoa to be boiled in the water for one hour.

Amongst the innovations was a section on herbs and spices, such as the use of bay leaves for flavouring stews, pickles, prunes and soused herrings; carraway seeds for flavouring cakes and buns; fennel for flavouring sauces – usually served with fish; and mace for minced meat or fish dishes. Potatoes still featured prominently in the *Guide,* with ten suggested ways of serving them (boiled, baked, fatless roast, croquettes, au gratin, steamed, jacket, mashed, savoury and sauté). Porridge recipes were limited to a mere three – for fine, medium and coarse oatmeal. The range of other dishes had grown enormously and included items such as mulligatawny soup, baked herrings, cottage pie, Cornish pasties, toad in the hole, Vienna steaks, roast pork and stuffing, Windsor pudding, apple turnovers, gingerbread, chocolate sauce and doughnuts.

Mulligatawny Soup

10 gallons stock	4 lb. onions
12 oz. curry powder	4 lb. carrots
3 bay leaves	3 lb. barley
1 lb. dripping	1 lb. flour
seasoning	

Method: — Cut the vegetables into small pieces and fry in a little fat. Add the curry powder and flour to the vegetables and fry a little longer. Add the whole to the stock and stir until it boils. Add the barley and bay leaves, and cook for 1½ hours. Season. Remove the bay leaves before serving.

Vienna Steaks

25 lb. meat	4 oz. chopped parsley
6 lb. breadcrumbs	1 oz. mixed herbs
3 lb. onions	seasoning

Method:—Fry the chopped onions in the oven and allow to cool. Mince the raw meat and mix all the ingredients. Mould into 100 portions and cook them in the oven for one hour.

Cornish Pasties (Method No. 1)

12½ lb. meat	3 lb. onions
25 lb. potatoes	3 lb. turnips or swedes
seasoning	½ lb. chopped parsley
short pastry	

Cook the meat and cut it into dice. Cook the potatoes, onions, and turnips and slice. Mix the ingredients together. Make the pastry. Roll out and cut into rounds the size of a tea plate, place the meat and vegetable mixture in the centre, damp the edges and fold over, tuck in the ends and bake in the oven.

Windsor Pudding

2 lb. currants	2 lb. sultanas
1 oz. spice	4 lb. carrots
2 lb. raisins	4 lb. potatoes

Method:—Grate the raw carrots and potatoes and add them with the other ingredients to suet pudding mixture. Steam for 4 hours.

Doughnuts

7 lb. flour	2½ oz. yeast
2 oz. salt	3 pints water

Method:—Sieve the flour and salt, dissolve the yeast in half the water, then mix into it sufficient flour to form a thin batter and add it to the flour, together with the remaining water. Work the whole into a smooth dough, and leave to prove for 1 hour in a warm temperature. Knock back and leave for a further 30 minutes: knock back again and divide into 100 portions. Prove for a further 20 to 30 minutes.

Fry the portions of dough in deep fat, well drain them and roll in sugar to which a small quantity of mixed spice has been added.

A selection of the much wider range of recipes on offer in the *Guide for Cook and Baker Officers*, first issued in 1949.

TRAINING

As well as the production of a cookery book, the 1898 Departmental Committee called for the systematic training of all prison cooks, bakers and millers, and for those involved in the inspection of food supplies. By the time the committee's report was published, a training scheme had already been set up by the Prison Commissioners. Training courses for prison cooks and bakers were introduced in 1898 as part of a wider initiative to set up 'training schools' to be given to all newly appointed prison personnel, including warders, hospital attendants, and clerical staff. The first school of cookery was held at Wormwood Scrubs prison under the supervision of the inspecting and examining chef from the National School of Cookery.[210] Following the training courses, it was noted that reports had been received 'from all quarters as to the improvement that has taken place in the quality of the prison cooking'.[211]

fourteen

Prisons Enter the Twentieth Century

By the end of the nineteenth century, the prison system had undergone enormous changes. Gaolers no longer lived off fees extracted from their prisoners. The hulks had long gone and transportation had ended. Unproductive labour such as the tread-wheel had been abolished. Some well-known prisons had disappeared – the Marshalsea closed in 1842, Millbank was demolished in 1890 and Newgate was to go the same way in 1902. New prisons, still in use today, had taken their place, including Parkhurst (opened in 1838), Pentonville (1842), Dartmoor (1850), Wandsworth (1851), Holloway (1852), Brixton (1853) and Wormwood Scrubs (1883). In 1818 there had been 338 prisons in England and Wales.[212] By 1900, only sixty-one prisons remained – fifty-six local and five convict – although the total capacity remained virtually unchanged at around 24,000 inmates.[213]

Despite this dramatic reduction in prison establishments, the number of those serving prison sentences had actually risen. In 1818, about 107,030 persons had been put in prison, while in the year up to March 1901, 148,600 were sent by the ordinary courts to local prisons, with a further 12,576 imprisoned as debtors. In the same period, convict prisons received 797 new inmates, and 785 convicts were placed in local prisons. However, the rise in prison sentences was much smaller than the growth in the overall population (from 11.8 million in 1818 to 32.6 million in 1900). Most of those in local prisons were now serving very short sentences – an average of thirty-six days, with many being inside for two weeks or less. Very few sentences were longer than three months.[214]

Some of those most affected by the changes in the penal system were young offenders. In addition to the existing reformatories and industrial schools for those under 16, the Gladstone Committee had proposed that a special institution be set up to deal with offenders aged from 16 to 21. An experimental scheme was set up at Bedford in 1899, and then extended in 1901 using part of the convict prison at Borstal in Kent. The young inmates were kept apart from the adult prisoners and given a routine which included physical exercise, school lessons, work training, strict discipline and follow-up supervision after their discharge. The formal adoption of the Borstal system came in the 1908 Prevention of Crime Act. A second borstal institution was established at Feltham in 1910 (in the premises of the former Middlesex Industrial School), and another at Portland in 1921, with one for girls being set up at Aylesbury prison in 1909. Some existing prisons implemented a 'modified borstal' system, providing accommodation and treatment for those serving short sentences.

Changes were taking place for other groups too. There were moves to concentrate female prisoners in a small number of dedicated institutions. Holloway became an all-women's prison in 1902, while outside London prisons such as Liverpool began to develop in this role. Following the 1898 Inebriates Act, a number of special inebriate reformatories were set up for 'habitual drunkards' who committed offences while under the influence of alcohol. Some of these were operated by the National Institutions for Inebriates, a charity run by clergyman and former missionary the Rev. Harold Burden, which took over former workhouses for the purpose at Lewes in Sussex and at Guiltcross in Norfolk.

For those convicted of the most serious crimes, such as murder, hanging remained the ultimate sanction until its abolition in 1965. However, the use of the death penalty was already in dramatic decline. Those sentenced to death in 1818 numbered 1,254 of which ninety-seven were actually executed.[215] In 1900, only twenty received the death penalty, with around three quarters of those actually facing the hangman. The spectacle of public executions ended in 1868 and now took place behind closed doors. From 1908, the minimum age for execution was raised to 16.

A women's prison cell at Holloway prison in 1901. The occupant is engaged in sack-making. Her plank bed can be seen standing on end at the left. From 1902, all London's female prisoners were held at Holloway.

The 1901 scene outside Holloway where relatives or friends wait to meet those being discharged from the prison.

An aerial view of London's Wormwood Scrubs, opened as a convict prison in 1883 then used as a local prison from 1890. It used a 'telegraph-pole' layout, a design which had been popularised in the pavilion plan hospitals of the period promoted by Florence Nightingale. The cell blocks, linked by covered passageways, ran north–south to receive sunlight at each side during the day.

Internally, the Wormwood Scrubs cell blocks resembled the galleried wings of older prisons. This view, from around 1900, shows prisoners returning to their cells for dinner.

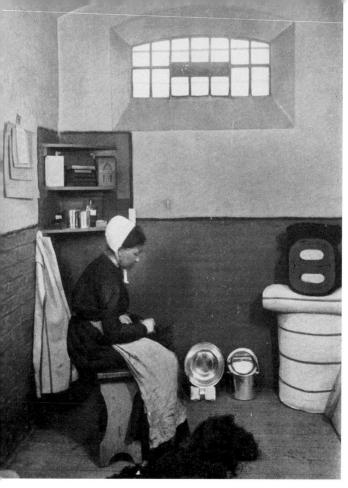

Left: A women's cell at Wormwood Scrubs in 1896 with bedding stowed away at the right. The corner shelves contain a few books from the prison library. The prisoner is picking oakum – teasing apart old rope into its raw strands.

Below: The 'babies' parade' – female prisoners with their infants taking outdoor exercise at Wormwood Scrubs in 1896. Nurseries for such children were established in a number of prisons in the nineteenth century.

An early version of the 'Black Maria' used to carry prisoners to and from gaol. The prisoners were placed in cells at each side of the vehicle and were accompanied during their journey by a constable.

Male prisoners taking a turn around the exercise yard at Holloway in 1901 – their perambulations apparently proving something of a spectator sport. When the prison became women-only in the following year the men were moved to Brixton, originally opened in 1853 as a convict prison, but which had served as a military prison since 1882.

The interior of Newgate's execution shed. Local prisons could requisition a ten-piece hanging 'kit' from Holloway or Pentonville. It comprised a rope, a pinioning apparatus, a cap, a bag holding sand to the weight of the prisoner in his clothes, a piece of chalk, a few feet of copper wire, a six-foot graduated pole, pack-thread just strong enough to support the rope without breaking, a tackle to raise the bag of sand or the body out of the pit, and a chain with a shackle and pin. And, presumably, some instructions.

THE DISTINCTIVE DRESS OF VARIOUS CLASSES OF CONVICTS.

All the clothing up to number 5 is yellow. Reading from left to right the clothing indicates:—(1) First stage (first twelve months); (2) second stage (two years), black stripes on cuffs; (3) third stage (three years), yellow stripes on cuffs; (4) fourth stage, intermediate man, blue stripes on cuffs, chevron on cap and arms; (5) star man, blue stripes on cuffs, star on each arm and on cap; (6) grey dress worn by long-sentence men who earn 2s. 6d. a month and spend 1s. 3d. on comforts; (7) blue dress for good character; (8) black parti-coloured dress worn as punishment for striking an officer; (9) yellow parti-coloured dress, the penalty for running away; (10) canvas dress for those who destroy the ordinary clothing of their class.

A comparison of the ten different styles of convict uniforms in use in around 1900. The arrow motif was also included in studs on the underside of the men's boots.

DEVELOPMENTS AFTER 1920

In the first four decades of the twentieth century, the prison population dropped from a daily average of just under 15,000 in 1901 to just over 10,000 immediately prior to the outbreak of the Second World War in 1939.[216] As a result, there was virtually no new prison building.

Things were not standing still inside the prison system, however. Reforms during the 1920s and 1930s began to make prisons much more humane places. From 1921, the 'convict crop' haircut was abolished, together with the broad arrows on prison uniforms; transfers between prisons were now in civilian clothes; prisoners could have a shave before attending court; the bars or wires separating inmates from their visitors were removed and replaced by an ordinary table; there were relaxations in the rules preventing talking between prisoners.[217] Compulsory chapel attendance was abolished in 1924, and the month-long initial solitary confinement of new prisoners ended in 1931. Other changes in this period included the introduction of educational courses run by voluntary teachers, film shows, lectures, amateur dramatics and radio sets. An earnings scheme introduced in 1933 allowed inmates to buy goods from prison canteens.[218]

A significant trend in prison accommodation began in 1930 with the opening of a new 'open' Borstal at Lowdham Grange, near Nottingham. A group of forty boys marched the 132 miles there from Feltham, initially living in tents and huts while they built their own institution, which lacked the usual walls or barbed wire perimeter. In 1934, the first open prison for adults was established at New Hall Camp, near Wakefield. During the day, inmates at open prisons were able to work in the open air on a farm or outside at local factories. For juvenile offenders, 1932 brought an end to reformatories and industrial schools and their replacement by a single system of approved schools.

Young offenders doing farm work at Lowdham Grange borstal in the 1940s. The borstal was largely self-sufficient in items such as milk, eggs and vegetables.

A major shake-up of the prison system came soon after the Second World War in the shape of the 1948 Criminal Justice Act which, amongst other things, abolished penal servitude, hard labour and whipping. The Act also introduced a new sentence of corrective training for younger offenders and established two new types of institution – the detention centre (providing a 'short sharp shock' for first offenders between 14 and 21) and the remand centre (for those awaiting trial or sentence).

At Norwich prison, an experiment began in 1956 where prison warders were encouraged to get to know their prisoners on a more personal level. This was accompanied by a move towards dining in association for all convicted prisoners and an increase in the time spent out of cells at work. The so-called 'Norwich system' achieved beneficial results for both staff and inmates and its use was taken up by other local prisons.

THE GROWING PRISON POPULATION

An increase in crime rates in the years following the Second World War eventually resulted in a major programme of new prison construction with Everthorpe, in 1958, being the first new closed prison to be built since Victorian times. Following the publication in 1959 of an influential parliamentary White Paper *Penal Practice in a Changing Society*, around forty new penal establishments were opened. 'New Wave' prisons, such as Blundeston, Coldingley and Long Lartin, employed a novel style of design based on the principle that cells were used only as bedrooms and so omitted built-in WCs or space for eating. Instead of the galleried radial wings of Victorian prisons, the new buildings generally consisted of several T-shaped blocks clustered around a central service building which contained classrooms, library, canteen, kitchens, gymnasium and chapel.[219]

After the 1960s, construction of new prisons steadily continued and experiments were made with a wide range of designs. The mid-1980s saw the influence of 'new generation' ideas from the USA, where small groups of inmates were housed in small triangular house blocks organised around a central communal area. At the opposite end of the spectrum, new prison buildings at Woolwich, Bicester and Bullingdon saw a return to the use of galleried wings reminiscent of Victorian prisons.[220]

Many new buildings during this period were for young offenders, supporting the aim of keeping them out of prison. Those receiving sentences of up to six months were to be placed in detention centres, with borstal training for those serving up to three years. Borstals were rebranded as Youth Custody Centres in 1983 then from 1988 became known as Young Offenders Institutions, after merging with the former youth detention centres which were abolished as a separate form of establishment.

As well as the erection of new buildings, there was a programme of refurbishment and reconstruction of old prisons. The most extensive project was at Holloway women's prison where, between 1970 and 1983, the Victorian buildings were completely replaced at a final cost of £40 million – more than six times the original estimate. The new layout was made up of a number of small separate cell blocks, linked by a corridor, and arranged around a 'village green', with communal facilities such as workshops, a swimming pool and chapel. However, its sprawling layout was subsequently criticised as being hard to supervise and control.[221]

Despite efforts to expand prison accommodation, it struggled to keep up with the growth in the prison population, which rose from just over 20,000 in 1950 to over 83,000 by 2009. Overcrowding was a regular feature of many prisons – in 1981, almost 5,000 prisoners were living three to a cell, in a space originally designed for one. Triple-sharing was abolished in 1994, although this was only achieved by an increase in the numbers of prisoners sharing with one other. Overcrowding has become markedly worse in recent times with prison numbers increasing by 85 per cent since 1993. In 2006, the UK government announced 'Operation Safeguard' – a contingency plan for situations where the shortage of prison places becomes acute. Under the scheme, temporary holding cells at police stations are pressed into use as additional prison accommodation. At the end of 2007, the government announced plans for three new 2,500-capacity 'super-prisons' as part of measures to create 10,500 new prison places. On 22 February 2008, the accommodation crisis finally reached breaking point when, for the first time ever, the total population exceeded the prison system's useable operational capacity.[222] In April 2009, following widespread criticism of the super-prison proposal, the Home Secretary announced a revised plan to erect five smaller prisons, each with a capacity of 1,500 – about the size of the country's large existing jail at Wandsworth.

fifteen

Prison Food After 1900

A FRESH LOOK AT PRISON DIETS

In 1924, the Prison Commissioners instigated a Departmental Committee to look at prison diets which, it was said, were too starchy and lacked both variety and green vegetables. The committee, reporting in 1925, agreed that the existing diets were 'somewhat low in fat and in fresh green food'[223] and proposed a number of improvements. As regards variety, a much expanded range of dinner dishes was put forward, based on trials that had proved successful at borstal institutions. They also recommended that prisons use any available ground for the cultivation of vegetables (potatoes, spinach, kale, cabbage, carrots, onions, parsnips, swedes and – where practicable – watercress), especially winter-cropping varieties and early potatoes.

Interestingly, some of the committee's suggestions were based on practical research conducted amongst cooks and diners. The use of raw vegetables, for example, was viewed as being particularly beneficial to health, but experiments with raw cabbage (shredded and pickled in vinegar) suggested it would probably be rejected by prisoners. Trials with bread, by now largely made with white flour, had concluded that a mix of 50 per cent white household flour and 50 per cent brown flour produced a loaf that was both nutritious and sufficiently palatable. Experiments with suet pudding, often complained of as being too stodgy, had shown that adding a small amount of yeast to the dough produced a light and tasty pudding. The same recipe (8oz flour, 2¼oz suet, ½oz yeast and water) was also used for dumplings.

The fat deficiency in existing diets was to be remedied by increasing the amount of milk, for example serving it with the porridge ration, and by an increased use of margarine which had been introduced during the 1914–8 war as a replacement for part of the bread allowance. It was suggested that margarine should be made more appealing by serving in individual pats stamped with a decorative design. Tea was now recommended as a standard part of breakfast, but with only 1½oz of milk to offset the cost of that now to be served with the porridge.

It was originally proposed that fish be largely removed from the dietary, as 'the type of fish obtained by contract is not very palatable; transport delays affect the freshness of the supplies; it is of small food value, and unsatisfying; and it taints the food utensils'.[224] However, a concession was made following a request from Liverpool prison, where the majority of women convicts were now detained, and where frying facilities could be readily obtained locally.

The committee noted that the now long-established Monday dinner dish of bacon and beans would appear 'somewhat repellent' to the average non-prisoner. The bacon often consisted of a solid lump of fat which prisoners were known to use for such purposes as greasing their hair and softening the leather of shoes. It was suggested that the dish be restyled as 'savoury bacon pie' using belly bacon, in which meat might actually be discerned. Replacing the beans by marrowfat peas, while likely to be popular with the inmates, was considered too expensive an option.

Finally, it was proposed that, for the first time, several baked dishes be included on the menu, although it was conceded that some prisons might have to adapt their bread ovens to enable this to happen.

The 1925 committee's proposals contained diets for local prisons (Diet I diet for men, Diet II for women) and convict prisons (Diet III for men, Diet IV for women), with various small additions for male convicts performing hard labour. The basic weekly diet plan is shown below:

Meal	Day	Item	DIET I	DIET II	DIET III	DIET IV
Breakfast	Daily	Bread	8oz	6oz	8oz	6oz
		Porridge	1 pint	½ pint	1 pint	½ pint
		Tea		1 pint	1 pint	1 pint
Dinner	Daily	Bread	3oz	2oz	4oz	2oz
		Potatoes	12oz	8oz	12oz	8oz
	Sunday	Preserved Meat	5oz	4oz	5oz	4oz
		Fresh Vegetables			4oz	4oz
	Monday	Beans	12oz	10oz	12oz	10oz
		Bacon	2oz	2oz	2oz	2oz
		Fresh Vegetables	4oz	4oz		4oz
	Tuesday	Soup	1 pint	1 pint		1 pint
		Mutton			5oz	
		Fresh Vegetables			4oz	
	Wednes–day	Suet Pudding	12oz	10oz		10oz
		Golden Syrup				2oz
		Pea Soup (pork)			1 pint	
	Thursday	Beef	5oz	4oz	5oz	4oz
		Fresh Vegetables	4oz	4oz	4oz	4oz
	Friday	Soup (beef)	1 pint	1 pint	1 pint	1 pint
	Saturday	Suet Pudding	12oz	10oz	12oz	
		Mutton				4oz
		Fresh Vegetables				4oz
Tea and Supper	Daily	Bread	8oz	6oz	12oz	6oz
		Cocoa	1 pint	1 pint	1 pint	
		Tea				1 pint
		Margarine	½oz	½oz	½oz	½oz
		Cheese			1oz	

The outlined weekly menu does not include all the different dinner dishes proposed by the new scheme. In Diet III, for example, it was suggested that a total of eighteen different dishes be used within each twenty-eight day cycle, as follows:

Diet III – Summary of Dinners for 28 Days			
Dish	Times issued	Dish	Times Issued
Beans and Bacon	2	Meat Pie	1
Preserved Beef	2	Meat Pudding	1
Preserved Beef and Pickles	2	Mutton (roast)	1
Beef (roast)	1	Pork (boiled) and dumplings	1
Beef and Treacle Pudding	1	Sea Pie	4
Haricot Mutton	1	Shepherd's Pie	3
Hot Pot	1	Soup (beef)	1
Irish Stew	1	Soup (pork)	1
Savoury Bacon Pie	2	Stewed Steak	2

SPECIAL DIETS

In addition to its provisions for the main categories of inmate, the 1925 review included a number of special diets. For the first time, special menus were provided for 'Oriental Prisoners', of which two groups were differentiated – 'Mahommedans' and 'Moslems'. The Mahommedan diet included the standard breakfast and supper offerings, but for dinner provided 8oz of potatoes and 4oz of bread each day, plus fish (on Sunday, Monday, Wednesday and Friday), boiled rice (Tuesday and Thursday), or rice pudding (Saturday). Moslem prisoners again had the standard breakfast and supper issue, with boiled rice and rice pudding for dinner on alternate days, together with the standard bread and potatoes of the ordinary diet. For Jewish prisoners, dinners containing pork were replaced by meat pudding, sea pie, shepherd's pie or stewed steak, and treacle pudding. Kosher meat could also be issued to Jewish prisoners during Passover, where the numbers were deemed sufficient to justify it.

Anyone satisfying the governor that they were vegetarian could have meat dishes replaced by items such as rice pudding (1½oz rice, 1oz milk and ½oz sugar per 6oz of pudding), flour pudding (2oz vegetable fat and 8oz flour per 1lb pudding) and vegetable soup (2oz fresh vegetables, 2oz pearl barley, beans, or peas, ½oz onions and ⅙oz flour per 1 pint soup).

Other special provisions, such as the hospital diet for sick inmates and the punishment diet for prisoners being disciplined for breaking prison rules, were largely unaltered.

One 'diet' that was never spelled out in dietary scales was the 'hearty breakfast', traditionally eaten by those about to face execution. However, by the 1930s, it had become formalised in section 196 of the 'Prison Rules and Orders':

Prisoners under sentence of death will be placed generally on an ordinary hospital diet with any addition (e.g. an egg or bacon for breakfast, or an egg or cheese for supper, and a pudding for dinner) which the Medical Officer considers advisable. Half a pint of beer may be allowed a condemned prisoner at dinner, and again at supper. Ten cigarettes or ½oz of pipe tobacco per diem will be allowed … the prisoner should be allowed to smoke in his cell as well as at exercise.

WORLD WAR II AND BEYOND

Improvements in the quantity and variety of prison food were halted by the Second World War. Following the introduction of rationing in 1940, a personal ration scale was drawn up for each prisoner. Set meals were abolished and it was left to the cook to serve the rations in the most suitable manner he could devise. The use of curry powder, herbs and dried fruit (or fresh fruit if in season) was suggested as a means of adding interest and variation to the food.[225]

In 1942, Dr Magnus Pyke investigated the nutritional value of the diets at a range of prisons. Although broadly satisfactory, some deficiencies were discovered, most notably in the amounts of fat and vitamin A. As a result, inmates were provided with extra rations of sausage meat and carrots. Vitamin C was also often lacking – often resulting from cooked food being kept too long in hot cabinets. Pyke recommended changes in the cooking procedures and an increased issue of green vegetables from Christmas to the spring to compensate for the declining vitamin C content of stored potatoes.[226]

The post-war years saw gradual improvements both in the food and in the way it was cooked and served. By 1949, 'supper' had become 'tea', with the evening cocoa served as a separate 'supper' at around 8 p.m. In the same year, the cylindrical tins long-used for serving prisoners dining in association began to be replaced by an issue of two dinner plates, a side plate for bread and a drinking mug. Old wooden dining tables and forms were replaced by tables with inlaid linoleum tops and wooden chairs. For those dining in their cells, a 'cafeteria compartment tray' made from a cream-coloured plastic was developed. Three years later, the cafeteria system with melamine trays came into general use. At one prison, 1,000 men could now be served in less than twenty minutes.[227] New kitchen equipment installed at various prisons included fish fryers, dough-mixing machines, meat slicers and stainless steel margarine stamps to replace the long-used wooden ones.[228]

In 1956, breakfast was supplemented by an additional dish, initially with sausage meat, cheese, bacon or syrup replacing part of the bread or oatmeal ration. A few years later, chips had begun to make an appearance on prisoners' plates. A typical week's menu from Durham prison in 1963 illustrates these changes:[229]

Breakfast	Dinner	Tea	Supper
Bread, margarine, tea, porridge, ham.	Soup, bread roll. Lancashire hot pot, peas. Fruit pudding and custard.	Bread, margarine, tea, sugar, fried fish.	Cocoa, cheese biscuits.
Bread, margarine, tea, porridge, bacon and potato savoury.	Soup, bread roll. Meat pie, peas, potatoes. Semolina pudding.	Bread, margarine, tea, preserved pork, figs and custard.	Cocoa, ham sandwich.

Bread, margarine, tea, porridge, sausage meat savoury.	Soup, bread roll. Stew and dumplings, peas, potatoes. Fruit pudding, custard. ½ pt. tea.	Bread, margarine, tea, cheese savoury, tomato, preserved beef.	Cocoa, soup.
Bread, margarine, tea, porridge, fried bacon, fried bread.	Soup, bread roll. Roast beef, roast potatoes, Yorkshire pudding, peas, gravy. Rice pudding. ½ pt. tea.	Bread, margarine, tea, sugar, cream bun, jam, fresh fruit.	Cocoa, preserved beef spread.
Bread, margarine, tea, porridge, sausage, fried bread.	Soup, bread roll. Liver, onions, peas, potatoes. Date pudding and sauce.	Bread, margarine, tea, sugar, ham and chips.	Cocoa, rock cake.
Bread, margarine, tea, porridge, bacon and potato savoury.	Soup, bread roll. Mince and batter pie, roast potatoes, gravy. Sago pudding.	Bread, margarine, tea, sugar, kippers.	Cocoa, Fruit scone.
Bread, margarine, tea, porridge, sausage, fried bread.	Soup, bread roll. Roast beef, roast potatoes, Yorkshire pudding, peas, gravy. Bread and butter pudding, custard.	Bread, margarine, tea, fried bacon, fried beans.	Cocoa, meat spread.

Food produced by prisons themselves increasingly formed a significant source of supply for prison kitchens. By the 1970s, agricultural activities were managed by what had become the Prison Service's Farms and Gardens Group, which controlled some 12,500 acres of land of which 11,000 were devoted to commercial farming and horticultural enterprises. As well as supplying milk, vegetables, fruit, pork and bacon for prison consumption, in 1971 it provided work and training for more than 1,800 prisoners.[230]

PRISON DISTURBANCES

Despite the gradual improvements in its variety and quality, food was still often prominent among prisoners' complaints. Occasionally, these and other grievances resulted in violent disturbances by the inmates. One of the earliest mutinies took place at Dartmoor on the morning of Sunday 24 January 1932, when around forty convicts ran amok in the exercise yards. Within a few minutes, around 150 men were beyond the control of the prison officers. The mutineers managed to take control of the prison for more than an hour and set fire to parts of the building. Order was only restored with the help of local police. During the subsequent inquiry, a number of factors appeared to have contributed to the disturbance, amongst them being the porridge and potatoes, both of which had suffered problems in the days leading up to the mutiny. In one instance, the porridge was 'like water with grains floating in it'.[231] At a trial of the ring-leaders, one prisoner described the food at Dartmoor as food 'unfit for human consumption'.[232]

A series of serious disturbances took place in the 1970s and 1980s – one at Hull in August 1976 resulted in £750,000 of damage, while another in April 1986 spread to forty-six prisons, with damage amounting to £5.5 million and over 800 places being lost. In between these major episodes, there was often a simmering discontent, with prison canteens often being the focus of trouble. One former prisoner recalls that during the late 1980s 'prison confrontations at food serveries [were] a normal part of the daily routine in all closed jails. Spontaneous food strikes and sit downs happened often, pitched fights where trays of food, tables and serving instruments were sent flying were rarer.'[233] In April 1990, another rash of major disturbances took place at a number of prisons including Strangeways and Dartmoor. In the subsequent inquiry, food emerged as one of the main topics of complaint, often being described as inedible and monotonous, with too many variations on stew.[234] The often slow transport of meals in heated trolleys from kitchen to cell was noted as being a problem, as were the outdated facilities and poor hygiene in many prison kitchens, some of which were required to produce up to 1,700 meals three times a day. The report recommended that the Prison Service review its practice in a number of areas, including prison dietary scales, catering officers' budgets and the provision of communal dining facilities. It was also suggested that officers' attendance hours, which largely determined prisoners' mealtimes, be examined with a view to serving meals at more sensible hours.[235]

THE PRESSURE FOR CHANGE

In the past thirty years, the operation of the prison service, including matters such as catering, has come under close scrutiny from a number of sources. In 1981, the new Chief Inspector of Prisons (CIP) began to issue annual reports on the work of the prison service. A few years later, the independent National Audit Office (NAO) began to scrutinise the effectiveness and 'value for money' of various aspects of prison operation, with the NAO's reports being reviewed by parliament's Public Accounts Committee. Much of what the CIP and NAO had to say was often far from favourable, but their reports also gave valuable insights into the increasing problems faced by a service struggling to adapt to the changing expectations and demands placed upon it.

The CIP report for 1989 had a catalogue of criticisms regarding prison catering arrangements. That many inmates were required to eat their meals from plastic plates in overcrowded cells beside a lavatory that could not be flushed was considered a 'degrading and unacceptable practice'.[236] Typical meal times (breakfast at 7.30, dinner at 11.15 and tea as early as 3 p.m., when the supper bun or cake was also served) created gaps between meals that were too short during the day and too long – up to seventeen hours – at night. The range and quality of the food, and also its preparation, left much to be desired. At Durham, a glut of cabbages had led to their frequent appearance on the menu, while at Holloway the inspector was shown an unwashed lettuce and a vegetarian pancake that was not cooked properly.

One source of increasing strain on prison kitchens was the rise in the number of special diets for which they were required to cater. This included not only the various religious diets, such as the standard provision of Halal meat,[237] but also the increasing number of health-related ones, such as egg-free, fish-free, cheese-free, spice-free and pulse-free diets.[238] This issue was particularly common amongst female prisoners – in 1996, Holloway women's prison was providing around fifty special diets covering 40 per cent of the inmates. Even where special dietary provisions were made, the prisoners were not guaranteed to stick with them. At Strangeways, with 300 vegetarians amongst its 1,700 inmates, it was found that for the most popular meals, such as chicken or whole gammon steak, many of the vegetarians suddenly became meat-eaters, throwing the budgetary allocations into disarray. When the kitchens tried to offer a choice, the prisoners expected 1,700 of each dish to be available rather than 850 of each.[239]

Many of the issues to do with choice, diets and wastage were addressed by the introduction of a menu pre-select system, where inmates fill in a form to choose the meal preferences in advance, typically with at least three choices per meal of which one was vegetarian or vegan. The system, first used at Full Sutton prison, proved popular both with prisoners and caterers and was taken up nationally in 1995; about two years later around half of the country's prisons had adopted it.[240]

In 1996, a 'cash-catering' scheme was implemented where a fixed amount of money was allocated for each prisoner's daily food. Prison caterers were given more discretion in sourcing the food they needed, but were still required to place 26 per cent of their expenditure with the Prison Farms and Gardens Group. The scheme aimed to help control food costs and allow better comparisons between different prisons. However, in 1997 the NAO was still reporting considerable variations between prisons in such items as the portion sizes of meat being served. At Downview, prisoners were receiving 6-ounce gammon steaks, while at Cardiff the corned beef hash contained less than 3oz of meat per portion. One meal at Woodhill prison provided a meat content of only 1½oz per prisoner.[241] A simple-minded cash-catering approach could also contribute to such problems – the Halal and Kosher meat required by Muslim and Jewish prisoners was generally more expensive, resulting in them receiving smaller portions than those eating the standard meat issue.

THE PRISON SERVICE CATERING MANUAL

In 1999, in an effort to raise the standards and consistency of its catering provision, and to keep costs in check, the prison service issued its new catering 'Bible', *The Prison Service Catering Manual*, often referred to by its official publication code PSO 5000. Now revised several times, the manual includes major sections on food safety management, meal provision, healthy catering for a diverse prisoner population, and food and safety management for food at the point of service.

PSO 5000 is based on the requirement that 'the food provided shall be wholesome, nutritious, well prepared and served, reasonably varied and sufficient in quantity'.[242] The manual includes extensive information on hygiene and on the storage, handling and preparation of food, the training of staff and financial management.

As regards meal provision, the manual's recommended starting point is a regular 'market survey' of prisoners to establish their tastes and preferences. Based on this information, a pre-select weekly menu is then devised from which prisoners record their choice by filling out paper slips. The menus should include a description of each dish, with each meal including options visually identified as vegetarian, Halal and 'healthy eating'. Items containing genetically modified ingredients are also indicated.

Advice is provided on an extensive range of religious diets including those for Buddhists, Christians, Mormons, Ethiopian Orthodox, Greek Orthodox, Hindus, Jains, Jews, Muslims, Sikhs and even Pagans ('Many will require a vegetarian diet. Some may request a vegan diet').

The manual also emphasises the importance of a healthy diet, with advice on how to make dishes more healthy, for example by reducing the fat, salt and sugar content, minimising the use of deep fat frying and substituting less healthy foods by healthier options, for example by using fruit to decorate desserts rather than piped cream.

On the long-standing issue of meal times, the manual specifies that there should be at least 4½ hours between the start of one meal and the next, with fourteen hours being the maximum that a prisoner should go without food. The recommended meal times are currently: breakfast 07.30–09.00, lunch 12.00–14.00, and evening meal 17.00–19.00.

PSO 5000 undoubtedly resulted in a significant improvement in prison catering standards, as acknowledged by the NAO's subsequent review of the service published in 2006. The report recognised that the quality, range and choice of meals had improved over the previous seven years, and that complaints had fallen. However, many problems remained to be addressed. In some prisons, meal times were still being set to fit in with staff shift patterns, with meals being served earlier than the recommended times, and with some excessive overnight gaps between meals.[243] Lengthy delays also existed in the serving of food after its preparation – in more than a third of prisons visited, this was longer than the recommended maximum of forty-five minutes. At Altcourse prison, one prisoner claimed that dinners were cooked at 9 a.m. then left sitting in heated trolleys until being served up to four hours later.

THE END OF PORRIDGE

One historic change recorded in the 2006 NAO review, unpopular with many prisoners, was the demise of the traditional porridge breakfast – dropped at over half the prisons they visited, it was said, because cooked breakfasts were no longer part of contemporary eating habits.

In place of porridge and the cooked breakfast was the 'breakfast pack', containing items such as cereal, UHT milk, bread, butter, jam, a tea-bag, and sachets of whitener and sugar. The pack's shortcomings were described with contempt by one inmate at Leeds prison, 'you get the breakfast the night before which is a packet of cereal with one little cup ... it's about that big, it's not big enough'. Not only was it a cold meal, but it was eaten by some prisoners the same evening, leaving a long wait until the next day's lunch. The breakfast packs, which cost 27 pence, were also disliked by some catering staff because of their perceived frugal content and nutritional value.[244] Like it or lump it, the twenty-first-century prison menu had arrived:

Sample pre-select menus for meals at Kingston Prison (Portsmouth), April 2005.[245]			
Day	Breakfast	Lunch	Tea
Thu	Breakfast pack Milk (semi-skim) Bread Roll	Bread and Soup	
		1 Vegetarian Pasta Bake, Boiled Potato, Mixed Vegetables	A Vegetable Supreme, Mashed Potato, Green Beans
		2 Chicken and Mushroom Pie, Boiled Potato, Mixed Vegetables	B Chicken Supreme, Mashed Potato, Green Beans
		3 Halal Jamaican Beef Patti, Boiled Potato, Mixed Vegetables	C Halal Chicken Curry, Boiled Rice, Green Beans
		4 Corned Beef and Pickle Roll, Crisps	D Grilled Gammon, Mashed Potato, Green Beans
		5 Jacket Potato and Coleslaw	E Pork Pie Salad
			X Eves Pudding
			Y Fresh Fruit

Fri	Breakfast pack Milk (semi-skim) Bread Roll	Bread and Soup	
		1 Vegetable Spring Roll, Chips and Peas	A Bean and Vegetable Curry, Boiled Rice, Cauliflower
		2 Breaded Fish, Chips and Peas	B Chicken Chasseur, Boiled Rice, Cauliflower
		3 Cheese and Beano Grill, Chips and Peas	C Halal Beef Casserole, Boiled Rice, Cauliflower
		4 Cheese and Tomato Roll, Crisps	D Fish in Parsley Sauce, Boiled Rice, Cauliflower
		5 Jacket Potato and Tuna	E Vegetable Quiche Salad
			X Sponge Pudding and Custard
			Y Fresh Fruit
Sat	Breakfast pack Milk (semi-skim) Bread Roll	Bread	
		1 Veg Sausage x 2, Fried Egg, Hash Brown x 2	A Soya Lasagne Garlic Bread and Salad
		2 Chicken Sausage x 1, Bacon x 1, Hash Brown x 2, Fried Egg	B Minced Beef Lasagne Garlic Bread and Salad
		3 Halal Chicken Sausage x 2, Hash Brown x 2, Fried Egg	C Halal Beef Italienne Garlic Bread and Salad
		(1-3 served with Tinned Tomato and Toast)	D Rice and Bean Stuffed Peppers Salad
		4 Turkey Salad Roll, Crisps	E Cheese Salad
		5 Jacket Potato and Corded Beans	X Sultana Scone
			Y Fresh Fruit

NOTES

Vegetarian Cottage Pie made here as bought in product is not Vegan friendly.

Jacket Potato is served with its filling only.

Crisps go with Lunchtime Rolls only.

Soya Lasagne keep portions back for Vegans and top with Tomato Sauce instead of Cheese Sauce.

Garlic Bread not suitable for Vegans.

Vegetable Supreme to be made with Soya Milk and Vegan Margarine.

Vegans to be given a portion of Mushrooms in place of Fried Egg on Saturday.

INMATE COOKS

Unskilled inmate labour has long been used in prison kitchens to help prepare the daily output of meals. In more recent times, however, there has been increasing provision for prisoners to acquire their own culinary skills. In one early scheme, at Cardiff prison in 1905, a cookery demonstrator from the local university gave female inmates lectures on matters such as how to provide and prepare meals, and the most nourishing and economical foods.[246] Training in skills such as cookery and needlework became a standard part of the regime at borstal establishments, with the aim of helping inmates earn their own livelihood after release. Men, too, were included. At Wormwood Scrubs in 1909, eleven young male offenders held under the modified borstal system gained cookery certificates from the National Food Association.[247] By the 1930s, borstals were offering six-month-long training courses in 'simple cookery', leading to an examination by the Universal Cookery and Food Association.[248] A course was also offered in 'nautical cooking' – presumably aimed at young men – with a 'bread-bakery and yeast-goods' class replacing it in 1953.[249]

By the 1950s, evening cookery classes were being held in many prisons and continued to grow in popularity – Pentonville's 1992 cookery course was reported as being heavily oversubscribed.[250] Formal qualifications continue to be seen as a valuable result of such training with several prisons now entering candidates for National Vocational Qualifications in Food Preparation and Cooking. At High Downs prison, regular 'gourmet lunches' are held where those in training can try and impress potential outside employers with menus such as pumpkin soup with chive and Gruyere croutons, followed by roast fillet of beef with watercress puree and truffle and brandy sauce, or pan-fried Dover sole on roasted aubergine with tomato and olive tapenade rounded off with chocolate and raspberry bavarois.[251]

A lesson in how to make scones for inmates at Askham Grange female training prison in around 1950.

Improvements in prison food have not always met with universal approval. Even the culinary treats traditionally served on Christmas Day have sometimes sparked controversy. The exact details of the Christmas fare served to inmates rarely feature in official records, since it was – and still is – largely a matter of local discretion. The 1946 Christmas menu at Camp Hill prison, recorded by a former inmate, was said to be typical of its time:

Breakfast: Fried egg, with two rashers of bacon and fried bread. Sweetened porridge and tea. The usual 'cob' and a double ration of margarine.

Dinner: Roast beef and/or mutton. Roast and/or boiled potatoes. Greens. Christmas pudding, sauce, custard. Mince-pies, sweet tea. A packet of pressed dates or figs to each man, with a packet of ten cigarettes. Apples, nuts.

Tea or Supper: Bread. Double ration of sugar and margarine. Cocoa. Christmas cake with marzipan and icing. Mince pies, nuts, jam.[252]

The Christmas 'extras' at Camp Hill were largely self-funded and relied on the prison cook saving up a small part of the normal rations for several weeks beforehand. Christmas donations from outside were not welcome, however. Prison standing orders required that:

> All offers of fruit, cake, &c., for the prisoners at Christmas will be courteously declined; intending donors may be informed that a special dinner is given to all prisoners on Christmas Day, and it may be suggested that the money ... could, with greater advantage, be given to a Prisoners' Aid Society.[253]

In more recent times, providing prisoners with seasonal indulgences is a topic that has often received critical comment in the popular press. A typical example in *The Sun* newspaper, under the headline 'Feasts for the Beasts', bemoaned the Christmas 'pampering' of inmates at Wakefield prison where a number of convicted murderers and sex offenders were being held.[254] The Christmas Day lunch menu in 2008 reportedly included a choice of turkey with chipolata sausages, roast lamb with mint sauce or Halal roast beef with horseradish, together with roast potatoes, stuffing and onion gravy. The dessert alternatives were Christmas pudding and rum sauce or fruit cocktail with melon. Boxing Day options included buttered corn-on-the-cob or lemon and peppercorn escalopes, followed by half a roast chicken and mushroom sauce, roast beef with horseradish or gammon steak with pineapple. New Year's Day was celebrated with apple and cranberry roast grill, salmon in a dill sauce, roast pork with apple sauce or braised steak. The pudding menu included luxury chocolate ice-cream and strawberry cheesecake.

In 2007, following a request under the Freedom of Information Act, the Home Office released details of the previous year's Christmas Day menu (below) at Exeter prison which was calculated to cost £2.50 per head:

Breakfast:

Cereal, Scrambled Egg, Tinned Tomatoes, Grilled Sausage, Toast / Marmalade, Beverage pack

Lunch: (Pre-select)

Roast Turkey, Bacon Roll, Stuffing

Salmon Fillet and Parsley Butter

Vegetarian Nut Roast

Halal Chicken Kiev

Chicken Roll Sandwich

Chicken Roll Salad

(All served with Roast Potatoes, Brussels Sprouts, and Baby Carrots)

Christmas Pudding and Vanilla Sauce

Coffee

Dinner: (No Pre–select)

Sliced Gammon Ham

Spicy Chicken Pizza

Cheese and Tomato Pizza

Chips

Pasta Salad

Christmas Muffin

Mince Pie

The members of the 1878 Committee on prison dietaries, for whom a Spartan diet provided 'an opportunity for the infliction of salutary punishment', were no doubt turning in their graves.

MANUAL

OF

COOKING & BAKING

FOR THE USE OF

PRISON OFFICERS.

PRINTED AT H. M. CONVICT PRISON, PARKHURST.

1902.

(8553)

CONTENTS.*

A 2

CHAPTER VII.

CHAPTER VIII.

⋆ Please note that page numbers indicated here reflect this book and not the original *Manual of Cooking and Baking*

PREFACE.

IT having been one of the recommendations of the Departmental Committee on Prison Dietaries that a Manual of Cooking should be in the hands of Prison Cooks, the following instructions have been prepared to form a culinary guide for every-day reference for the Cook and Baker.

A chapter on the selection of food-stuffs has been added with the desire that it may prove useful, not only to the Cook, but to all those who have to inspect and supervise prison food supplies.

By Order,

E. G. CLAYTON,

Secretary.

PRISON COMMISSION,
January, 1902.

MANUAL: COOKING & BAKING.

CHAPTER I.

ELEMENTARY OBSERVATIONS.

COOKERY, though essentially a manipulative art, requires also a certain amount of scientific knowledge in order to understand the rudiments which underlie the art. For if performed unsystematically or on the so-called rule of thumb principle, it is rarely uniform, and the results obtained are too often unsatisfactory and disappointing. It is a handicraft which cannot be learnt merely by scientific or theoretical training, but also needs much assiduous and constant practice, on well recognised methods, before any degree of proficiency can be attained. Most of the natural substances used as food, when raw, are difficult or even impossible to digest, and it is only by sundry manipulations, such as the application of moisture and heat, or in other words by cooking, that they are rendered palatable and digestible.

For cooking to be a success it is important that

the cook should not only know how to select the various ingredients used, and when rightly selected how to prepare them, but he should also possess some acquaintance with the composition of the various food materials employed and understand the changes brought about by the application of heat, &c.

Food is necessary to repair the waste that is constantly going on in the body and also to maintain its natural warmth. Food stuffs have therefore been described as (1) Tissue-formers and (2) Heat-producers. This division however is somewhat misleading and inaccurate, for most foods are not absolutely restricted to one or other of these functions, but may combine the two actions, though in very different degrees.

But as man derives his food from the animal and vegetable kingdom as well as from the mineral world, foods can be more scientifically divided into (I) the Organic, as belonging to the active or living world, and (II) the Inorganic, as belonging to the non-living world ; these broad divisions, being classified into five groups, according to their chemical constituents, in the following way :—

I. ORGANIC.

> (a) *Nitrogenous substances, or Albuminoids ;* so called because their type is that of the albumen (white) of egg, as for example the syntonin and gelatin of meat, the gluten of flour, and casein, the chief constituent of cheese. All these contain the four chemical elements, carbon, hydrogen, oxygen and nitrogen, sometimes also phosphorus and sulphur.

> (b) *Carbohydrates,* which are such substances as starch, sugar, dextrine, &c., and they derive their name from the fact

that they are composed of carbon and water.

(c) *Fats;* Oils, and all vegetable and animal fatty matters, such as butter, cream, suet, lard, &c., come under this head; these contain carbon, hydrogen, and oxygen, but the oxygen is less in amount than in the carbohydrates.

II. INORGANIC.

(d) Salts.

(e) Water.

The Albuminoids are to be found chiefly in the flesh of Meat, Fish, Poultry, Milk and Eggs, and also in certain fruits, as Lentils, Peas and Beans.

The Carbohydrates are to be found chiefly in Flour, Oatmeal, and other Cereals, as Maize, Rice, Barley, and in Vegetables, especially Potatoes, and Fruits.

It is not to be assumed that the foods which principally contain albuminoids do not contain fats, salts, and a certain amount of carbohydrates, or that those consisting chiefly of carbohydrates do not contain some of the other alimentary substances; for example, meat, besides albuminoids, contains more or less fat and salts, flour contains a nitrogenous body called gluten and a small amount of fat as well as the starchy matter. Milk contains all the elements of a typical diet, hence it is called a "complete food." Eggs form another example of the natural admixture of the various alimentary principles.

Except in infancy and in sickness, man does not live exclusively on milk and eggs, for many reasons; and for the purposes of ordinary life we find it more expedient to amalgamate and partake of various kinds of foods. A "mixed" diet is the universal practice.

EFFECTS OF COOKING UPON FOOD-STUFFS.

Man is the only animal that cooks his food; let us see the reasons for his doing so. It has already been said that cooking renders food more easily digested; it does more, it makes it pleasing to the eye, and agreeable to the palate and olfactory organ, thus increasing the desire to take the nourishment necessary for the body. The exposure of food to a high temperature also affords security, by destroying parasitic or other minute living creatures or germs which may accidentally be present in it. Food taken warm promotes and stimulates the digestive action of the stomach.

The various methods of cooking consist chiefly in exposing the food to various degrees of heat, according to the character of the article to be cooked and the effect which is aimed at.

Meat possesses great advantages as a form of food, and is an article of diet which cooking makes either most desirable or quite the reverse. In the raw state it is tough and tenacious, and torn apart with difficulty; but when subjected to the proper degree of heat, for a sufficient length of time and no longer, the connective tissue which binds the muscular fibres together is softened and gelatinized, the muscle fibres themselves, though becoming more firm and solid, owing to the coagulation of the albumen, lose much of their toughness, and are far more readily divided or masticated by the teeth; sundry extractive matters and juices are also set free and developed, which are agreeable both to the taste and smell. These juices are often described as "osmazome," and are the substances which give the flavour to meat. The different way of applying the heat varies according to the object required, and it is only by constant practice and study, that the correct degree of heat necessary for cooking can be acquired; for example, in roasting, the object is to retain the juices of the meat as much as possible, to have the surface nicely browned, and the interior of the joint sufficiently cooked. In order to attain this, the joint is at first exposed to a strong heat, and afterwards removed further from the fire and cooked slowly; by these means the albuminous matter in the external layers of the joint is *rapidly* coagulated, and forms a protective crust which prevents the escape of the juices; the subsequent lower temperature for a longer time coagulating the albumen slowly without any great shrinking or hardening of the flesh. Again, in boiling, the method varies according to the object desired. When a joint is required to be boiled, it is plunged into water which is already boiling, and kept on the boil for about ten minutes, to coagulate rapidly the external surface; the heat then is reduced to from 150° Fah., to 160° Fah., that is, *slow simmering heat*, until the joint is sufficiently cooked. Should broth be required, the meat is cut into several small pieces and put into cold water, and the temperature gradually raised to about 185° Fah., the object here being to allow the juices of the meat to pass into the fluid, the meat itself being tender and still retaining much nourishment. In the preparation of soups, when the meat, &c., is not served, prolonged and continuous, but *not too fast* boiling is required in order to fully extract the gelatine. The addition of salt to the water will help in this extraction. Boiled in this manner the nutritive principles of the meat pass out as completely as possible, the residue, fibres, &c., left being only a tough, tasteless, stringy mass. It is thus seen that in boiling either the meat must be sacrificed to the broth, or the broth to the meat.

The effects of cooking on fish are very similar to

those on meat; it is more easily digested when boiled.

When an egg is boiled, the albumen (white) is coagulated, and it is thus rendered more suitable for food.

Mechanical sub-division and the action of high temperature are the chief processes which are applied to the preparation of vegetables. By these processes they are softened, their structures loosened and rendered more easy of mastication; the heat causes the starch granule to swell up, its outer envelope is ruptured, and its contents set free, so that they can be more readily acted on by the digestive secretions. Also certain substances are extracted into the water in which the vegetables are boiled; thus vegetables of the cabbage tribe give a very disagreeable odour to the water in which they are boiled, and this must be thrown away as soon as possible.

From the above brief account of the effect of cooking upon food it will be understood that it is partly a mechanical and partly a chemical action which is brought about.

CHAPTER II.

GENERAL INSTRUCTIONS.

The Cook or Baker will be held responsible for the proper carrying out of all the work connected with his department. He should so distribute the work amongst the prisoners under his charge, as to provide for the due preparation of the diets for the day, and to arrange the work that each man will know exactly what he has to do. He will be personally responsible that no misappropriation of any kind takes place; that the preparation of food materials and their cooking is conducted according to the official rules; that no waste of any kind occurs; and that the rations are accurately weighed or measured, distributed and served. The cook must endeavour to keep the rations warm whilst they are being dished up, and make the best use of the accommodation provided for this purpose. In many prisons this is achieved by placing blankets over the trays which contain the diets. It is most essential when this custom prevails to have a sufficient number of blankets, so that they can be frequently sent to the laundry. They ought to be washed once a week.

The Bread must be served in special baskets, and not put on the top of the hot potatoes,—an objectionable practice.

The Cook or Baker will be held responsible for the economical consumption of fuel, that is, coal, coke, gas, steam, or wood; and it is his duty to regulate the fire or other heating power, so as to use no more than is needed for proper cooking or baking. The cinders from the coal-fire should be sifted for future use. When leaving his boiler on going off duty he must hand it over to an officer only. See the authorized regulations and instructions for the working and management of steam boilers.

It cannot be too strongly impressed upon Cooks and Bakers that the most scrupulous cleanliness must be maintained in kitchens and bakehouses, both the buildings themselves, and every article in them, should be spotless.

The windows of the kitchen and bakehouse are to be cleaned once a week, and the floors scrubbed daily; and if the floor of the kitchen has become greasy the surface should be sprinkled with fine sand. Care should be taken, when the sand is washed off, that the sand and water are not thrown down the sinks, as this is liable to choke the drains, or interfere with the traps disconnecting the drains. The time chosen for this scouring of floors is usually in the afternoon, when the chief cooking of the day is over. The walls should be brushed down frequently, and the proper time for this is the early morning before they become damp with the steam; the dust, &c., being swept up immediately afterwards. Tables must be washed and scoured at least once a day. Tables should be turned over and scrubbed underneath at least once a week. Shelves, drawers, and cupboards must be kept clean and free from dust, and they should be occasionally scrubbed out with hot water and soda.

The steamers and boiling vessels must be well washed daily inside and outside, with hot water and a small quantity of soda. The copper coverings or lids must be kept thoroughly clean and brightly polished; a flannel dipped in a little whiting or *wood* ashes is a good method to secure this.

The baking and cooking ovens must be well swept

out every day and the latter washed out once a week.

All cooking vessels and utensils must be washed and scrubbed thoroughly as soon as possible after being used. New utensils must be cleaned before being used. Saucepans, &c., should be nearly filled with water, which is then well boiled with a piece of soda, later they should be well scoured and rinsed with hot water, well dried, and then put away in their respective places. If a saucepan has been burnt, put some cold water in with a piece of soda, boil for awhile, then scrub out thoroughly with a saucepan brush. Saucepans and covered vessels should not be kept covered, but exposed freely to the air, the lids hung up neatly; the practice of keeping cooking utensils in cupboards until required for use is to be discouraged.

Dinner tins and such like articles must have all the pieces of food, &c., cleared out before they are put into the water for washing them. Each tin should be thoroughly scalded, washed, rinsed in a second water and turned upside down to drain, and should later be dried with a dry cloth before being stacked away. If this is done carefully and systematically, the tin-ware will keep bright for a considerable period. It is very essential for the cook to supervise prisoners washing up, and see that *plenty of water is used and changed frequently ;* it is impossible to wash up in a puddle of dirty water, with pieces of food floating in it, as is too often attempted.

Knives and forks should be washed separately from the utensils in which food is served. Those with wooden, bone, or horn handles, should not be thrown into hot water, the blades, &c., only being dipped into the hot water, and wiped with a cloth whilst hot.

Should the steel work of the grate, &c., become tarnished or rusty, rub the surface with a raw potato cut in half, and dipped in ashes.

All kitchen refuse must be collected and put into vessels provided for the purpose. It is essential that the refuse should be removed from the vicinity of the kitchen, and if possible from the prison buildings, daily.

The vessels for the reception of refuse must be frequently scalded out with hot water to prevent any smell and to preserve them in a good sanitary condition; and the outsides of them may be whitewashed to give them a tidier appearance.

It will seem from the above that the work of a kitchen must be conducted in an orderly way and on a system, otherwise it will be impossible to get through the day's work in a satisfactory manner. "Clear, clean, and tidy up as you go," will considerably diminish the labour.

CHAPTER III.

OBSERVATIONS ON THE CHOICE AND SELECTION OF FOOD MATERIALS.

Great skill and much scientific knowledge is required to make a true analysis of Food Materials, and to form a correct opinion on their quality, purity, and composition, but with practical experience, and by exercising reasonable intelligence and care, a fairly accurate estimate can generally be made.

The following observations and hints are intended as a guide and help to officers in their inspection of the various food-stuffs used in the Prison Dietary, and in forming a decision thereon.

It is obvious that officers whose duty it is to inspect food, should make themselves fully acquainted with the general conditions and terms of the contract, and with the specifications with regard to the supply of the various articles.

A copy of the specifications should be kept in a conspicuous place in the Store-room, or other convenient site, for ready reference.

MEAT.

To form a correct idea as to whether meat delivered is fit for issue, and complies with the conditions of the contract in every respect, is not always a very easy matter; but a careful consideration of the following remarks will help considerably in forming a conclusion.

Meat may be roughly divided into four classes.

(*a*) *Home-bred and killed*, including every kind of bull, ox, cow, heifer, sheep, and pig.

(*b*) *Foreign-bred, but killed in England*, principally beef. This class is generally of good quality, having been well fed. The rigid inspection on arrival in this country is sufficient protection against the importation of diseased animals. There is often a deficiency in fat owing to wasting during the sea voyage. Occasionally there are signs of bruising, or even laceration of the flesh, due to injury from bad weather; meat in this latter condition should not be accepted.

(*c*) *Refrigerated meat*, chiefly American and Canadian, which is *killed and dressed abroad*, wrapped in canvas and hung up in cool chambers at a temperature of about 36° to 40° Fah. The meat of this class is generally like that of *b* class, as the animals are killed in prime condition, and the rigid inspection is a guarantee against the importation of unsound meat. Refrigerated meat differs slightly in appearance from freshly killed meat; it can be distinguished by :—

(1) The bruised condition of the shanks owing to the chain which is passed round the hind legs during the process of slaughtering.

(2) The fat of the meat is pink, owing to its being stained by the juice of the lean which escapes.

(3) The outside of the meat will present a dull, *dead* colour, when compared with the lustre on the outside of good fresh meat, also occasionally the marks of the canvas covering can be seen.

(4) The dressing is not always so clean and neat as in English dressed meat, and the pizzle and root are not always entirely removed.

If there is the slightest smell to be discovered on the outside, the flesh should be cut into and examined.

(*d*) *Frozen meat*, principally mutton, which has been brought over chiefly from Australia and New Zealand in an actually frozen condition. It can be easily distinguished, before it is thawed, by its hard cold touch. The fat is not stained as in refrigerated meat. When thawed, it can be distinguished by :—

(1) The outside having a wet, parboiled appearance, there will be oozing and dripping of liquid from the meat.

(2) The fat is of a deadly white colour.

(3) The flesh has a uniform pink appearance, owing to the diffusion of the colouring matter of the blood, not mottled as in fresh meat.

It may be well here also to offer the following points with regard to salt meat.

(1) If there is any doubt, a portion should be tested by cooking, which will often reveal deficiencies otherwise not recognisable.

(2) The salting may be well done, but the parts inferior. Examine those pieces at the bottom of the cask, and compare several pieces, to see if there is a fair proportion of good parts of the animal.

(3) The salting may be well done, and the parts good, but the meat old. Here the extreme hardness or toughness and shrivelling is the test. See if the year of salting is on the cask.

(4) The salting may be well done, but the meat bad. If the meat has partly putrefied, no salting will entirely remove its softness, and there may be an offensive smell or greenish colour.

(5) The salting may be badly done either from haste or bad brine. Signs of putrefaction will be present: the meat is paler than it should be and has a bad odour, &c.

When inspecting meat, it should be hung up, so that it can be seen on all sides without handling.

Twenty-four hours after being killed is the best time for the inspection.

The following points must be attended to :—

(*a*) Quantity of bone, (*b*) Quantity and character of the fat, (*c*) Condition of the flesh, (*d*) Condition of the marrow, (*e*) Age of the animal, (*f*) Sex.

(*a*) In lean animals the bone is relatively in too great a proportion; 17 to 20 per cent may be allowed.

(*b*) The fat is a most important item. The exterior of a carcase should be covered with a bright healthy looking fat. In a fat ox it may be as much as one third of the flesh, it should be firm and white, or pale straw colour.

(*c*) Condition of the flesh. The muscles or flesh should be firm, and yet elastic; not tough. It should be of a bright florid hue. In certain parts there should be an absence of fat, whilst in others, as in the loin, fore rib, and mid rib, it should have a marbled appearance from the ramifications of little streaks of fat. Its absence in those parts indicates age or poverty of condition. When pressed with the finger no mark should remain. Good meat should not become moist when kept for a while, but when exposed to the atmosphere for a short time it should be tolerably dry, and there should not be any dripping of water from its meshes, the colour should also remain bright. On the other hand, if the cut side of raw meat becomes of a black hue and shrivelled up after exposure for about an hour, it may be taken as a pretty sure sign that the meat is not good. The interior of the muscle should be of the same character as the outside, there should be no softening or fluid, but it should be smooth and silky to the touch, and juicy; this is particularly noticeable if the animal be young; if old, the lean is coarse looking, stringy in texture, and practically without juice. Meat should not have an unpleasant odour; if it has a sour or putrid smell, it is not fresh The best place to test this is to smell near the bone; it is also a good plan to push a *clean* knife into the flesh up to its hilt; the resistance to the knife should be uniform, and any bad smell can be detected on the blade of the knife when it is withdrawn. That possessing a putrid smell should be rejected.

(*d*) Condition of the marrow. The marrow in the hind legs should be solid 24 hours after the animal has been killed. The colour should be light rosy red; if dark with spots of black, the animal has been sick or putrefaction has commenced. The marrow of the fore leg bones is more fluid, otherwise it should present the same characteristics.

(*e*) Age of animal. In the young the bones are small, soft, porous, and pinkish in colour. The older the animal, the larger, harder, denser, and whiter in colour, the bones become. The inner side of the rib bones is a good place to look for these characteristics. The condition of the joints will indicate information on the point of age. In the joints of young animals the prominences on the ends of the bones are more pronounced, more vascular, more gristly, and so softer than in old animals, when they are smoother, more compact, and whiter.

(*f*) Sex. Under this head must be considered the differences between ox and bull-beef, and old-cow and heifer; the latter is really of more importance than whether male or female.

Bull-beef may be distinguished from ox-beef by the size of erector muscle, pizzle, and pelvic bones; the absence of a plentiful supply of "cod" and "kidney" fat, a general massiveness of the bones and muscles, and almost a total absence of that coating of fat on the exterior of the carcase which is the characteristic of well-fed ox-beef. The lean will be very coarse and stringy in texture, dark in colour, with an absence of juice and marbling by fat. The feel to the finger and thumb will convey an india-rubber-like consistency, instead of displaying the marbled, juicy, and florid coloured appearance of the ox, which is also smooth and silky to the touch.

The fore-quarter of the bull is very large, the collar or crest requires the whole hand to grasp it, whilst in the ox it can be grasped with the forefinger and thumb. If the neck has been removed suspicion will at once be aroused.

The distinguishing features between old-cow and heifer or young-cow, are that in the latter the udder is but slightly developed, but consists principally of soft fat; if the cow has had one calf, the surface of the udder will be slightly soft, but larger and more developed; whilst in the old-cow, the udder will be tough on the surface and brown in colour, the ducts through which the milk has come will be plainly visible, and the general substance will be spongy and only partially fat. There is a practice of first cutting away the udder altogether while the carcase is warm, pulling the skin over the site, and skewering in fat instead. This can be detected by removing the skewers. This trick is never resorted to unless the animal has had more than two calves, accordingly the meat can be safely rejected as coming under the age clause in the terms of the contract. The pelvic bone or aitch bone is very thin in an old cow, especially at the end nearest the udder.

In the fore-quarter, the ribs of the heifer or young cow show the pinkness of youth; in old cow they will be white and more bleached as age advances, and there is a general want of fat.

The meat of a heifer is like that of a young ox, and very difficult to distinguish from it; whilst that of an old cow is coarse, stringy to the touch, dark in colour, and with an absence of moisture. The fat is plentiful on the exterior, coming right to the shoulder; in the cow it is yellow in colour and scanty.

The differences of sex in sheep can be told in much the same way as in cattle. The ram in relation to the wether presents very much the same appearance as the bull to the ox. In old ewes the kidney fat will be much veined, the udder large and spongy, the holes through which the milk has come being visible.

Most of the above remarks refer more especially to beef, as being more in use in prisons than mutton. Good mutton is of deep red colour when cut, the fat should be white and should not be coarsely ingrained with the lean. Small-boned mutton is generally the best and most profitable. The fat, in addition to being of a good white colour, should be firm. The greater portion of contract mutton is too fat, the proportion of fat to lean being so great as frequently to give rise to complaint. The way of detecting the amount of fat on a carcase without cutting it through, is to look at the shoulders; if a bluish tinge is discernible the proportion of fat is not too great. If, on the other hand, this tinge is absent, the carcase is too fat. Should the contractor refuse to remove the surplus fat, the carcase must be rejected. When joints only are received, the consumption being small, if too fat, the butcher should be asked to trim them or make allowance.

Frozen mutton is not in the meat contract, but it may be well to mention that it has many of the same peculiarities as frozen beef. It lacks the external bright appearance of freshly killed meat. It is more often frozen in the whole carcase than is the case with beef, and therefore retains the nutriment of the meat better. Frozen mutton should be carefully examined by cutting into the thickest parts and observing the cut surfaces; as if frozen before the natural heat of the animal has passed off, the outside only may have been frozen and the interior may be putrescent.

GENERAL HINTS.

The general conditions of the Meat Contract state that the meat shall be of unexceptionable quality and properly fed. This gives ample scope, for it is impossible to lay down any hard and fast line as to what a quarter of beef should weigh, though a well-fed quarter of ox should, ordinarily, weigh not less than 150 lbs., and the same if heifer not less than 135 lbs. The question of the contract price is not to be considered.

It is suggested that the Contractor be requested to bring the fore and hind quarters alternately. If smaller quantities are required, these should be in something like a fair rotation,—as, for instance, first day, the top piece (comprising the thick flank, buttock, and aitch bone); second day, the remainder of the flank (viz., rump, loin, and thin flank); third day, half the fore-quarter, fore rib, middle rib, and part of the brisket; fourth day, remainder of fore-quarter (viz., clod and sticking, chuck and leg-of-mutton piece, and remainder of brisket). An arrangement of this kind will ensure the whole of the joints being obtained in turn, and in pieces of fair size, giving an opportunity of judging the quality. On no account should the meat be received in small bits.

Hospital meat is not to be cut off from the meat supplied for the general use of the prison. As regards mutton the Contractor is paid a higher price for this meat, and should provide separate best joints.

All meats, after being inspected and weighed, should, unless immediately wanted, be hung up in the store-room.

Suet should be fresh, sound, clean, and dry; if the caul is sent it should be unrolled; only the head of this part is allowed, the apron portion being thin and membranous.

The strictest order and cleanliness must at all times be observed in the store-room.

The cart bringing the meat, and also the person who delivers the meat, ought to be clean. The hands and clothes of officers and prisoners who have the handling of the meat must be scrupulously clean.

Baskets, Boxes, Trays, Slabs, and Hooks, must be kept well scoured and spotlessly clean.

BEEF.

MODE OF CUTTING UP.

An ox, cow, or heifer, is divided (jointed) as follows (see plate):—

1. *Fore Ribs*, suitable for roasting.
2. *The Sirloin*, ditto.
3. *The Rump*,—braising, grilling, &c. (best part for steak).

[These are known as the best joints, and, being more expensive than the rest, are not, as a rule, supplied by the contractors at contract price.]

4. *The Aitchbone*, sometimes called the Round; it is below the rump, at the hind part, is suitable for roasting and boiling, or when salted, it may be boiled or stewed.
5. *The Mouse (Buttock)*, which includes part of the thigh bone, suitable for braising, boiling, grilling, and stewing. This piece is also salted at times.
6. *The Leg*, also called the Veiny-piece, suitable for stewing, used for stock or soup.
7. *Thick Flank*, generally boiled or stewed.
8. *Thin Flank*, generally boiled.

9. *Nine Holes*, includes part of the Brisket, chiefly salted or pickled, when it is boiled; also

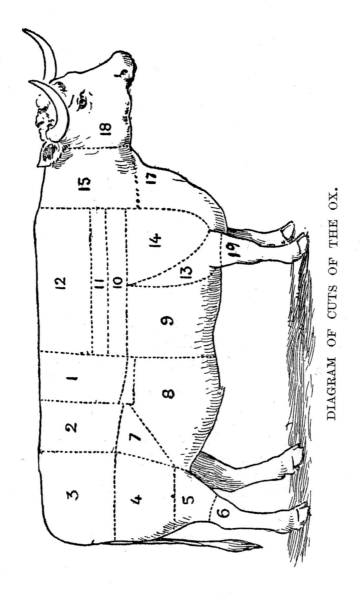

DIAGRAM OF CUTS OF THE OX.

used plain for boiling and stewing purposes; this part is less fat than the brisket proper.

10. *Runners*, cut close to shoulder and head,

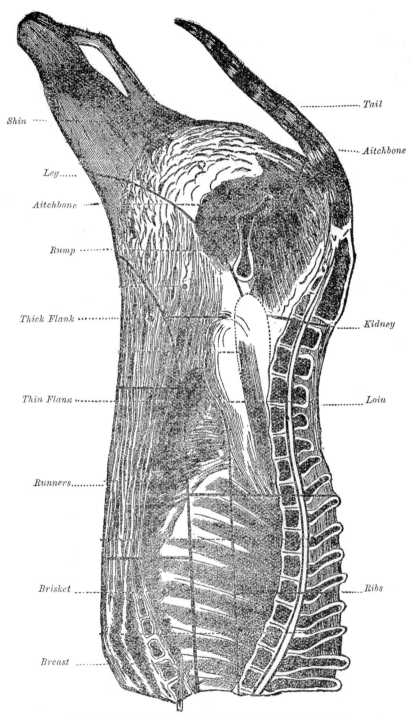

Shin

Leg

Aitchbone

Rump

Thick Flank

Thin Flank

Runners

Brisket

Breast

Tail

Aitchbone

Kidney

Loin

Ribs

SIDE OF BEEF, SHEWING PRIME JOINTS.

used for boiling, stewing, also for pies; the thin end is sometimes salted and boiled.

11. *First Runners*, used for boiling or stewing.

12. *Spare Ribs*, generally roasted or baked, and sometimes stewed.

13. *Shoulder*, sometimes called Mutton-piece or Leg-piece, suitable for roasting, baking, or stewing.

14. *Brisket*, generally salted and boiled. It is not suitable for either roasting or baking.

15. *Neck or Sticking-piece*, including part of the Head, used for soup, stews, and for mincing.

17. *The Clod*, suitable for stewing, or for soup and stock.

18. *The Head*, including Cheek, for stewing and boiling.

19. *The Hough or Shin (leg)*, generally used for soup and stock; the fleshy end is sometimes used for stews.

MUTTON.

MODE OF CUTTING UP.

A Sheep is divided into the following pieces. (see plate):—

1. *The Leg*, suitable for roasting, baking, or boiling. The leg of a wether is best for roasting or baking, and the leg of ewes is considered best for boiling.

2. *The Loin*, best and suitable for roasting or baking, also for grilling or broiling, and stewing when cut into chops.

3. *The Loin, Chump-end*, treated the same as

best end of loin, but more often stewed. *Two Loins, undivided, constitute a Saddle.*

4. *The Neck, best end,* suitable for roasting, baking, boiling, or braising, but generally made into cutlets, when they are grilled or fried.

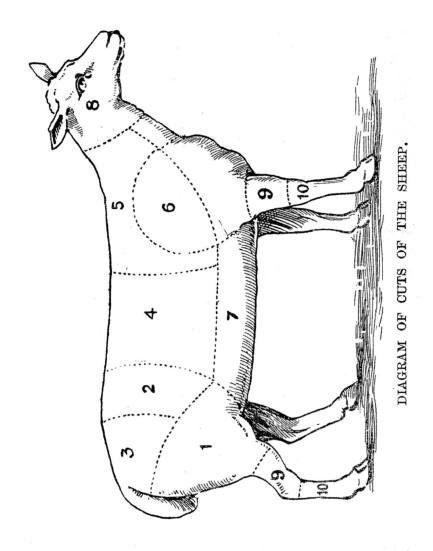

DIAGRAM OF CUTS OF THE SHEEP.

5. *The Neck, scrag end,* useful for stews and soups, also boiled.

6. *The Shoulder,* generally baked or roasted

whole; the blade-bone is frequently removed, when the shoulder is stuffed and roasted or braised. This joint is not suitable for boiling.

7. *The Breast,* suitable for baking or stewing.

8. *The Head,* including part of the Neck (scrag end), suitable for boiling, useful for broth.

9. *The Shank,* used for soup and broth, sometimes stewed.

10. *The Trotters,* made into broth with or without the head; they are also boiled and sometimes stewed

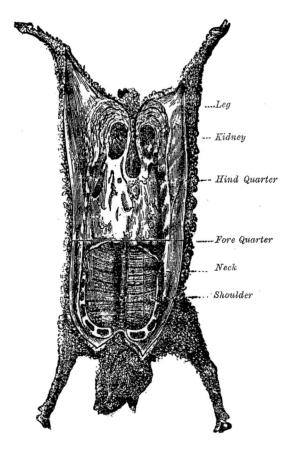

PRINCIPAL JOINTS OF THE SHEEP

FISH.

Fish is frequently required for Hospital use. Every precaution must be taken to see that it is absolutely fresh. Fish is not in contract (except at a few prisons), but is bought as occasion requires. A fresh fish is firm and stiff, the drooping or not of its tail is a fair criterion on this point. The eyes should be bright and prominent; the gills a bright red colour. Flat-fish, like plaice, sole, brill, or turbot, keep better than herrings, mackerel, or mullet. All fish should have been cleaned, be unbruised, unbroken, and free from smell, when delivered. Cod-fish is considered better if it is allowed to soak in salted water for a few hours before it is cooked, as this makes the flesh firmer.

When small flat-fish, as dabs, &c., are tendered, see that you get something beside head and fins; a proper allowance of weight should be made for heads, &c.

Stale fish is not only unwholesome, but sometimes poisonous. Fish smelling the least unpleasant should at once be rejected.

EGGS.

Two things with regard to eggs have to be considered: freshness and size. The first can to some extent be judged by the appearance; there being a characteristic aspect, a kind of lustre, difficult to describe, which indicates a fresh egg. The egg may be held up to the light in one hand and viewed through a tube formed by the other hand,—when, if the shell is not translucent, or if dark spots are observed, it is a sure sign that the egg is not fresh.

The size is judged of by the weight. The average hen's egg weighs 2 oz.

When eggs are used for cooking, each egg should be separately broken into a clean cup and smelt, so that a bad one can be rejected without spoiling other articles previously prepared.

Stale and small eggs must be replaced by others by the contractor.

MILK.

The amount and character of the milk yielded by a cow vary considerably. The quantity and richness depend largely upon the breed, and in the same cow upon its age, the age of the calf, the season of the year as influencing the character of its food, &c. But although the milk from individual cows varies, yet the mixing of the milk from a herd averages the general composition, so that the average secretion of a healthy cow may be taken as 20 to 25 pints daily, and as a general rule should contain not less than 12 to 13 per cent. of total solids, of which 3.2 per cent. is fat.

On receiving a consignment of milk, after ascertaining that the proper quantity has been delivered, the object is to determine whether it is pure and wholesome, and that it has not been adulterated or sophisticated. The milk should be stirred gently, and a fair sample taken from the centre of the can. A portion of this should be placed in a narrow glass, which is stood on a sheet of white paper.

The colour of the milk should be opaque white; a slight tinge of colour may be due to the food of the cows, or may be owing to the addition of annatto or turmeric,—a deep tinge is suspicious of this latter.

There should be no pronounced peculiarity of taste or smell.

The reaction should be neutral, *very faintly* acid or alkaline. Strong acidity is indicative of retrograde changes in the milk; strong alkalinity either disease in the cow or the addition of carbonate of soda.

The specific gravity is tested by a lactometer; it varies a little with the temperature. Normal milk usually averages 1030 at 60° Fah., 1031 at 39° Fah., 1029 at 70° Fah.

The cream is measured by a creamometer; the amount varies according to the breed of the cow and its food. It should not be less than 10 per cent. by volume of the milk.

There should be no deposit or sediment until the milk decomposes; if there be, it is probably chalk or starch.

When milk is boiled it should present no difference in appearance.

The chief adulterations are (1) the addition of water; (2) the removal of part of the cream, with or without the addition of water; (3) the addition of starch, gum, dextrine, flour, or glycerine; (4) the addition of the so-called preservatives, as bicarbonate of soda, borax, boric, and salicylic acids, and formalin. The addition of water lowers the specific gravity and, speaking generally, there is a loss of three degrees for every 10 per cent. of water added. On the other hand, removing the cream (skimming) raises the specific gravity; so that milk which has been creamed and watered may have a normal specific gravity; the specific gravity therefore must be taken in conjunction with the amount of cream.

Watering alone is detected by a lower specific gravity and a diminished quantity of cream.

Creaming alone is detected by a heightened specific gravity and a diminished quantity of cream.

When both are resorted to, the cream will be small in amount; but the specific gravity may be normal, and adulteration can only be detected, if kept within certain limits, by a comparison with the milk, freshly drawn from the same source.

The power of inspecting the dairies, &c., of the contractor is given to the Governor and other authorities by the terms of the contract.

To determine the total solids of the milk, a measured quantity is weighed, and evaporated to dryness; the residue may then be weighed and the total solids calculated; but for this and the detection of other adulterations expert knowledge is required. If there is a deposit at the bottom of the milk cans, the attention of the Medical Officer should be called to it.

Milk should always be scalded before being issued, and the utmost care and vigilance are required to ensure perfect cleanliness of all utensils in which this is done. A special apparatus called a Sterilizer is in use in some prison kitchens, and it is essential that officers should make themselves acquainted with its use and pay strict attention to the Rules laid down for their guidance.

BUTTER.

When the cream of milk is churned, that is, violently agitated in a suitable apparatus, the fat globules get clotted together, entangling in their meshes some casein and water. The butter so formed is then pressed, in order to squeeze out some of the water, and salt is added to keep it.

The aspect, smell, and taste are points that should be considered in inspecting a consignment of this article.

The amount of water in good butter is about 12 per cent.; if much below this it is suspicious as suggestive of the addition of foreign fat. The addition of water or milk is sometimes made by beating up the butter in these fluids; if excessive it can be detected by melting the butter in a test tube, when the fluid will show beneath the oil.

The amount of casein or curd is generally about 1 per cent.; it should not exceed 3 per cent. In bad butter it is much more than this. It is the decomposition of the casein that is chiefly the cause of rancidity in butter, and therefore the greater amount of casein the more the chance of rancidity.

The fat forms 83 to 90 per cent. of the butter. The proportion of the fats and residue, chiefly casein, can be roughly estimated by putting a known quantity of the butter into a glass vessel, previously weighed, melting the butter by placing the glass vessel in hot water, then pouring off the oil into another vessel whose weight is known, and thus the amounts can easily be calculated by re-weighing.

These butter fats consist of certain volatile and non-volatile fatty acids, all in combination with glycerine, the former being also soluble, the latter insoluble, in water. The volatile and soluble fatty acids should not be lower than 5 per cent., usually in good butter they are nearly 8 per cent. It is the presence of these volatile fatty acids which give to butter its peculiar and distinctive characters, and the determination of the amount present which enables the analyst to distinguish butter fat from margarine fat.

It may be of interest here to say that Margarine is manufactured chiefly from beef-fat. The beef-fat

C

is finely minced and heated in tanks sufficiently to melt the fat, which rises to the top, and this is run off as a clear yellow oil. It is then partially cooled, which allows a portion of a substance called stearin to coagulate, the oleo-margarine is separated, filtered, pressed, mixed with milk, coloured with annatto, and cooled with ice. If properly manufactured, margarine is a wholesome article of diet; but this is no reason for its being sold as butter. It contains a much smaller amount of the volatile fats than true butter, and, as said above, it is this difference which is made use of in analysis.

Salt is added to nearly all butter; in fresh butter it should not be more than 2 to 8 grains in the ounce (0.5 to 2 per cent.); in salt butter not more than 35 grains in the ounce (8 per cent.). An excess of salt means, usually, too much water and curd.

CHEESE.

In the manufacture of Cheese, casein, its chief constituent with some fat, is precipitated from milk by rennet, at a suitable temperature. The curds are then pressed to squeeze out the whey and to reduce the mass to the required shape.

When cheese is kept it undergoes a change known as "ripening," which is essentially a decomposition. Later, various moulds, blue, green, or red, occur, during which the fats augment at the expense of the casein, and certain extractives and volatile acids are produced. The aroma of cheese arises to a great extent from this decomposition. The maggots or larvæ of a fly (mites) are frequently present in cheese undergoing decomposition. These products are harmless, indeed they are much appreciated by some.

Cheese is not much adulterated; substances, of

which the chief is starch, are added sometimes to increase the weight. Starch can be detected by applying a weak solution of iodine to the cut surface, and is indicated if a violet colour results.

The quality of cheese is known by the taste. Prisoners, as a rule, like a fairly full-flavoured cheese, and one not decayed or so dry as to crumble, so that the whole cheese should be free from many cracks, and the cut surface should have a homogeneous, uniform appearance.

BACON.

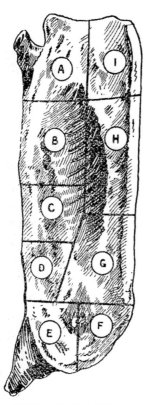

SIDE OF BACON.

Except for occasional use in the hospital, Bacon in prison is demanded to supply fat in the beans and bacon dinner; accordingly the contract requires "short-cut middles," fat and boneless, to be supplied; and not the streaky portions, which are generally chosen from the breast or flank for "rashers," or from lean portions like the gammon.

The fat should be white, firm, and fairly dry, not spotted or streaked with yellow, nor flabby, wet, and loose in texture. The rind should be thin and bright in colour.

It is well not to keep too large a stock, and when placed in the store-room, bacon should be hung up.

c 2

A. Fore-end or Shoulder, Hock (about 8 lbs.)
B. Thick, streaky (about 7 lbs.)
C. Thin, streaky (about 4 lbs.)
D. Flank (about 4 lbs.)
E. Gammon, cushion.
F. Gammon, corner.
G. Loin and flank (about 7 lbs.)
H. Ribs, back (about 6 lbs.)
I. Collar (about 7 lbs.)

FOWLS.

Fowls are at times required for the use of patients in the hospital. They ought to be young, fresh, in good condition, and weigh not less than $1\frac{3}{4}$ lb. when trussed. Signs of age are shown by stiff, horny feet, long spurs, dark-coloured hairy thighs, stiff beak and bones.

There should be no smell nor discolouration of the skin. The back generally discolours before the breast. The feet should be limp and pliable, not stiff and dry, which indicate a stale bird.

The condition of the flesh should be firm and not flabby, and the bird should be plump; the breast bone is sometimes broken across to produce this appearance, if the bird be sent in by a poulterer. There should be some fat, which is a sign of health and good feeding, but there is no advantage in having one excessively fat, as this only wastes away in the cooking, and is not always agreeable to a sick person. The flesh is not marbled like that of the ox, but the fat is accumulated in a layer over the body.

From Christmas to April chickens are most difficult to obtain; and consequently during this period
of the year greater care and caution should be exer-
cised in inspecting those sent in.

VEGETABLES.

Cabbage, Turnip Tops, or Greens generally should
be young and tender, sound, clean and fresh, properly trimmed and without decayed leaves.

Carrots should be of a good colour, quite firm, have
a crisp appearance when broken across, and when
boiled be soft and tender.

Parsnips should not be too large, the texture
should not be woody, and they should cook well.

Turnips should be small, finely grained, juicy,
smooth and sound, not soft, porous, or stringy.

Onions should be sound, dry, clean, and have
been well harvested. They should be kept in a cool,
dry, airy place; during severe frost they must be
protected, piled together with a few sacks or mats
over them, and when the weather softens they should
be spread out again, or, if roped, hung up again.
Damp will start them into growth, which will soon
spoil them.

Potatoes enter largely into the prison dietary, and
it is very necessary they should be of good quality.
This is judged by the size of the tuber,—the contract specifying not less than eight to the pound,—
the appearance of the skin, firmness of the texture,
absence of fungus disease, and the characteristics
when cooked, which should be mealy or floury, not
close, waxy, or watery; nor should they turn black
on cooling.

Potato disease, which is very prevalent in wet

cold seasons, shows on the tuber as brown spots : it is really a fungus which penetrates the substance of the potato, causing it to rot and decay.

Potatoes, if frozen, rapidly decompose when thawed, but are not harmful to health if used before they putrefy, though they acquire a sweetish taste which is objectionable. They also deteriorate if allowed to sprout.

The varieties of potatoes are numerous, many having characteristic qualities of their own, and requiring a little different treatment in the cooking. The consignments of this vegetable should not, therefore, be mixed, even though the sorts are of good quality. They should also be of fairly uniform size for the day's ration ; for if some are small and the others large, cooking equally is difficult: · ⸺

Preserved or dried vegetables are sometimes used ; a sample should be cooked before definitely accepting a consignment.

For Rules for Cooking Vegetables see page 51.

PEAS.

Those used in the prison dietary are the variety known as "dried split peas." They should be of good size and colour, the convex surface smooth ; there should be freedom from worm-eaten, shrivelled, green, or very light yellow ones. Occasionally a good sample of pea may be a dull grey colour, from being sprinkled with pea flour ; a few placed in cold water will reveal their true colour in a few minutes. It is essential that the peas should boil quite soft. Old peas require soaking for some hours, before cooking, in cold water ; but if peas are young they will cook soft without this.

BEANS.

Those called " White Haricot Beans " are chiefly used. They should be of good size, but more important still, they should be uniform in size. The colour should be white, not yellow or black. The convex surface should be fairly smooth and not crinkled and shrivelled.

RICE.

The varieties of Rice are numerous. Patna is the variety generally used. The grain should be free from the husk, whole, clean, of good colour and size.

SUGAR.

Both moist and loaf Sugar are in use. The former is of the kind called " Demarara "; it should be light brown in colour, not gummy or wet, and should all dissolve without sediment.

TEA.

When there is doubt of any consignment of tea, the leaves may be damped and spread out and their characteristics inspected. The structure of the tea leaf is serrated or notched, but not quite up to the stalk. Dirt, sand, and other foreign matter should be looked for. The usual way, however, to test tea, is by making an infusion, which should be fragrant to smell, not harsh or bitter to taste, and not too dark in colour.

The chief adulteration of tea is now principally the admixture of old and exhausted tea leaves, which gives a bitter taste, and the addition of other leaves than those of the genuine tea plant, which requires expert knowledge for detection.

WHEAT.

So little wheat is now ground in prisons, that it will not require to be dealt with at any great length, but mention must be made of it in order to give some idea of the quality and composition of flour and whole-meal, which, in the shape of bread, forms a large element in the prison dietary.

Wheat being very rich in solids, and containing comparatively little water, presents much nutrition in a small bulk. Its chief defect as a food is that it contains only a small amount of fat.

There are several kinds of wheat, each of which has certain characteristics. The wheat grown in this country is usually known as White or Red, Hard or Soft, &c. The prison contract specifies for the supply of English, Colonial or Foreign Wheat, to be delivered separately, so that in grinding, a mixture of the different kinds may be used; this is found to be more satisfactory in the grinding, and to give a better and more uniform product. These wheats are not to weigh less than 62 lbs. to the bushel, the heavier the better. They are to be dry, clean, and sweet. Some estimate can be formed as to the dryness by thrusting the hand into the sack, when, if the wheat is dry, the hand will easily be passed in, but with some difficulty if damp. There should be no smell of damp or mustiness, and no evidence of insects, fungi, mouse, or other dirt. It should be free from other grains, like barley and oats or cockle seeds (small, short, thick, blackish grains), and smut,—a fungus which fills the wheat grain with a black, dusty powder. The grains should be well filled out, the envelopes should not be split open. Sprouted wheat is of a dark colour and bitter to the taste, and careful search will show where the sprout is broken off, or even a few grains with the sprouts on them. The shape, colour, and general appearance of the different kinds of wheat, whether English or Foreign, &c., will, after a little experience, be fairly easily learned. Foreign wheat is usually smaller, harder, darker in colour, and drier, than English wheat.

The mean composition of numerous analyses of wheats is given as follows (König):—

Water .... 13.54 per cent.
Nitrogenous Matter......... 12.42 ,,
Fat .... 1.70 ,,
Sugar .... 1.44 ,,
Gum and Dextrine .... 2.38 ,,
Starch .... 64.07 ,,
Fibre and Ash.............. 4.45 ,,

If wheat grains are soaked for a short time in water it will be easy to see that externally there are sundry yellowish coats or envelopes,—four are usually described,—and internally a central white portion, or, roughly, bran and flour. The proportions of the two are usually given as about 80 per cent. of flour, 16 per cent. of bran, with 4 per cent. of loss in the process of separation. The ground product of wheat is divided into different qualities according to its fineness, thus:—Fine or best flour; Seconds or household flour; then following sharps or middlings, pollards, and finally the coarse bran.

The outer coats of wheat grains contain more nutritive material (nitrogenous matter and fat) than the inner portions, for instance, the proportion of gluten in whole grain is 12 per cent, in bran 14 to 18 per cent., whilst in flour it is only 10 per cent.; hence arises the practice of using wholemeal, or all the constituents of the grain, in preference to fine white flour; but the bran or outer envelope itself is exceedingly hard and difficult to digest, accordingly a middle course is adopted in the prison dietary; 12 per cent. of the coarse bran and pollard is extracted, giving what is sometimes called a " decorticated" wholemeal.

It will be convenient to mention the character of white flour first. It should be almost a perfectly white, fine powder, with only the very slightest tinge of yellow; there should be no lumps, or, if there are, they should break down easily between the finger and thumb; the odour should be sweet, there should be no smell of mustiness, and it should be free from acidity to the taste, though the best flour is faintly acid to test paper. It should exhibit no trace of bran when pressed smooth with a polished surface; and it should have a certain amount of cohesion, sufficient to retain for some time the impression when a handful is squeezed. Microscopically there should be an absence of foreign starches, negativing adulteration with the flour of other cereals, as barley, oats, maize, &c. Fine white flour should all pass through a sieve with a mesh of 3,600 holes to the square inch.

Prison whole-meal, that is the products of the whole grain with 12 per cent. of the coarse bran eliminated, should present many of the characteristics of white flour, but of course is of a darker colour: more especially will this be noticeable if it be ground from a red wheat or foreign wheat. When it is flattened with a polished surface there should be found the white flour in good proportion, and the sharps and pollards should not be present to too large an extent or too coarse. The whole should pass through a sieve with a 16″ mesh to the inch, and if the flour be well ground, 13 ounces out of a pound of the whole-meal should pass through the 60″ mesh sieve. Occasionally, however, whole-meal will be sent in, and when this test is applied, it is found that only some 9 ounces of the pound will pass the 60″ mesh sieve; if the 7 ounces residue, however, be examined, it will be seen that a considerable amount of white flour remains in it, in granules of globular shape,—this is known as semolina; it is the portion just inside the cortical portion of the wheat grain of hard wheats, and is very rich in gluten (vegetable albumen), and it is much sought after for pastry-making, and does not render the whole-meal inadmissible.

Attention to the above points, and the character and quality of the bread made from it, will give a very fair estimate of the quality of any particular consignment. Microscopical and chemical examination must be left to the expert.

OATMEAL.

Oatmeal is a highly nutritious food, and, like wheat-meal, enters largely into the prison dietary. It is the richest of all the cereal meals in fat and nitrogenous matters. but contains less starch; and owing to the absence of certain adhesive properties in the gluten, which is possessed by the gluten of wheat, it cannot be made into bread, but is used to make porridge and gruel.

The coarse Scotch oatmeal in use in prisons is the

oat deprived of the husk, but retaining the envelopes of the oat grain, which correspond to the bran of the wheat grain.

It should be sweet, dry, and clean. The chief adulteration is with barley-meal, or the husk of the oat itself, or that of barley and wheat, which can be usually detected by careful inspection, but can only be definitely proved by microscopical examination.

The following table shows roughly the relative difference between Fine wheaten flour, Wholemeal flour, and Oatmeal :—

	Fine Wheaten Flour. per cent.		Whole-meal. per cent.		Oatmeal. per cent.
Water	13	...	13	...	8
Nitrogenous matter, chiefly gluten	10	...	12	...	14
Fat	1	...	2	...	6
Starch, &c.	74	...	71	...	65
Fibre and Ash	2	...	2	...	7

CHAPTER IV.

GENERAL DIRECTIONS FOR THE VARIOUS METHODS OF COOKING.

The various methods of cooking in H. M. Prisons comprise boiling, steaming, baking, roasting, stewing, broiling, and frying. The last three are mostly employed in connection with Hospital or Sick-room Cookery.

BOILING.

Boiling has two distinct objects which differ considerably from each other. The first is to retain as much nourishment as possible in the article so cooked; and the other is to extract as much as possible of the nourishing juices of the solid ingredients used, so as to amalgamate them into the liquid (water) in which the article is boiled. The latter is more largely practised in connection with Prison Cookery than the former. Water boils at 212 deg. Fah.; this degree is generally known as *boiling* heat, whilst simmering (slow cooking) is done at a temperature from 185 to 210 deg. Fah.

When a piece of meat is to be cooked to be served whole, it must be placed in boiling water and allowed to boil fast for at least ten minutes, in order to harden the albumen, so as to prevent the juices from escaping; the heat is then reduced, and the article to be boiled must be cooked at simmering heat, until tender; 15 to 20 minutes to the pound is the usual average time allowed for meat to be boiled. The scum which rises to the surface during the first stage must in every case be carefully removed, but fat must not be taken away when the skimming operation is performed. In the case of soups, when the meat, cereals and vegetables are cut up small, slow cooking is generally recommended, in order to extract all the goodness of the ingredients and to make them very tender. Most vegetables are cooked at actual boiling heat.

Salt, pickled, cured, or smoked meat, should, when possible, be allowed to soak for some time in cold water, and then placed in the cooking vessel with either cold or warm water, according to the nature and character of the meat, and then be brought quickly to the boil. The salt or brine is considerably extracted when cured, salt or smoked meat is thus treated.

STEAMING.

Cooking by steam is more gradual (slower) than by boiling, and is therefore for many reasons to be recommended. Steaming is cooking by means of moist heat; it is effected by the steam passing through pipes from the *boiler* into the coppers or cauldrons, (into a hermetically closed vessel or chamber).

Meat, potatoes, fish, soups, &c., are usually cooked by steam. In all cases the water or other liquid, such as stock, liquor, &c., is to be brought to the boil, and after a period of from fifteen minutes to thirty minutes the steam should be somewhat reduced, so as to allow the contents of the steamer to cook more or less slowly till the articles, solid or liquid, to be steamed are quite done and fit for serving. Exception to this rule is made in case of vegetables—potatoes and greens,—when full steam is required during the whole process of cooking.

BAKING AND ROASTING.

The success of every method of cooking depends largely upon the good management of the fire or heat. Both baking and roasting cannot be successfully performed without a good heat. Iron and brick ovens are used for the purpose of baking. The management of bakers' ovens and the baking of bread is dealt with under a separate heading, and is therefore not explained here.

Iron ovens, as well as brick or bakers' ovens, heated by coal or gas, are adapted for roasting, *i.e.*, baking meat, &c. In roasting or baking joints of meat in an oven, the great secret is that of preserving as much as possible the nourishing qualities of the meat, by preventing the essential juices from escaping. The usual time allowed for roasting or baking meat is 15 minutes per lb. and 15 minutes over; but the thickness of a joint, its shape, and the season of the year, have to be considered; and the cook must therefore use his judgment and bear in mind, also, that the meat from freshly killed animals takes longer to cook than meat that has been hung for a time; again, the meat of young and fat animals takes a little less time than that of old and lean animals.

The oven must be thoroughly hot before the meat is put in. The latter must, when possible, be placed on a trivet in the roasting pan; this will cause the joint to get much better cooked, and facilitate the basting, which operation is most essential.

" Basting" is to pour liquified fat or dripping over the meat during the process of roasting or baking. For this purpose some dripping should be placed on top of the meat, if the latter be not fat enough. The fat or dripping becomes liquified (dissolved) when exposed to heat, and will thus enable one to baste.

After the meat has been in a very hot oven from 15 to 20 minutes (the needful time required to brown the surface of the meat), the heat should be somewhat reduced, and a moderate heat maintained until the meat is done. If the oven is too hot the meat becomes scorched, and every care must be taken to guard against this. Some cooks dredge the meat with flour when it is half cooked: this is done to make the gravy better, but it is not essential. The average heat required for roasting is about 190 deg. Fah. for the first stage, and 160 deg. after. Perfection in roasting can only be attained by carefully studying the important points enumerated. It is difficult to give hard and fast rules as to the actual time needed for roasting or baking joints, as this depends on many circumstances which, as explained, continually change; for this reason Cooks must pay the strictest attention to the various details connected with this mode of cooking.

GRAVY FOR ROAST OR BAKED MEAT.

An ample supply of gravy should be served out with each ration of roast or baked meat. It is made as follows:—Pour away all the fat in the dripping pan (strain and preserve it for further use), add the required quantity of bone liquor, stock, or water, season with salt and pepper, stir over the fire until it boils, and simmer for five minutes, then strain and use as required.

STEWING.

By this method coarse and tough meat can be cooked tender, and be made nourishing. Stewing is considered the most economical mode of cooking, because more nourishment can be gained by this process than by any other, and is therefore the most profitable way of cooking. All articles to be stewed are to be cooked very gently, the heat should never exceed 189 deg. Fah. When cooked or preserved meats are to be stewed they should only be allowed to simmer just hot enough to get the meat hot through. Fresh meat should be first fried in a sufficient quantity of fat or dripping, and then allowed to simmer gently till tender in a small quantity of liquid—either stock, bone liquor, or water. Seasoning must in this case be added in moderate quantity at the commencement. In using fat for frying in the first stage only a sufficiency to prevent the meat from burning must be taken.

BROILING OR GRILLING.

A gridiron is required to broil or grill, between which the meat or fish to be broiled is placed. The gridiron must be kept very clean and well greased each time it is used. Broiling or grilling is to cook in front of or over a fire, which must be brisk and clear and proportioned to the article to be cooked. Mutton chops, cutlets, steaks, whiting, slices of cod, fresh haddocks and soles are the usual articles of food cooked in this manner. A steady fire is required for fish, which must always be *well* done. Frequent turning is most necessary. From 10 to 15 minutes are required to broil a moderate sized chop or steak.

D

The best way to test this is to press the meat with the handle of a knife, and when firm to the touch it is done. Underdone meat should only be so cooked when ordered by the Doctor. After the first 5 or 10 minutes all meat or fish to be broiled should be moved a distance from the fire, and be cooked more gently till done enough.

FRYING.

This process of cooking is defined as boiling in solid fats or oil. Lard and dripping (clarified fat) are best adapted for this purpose. Most articles to be fried are coated with either flour, egg, and bread-crumbs or batter, before they are put into the fat.

The fat used must be sweet and clean, and should be strained each time it is used. It can be used several times if care is taken, but when it is of a dark brown colour it is no longer fit to use.

Frying is performed at a much higher temperature of heat than any other method of cooking; it is done at 290 to 390 deg. Fah., according to the kind of fat used: oil rises to 400 deg.

To fry successfully the fat must in all cases be sufficient to well cover the articles to be fried, and must be thoroughly hot (smoking hot) before the article to be so cooked is placed in it. When the fat is hot enough to fry a blueish smoke will arise from it. Another way to test it is to drop a small piece of bread in it, and if it turns a nice brown colour within a few seconds the fat is ready for frying; if on the other hand the bread turns a dark brown it is a sign that the fat is too hot, and in that case it will burn and is not fit to be used until it has cooled a little. Special precautions must be taken to have the fat hot enough and yet not too hot, and to prevent it from burning—in both cases the results would prove failures.

RULES FOR COOKING VEGETABLES.

(*See also page* 37.)

Tubers, Roots, and so-called green vegetables, such as Cabbage, Greens, Turnip - tops, Savoys, Kale, &c., should be put into fast-boiling salted water, and be quickly brought to the boiling point again, and allowed to cook till tender at a more or less high temperature.

The following is the average time for cooking vegetables:—

> Potatoes, half-an-hour when small, 40 to 45 minutes when large.
> Cabbage, half-an-hour when small, 40 to 45 minutes when large.
> Carrots and Turnips, 45 minutes when young, one hour when old.
> Parsnips, 45 to 60 minutes.

Vegetables when once cooked should not be allowed to stay in the water, because this toughens them, and destroys colour and flavour. Green vegetables must always be well drained before they are served.

THE STOCKPOT.

Hitherto the stock-pot has played but an unimportant part in prison kitchens. It is, however, of the greatest importance that a stock-pot be constantly

D 2

kept in all kitchens. The object of a stock-pot is to produce a nourishing broth or liquor, which is used for various purposes instead of water, but mainly for gravies and soups. Either a large boiling pot, a copper boiler, or steam-vessel can be used for this purpose. Into it are put all kinds of bones from meat, provided they are fresh—trimmings of meat and vegetables. The bones must be chopped small, before they are put in the stock-pot, or cooking vessel; either cooked or raw bones and meat can be used, to these the necessary quantity of cold water is added (average quantity being three pints of water to one pound of bones and meat). The whole must then be allowed to come slowly to the boil, when the scum which rises to the surface must be carefully removed. Soup vegetables, such as onions, carrots, turnips, and also a cabbage or two if possible, previously washed and cleaned and cut up, are next added. Allow about 4 hours of gentle boiling. During the process of boiling the scum must be removed occasionally, but the fat rising to the surface must not be removed until the stock is finished. A little salt should be added with the bones, etc., as this will help to bring up the scum and impurities more quickly. After this the stock should be strained, and used as directed in the recipe.

The bones may be used again the next day, along with fresh materials, but the vegetables are useless for further boiling, they may be chopped finely and put with the stock when it is made into soup, and thus be made use of.

Stock when properly made, will provide an excellent basis for soups for the sick; in that case, rice, sago, or tapioca must be cooked with it. Average quantity, one ounce to a quart of strained stock. Seasoning to be added at the last.

CHAPTER V.

PRISON DIETS.

INGREDIENTS, METHODS, AND INSTRUCTIONS.

SOUP FOR LOCAL PRISONS.
(DIETS B AND C).

INGREDIENTS.—Sufficient to produce 1 pint of soup. 4 ozs. meat (clods, shoulder, leg, or shin of beef), 2 ozs. fresh vegetables (leek, carrot, turnip, turnip tops or cabbage); liquor, water (stock); 4 ozs. split peas; $\frac{1}{2}$ oz. onion; salt and pepper to taste.

METHOD.—When fresh meat is used prepare a stock as directed in the following recipe :—Remove the meat as soon as tender, free it from bones and gristle, and mince it up. Put the peas in a large pan with sufficient water to cover them, and let them soak for some hours, the time depending much on the age and condition of the peas. Young peas require little or *no* soaking, whilst others require from 8 to 12 hours. In the latter case it is best to put the peas to soak over night. Pour off the water, and put them into the copper with the required quantity of water and stock, let the whole come to the boil, remove the scum, and add the vegetables,—these must be previously peeled and washed, and cut up small (the onion should be peeled and minced). Turn the steam on full, *i.e.*, to boiling point, and allow contents of the copper to simmer from $1\frac{1}{4}$ to $1\frac{1}{2}$ hours. Stir frequently during the process of simmering. Now add the chopped meat, and cook for another quarter of an hour: stir occasionally. If any scum arises to the surface it should be carefully removed with a ladle, but *none* of the liquid fat must be removed. The salt and pepper should now be added: this must be incorporated very judiciously. In seasoning liquid it should be remembered that an overdose of salt or pepper will spoil the soup. Once the seasoning is added it cannot be taken out, but if underseasoned more can be added at the last moment if found necessary. Whilst the rations of soup are being served out, the contents of the copper must be stirred frequently, so as to make each portion of uniform quality and consistency. Except for skimming or stirring purposes the copper should be kept well closed (covered) during the cooking of the soup.

SUBSTITUTE (from May to September).—Instead of the above stated ingredients, use 4 oz. beef clod (or shoulder) leg or shin, 1 oz. pearl barley, 2 oz. fresh vegetables, 1 oz. of onion, $\frac{1}{8}$ oz. of flour, pepper and salt. Proceed in the same manner as directed in the foregoing recipe, using the barley in place of the peas. Mix the flour with cold water into a smooth paste or batter, and stir into the soup. Cook for 30 minutes longer after the flour is added. Season with salt and pepper. The soup must be frequently stirred.

VEGETABLE SOUP (BEEF).—CONVICT PRISON DIETARY.
(DIETS D, E, AND G).

INGREDIENTS.—To produce 1 pint of soup—8 oz. beef clod or shoulder, leg or shin, for male convicts on Diet E (6 oz. for male and female convicts on Diets D and G respectively), 1 oz. pearl barley, 2 oz. fresh vegetables, 1 oz. onion, $\frac{1}{8}$ oz. of flour, salt and pepper.

METHOD.—Bone the meat, cut it up into thick pieces, and chop or saw the bones into small pieces. Make a bone liquor by adding one quart of water to every lb. of bones, and a little salt, boil up and skim.   Cook for 6 to 8 hours, then strain.   Do not remove the fat.

Put the meat into the cooking vessel with 1 pint of water to every lb. of meat; when it boils remove the scum, then add the barley (previously washed) and the vegetables (previously prepared and chopped up finely) also the bone liquor.   Cook gently for about 4 hours.   Mix the flour with enough cold water to make a smooth paste or batter, and stir it into the soup.   Season with pepper and salt, and cook for another $\frac{1}{2}$ an hour.   The soup must be stirred frequently whilst cooking.   The cooking vessels must be kept closed as much as possible during the cooking process.

When serving out the rations the soup must be frequently stirred.

BOILED BACON.

Place the pieces of bacon to be cooked into the boiling or steaming vessel, add enough cold water to well cover the meat.   Bring it to the boil, then reduce the heat to 200 or 210 deg. Fah., and allow it to simmer gently from $2\frac{1}{2}$ to 3 hours, according to the thickness, condition, and size of the bacon.   The cooking vessel should be kept covered during the cooking process.

The liquor in which the bacon has been cooked must be allowed to get cold, the fat which is formed on the top should be carefully removed, clarified, and used as directed.   Cold fat, according to custom adopted, must always be issued proportionately with the bacon as part of the ration.   It is most essential that the bacon when cooked be left in the cooking vessel or copper for at least an hour and a half.

Soak the beans in cold water from 6 to 12 hours, according to requirements, drain them and cook them in the bacon liquor. Allow $1\frac{1}{2}$ hours at least for cooking. They should be cooked at moderate heat, so as to allow them to swell. Six ounces of raw beans will produce 12 ounces when properly cooked.

PEA SOUP (PORK).—Convict Prison Dietary.

(Diets D and E).

Ingredients to produce 1 pint of soup.—4 oz. salt pork, 4 oz. split peas, 1 oz. onions, $\frac{1}{4}$ oz. vinegar, salt and pepper, water.

Method.—Soak the peas overnight, by pouring over enough cold fresh water to well cover them. The actual quantity of water required depends upon the nature and dryness of the peas used.

Place the pork in the copper or other cooking vessel, add cold water, bring slowly to the boil, and remove the scum but not the fat. Then simmer gently for 4 or 5 hours. Pork so cooked must be left in the liquor in which it is cooked all night, and the fat on top of the liquor must not be removed. On the morning following, pour off the water from the peas, and substitute an equal quantity of fresh water; to this add the given quantity of chopped onions and a little salt. Bring to the boil, remove the scum, and cook slowly for about 2 hours. Stir occasionally to prevent the peas, etc., from burning.

The cooked pork must next be taken out of the copper, the bones removed, and the meat chopped finely. This is then added with the liquor to the peas, etc., and brought to the boiling point whilst stirring. If needed, add some boiling water to make up the necessary quantity of soup. Season to taste with salt and pepper. The vinegar is next added to give additional flavour. Allow the whole to boil (simmer) gently for another hour or so. It is then ready to serve.

Special note. The copper lids must be kept closed as much as possible whilst the process of cooking this soup goes on. Frequent stirring is also necessary.

MEAT LIQUOR (STOCK).

Break up the meat bones into small pieces, put them into the copper or cauldron with cold water, allow 1 quart of water to 1 lb. of bones, add a little salt, and bring to the boil. Skim, and simmer at a temperature of 200 deg. to 210 deg. Fah. from 4 to 5 hours. Strain off the liquor and let it get cold; the fat which is formed on the surface must be put into the soup. Measure out the quantity of liquor required for the soup, and add water if not found sufficient to make up the required quantity. The bones should be placed on a wooden tray, and any particle of meat adhering thereto must be removed, minced up small, and added to the soup.

LIQUOR (THICKENED) MADE FROM THE ABOVE.

INGREDIENTS.—To 1 pint of stock (a ration).—$\frac{1}{6}$ oz. flour, $\frac{1}{2}$ oz. onion, pepper and salt to taste.

METHOD.—Mix the flour with a little cold stock or water, and work into a batter (the liquid must be stirred gradually into the flour). Peel and mince, or chop finely, the onion, and stir the batter and onion into the stock, stir till the contents of the copper or cauldron reach boiling heat, and let simmer for at least twenty minutes longer, season lightly with pepper and salt. The liquor is then ready for use.

COCOA.

Cocoa as a beverage is more nourishing than tea or coffee, it possesses a stimulating principle called "Theobromine", similar to the "Theine" in tea and the "Caffeine" in coffee.

Admiralty Cocoa is issued in block, and is similar in consistency and quality to what is known as "Compound Cocoa" containing a certain percentage of arrowroot, sugar, and sundry fatty ingredients. It requires from 20 to 30 minutes boiling.

The best way to prepare cocoa is to put it in a boiling pan with enough water to make it into a paste; this can easily be done as it becomes heated. Cocoa must be well stirred whilst it is being cooked.

INGREDIENTS.—To make 1 pint of Cocoa, $\frac{3}{4}$ of an oz. of Admiralty Cocoa, $\frac{3}{4}$ of an oz. of sugar and 2 oz. of milk are allowed.

METHOD.—Break up the cocoa and put it into the cooking vessel with sufficient water to well cover it, stir till dissolved, then add the remainder of water, allow to simmer for 20 minutes, add the sugar and milk, boil again and serve.

TEA.

INGREDIENTS.—To produce one pint:—$\frac{1}{6}$ oz. tea, 2 oz. milk, $\frac{3}{4}$ oz. sugar.

METHOD.—The tea must be placed in a fine canvas or muslin bag, tied up loosely; or else put into a strainer. The correct quantity of water needed to produce the required bulk is put into a clean urn or cauldron (copper boiler or other vessel), bring it to the boil, drop in the tea, and allow it to remain in for about 10 minntes; after this remove the tea, add the milk and the sugar and keep *hot*, but not boiling, till it is time to serve it.

POTATOES.

Potatoes are as a rule best when cooked in their skins. They must be thoroughly scrubbed and washed in several waters. The best way to do this is by scrubbing them with a bass broom in a tank with sufficient water to cover them. After being well scrubbed rinse them thoroughly in fresh water, and drain them. They can either be steamed or boiled. If boiled, put them in a vessel containing sufficient cold water to well cover them, and add enough salt to flavour the water; boil fast till they are done, then drain, and let them dry for a few minutes; keep hot.

Steaming is, however, the better process, because the flavour of the potato is thereby improved, and the waste is somewhat less than by boiling. A little more time must be allowed for steaming than for boiling.

When it is necessary to peel potatoes, the rind must be removed as thinly as possible, because the best and most nutritious part of the potato is immediately under the skin. As the potatoes are peeled place them in a pan of cold water, and leave them there till required. If any parts of a potato are discoloured, or if any be found spotted in the inside, the defective part must be cut off and thrown away. Peeled potatoes are cooked in the same manner as those cooked in their skins.

Time allowed for cooking is generally $\frac{1}{2}$ an hour for boiling and $\frac{3}{4}$ of an hour for steaming. They should be arranged in the cooking vessels so that they cook evenly; very large potatoes should be picked out and cooked in a separate tray or vessel, as it will take somewhat longer to cook them than those of small or moderate size.

SUET PUDDING.

INGREDIENTS.—To produce 1 lb. of pudding when cooked. 2 oz. suet, $\frac{1}{2}$ lb. flour or whole-meal, $6\frac{1}{2}$ oz. or $1\frac{1}{2}$ gills cold water, a pinch of salt.

METHOD.—Free the suet from skin, and chop finely. Add the flour, and mix thoroughly, then add the salt, and mix with the water. Put it into greased tins or pans, and steam or boil for $2\frac{1}{2}$ to 3 hours, according to size of tins or pans used.

The best way to ascertain if the pudding is done is to insert a skewer; if the skewer comes out clean the pudding is done and fit for serving; if not, additional cooking (steaming or boiling) is required.

By way of change this pudding can also be cooked in the oven (baked).

GRUEL.

INGREDIENTS to produce 1 pint of gruel.—2 oz. coarse oatmeal (Scotch), 1 pint water, $\frac{1}{4}$ teaspoonful salt (or $\frac{1}{2}$ oz. sugar, Diet D).

METHOD.—Mix the oatmeal in a pan with sufficient *cold* water to form a paste. Heat up the remainder of water till it boils, and stir in the mixed oatmeal, add the salt, and allow it to simmer for at least 20 minutes. It is necessary to stir the mixture occasionally with a wooden spoon or bat, otherwise it is likely to burn.

PORRIDGE.

INGREDIENTS to produce 1 pint of porridge.—3 oz. coarse oatmeal (Scotch), $\frac{1}{2}$ teaspoonful salt, $1\frac{1}{4}$ pints water.

METHOD.—Put the oatmeal and salt into the pan in which the porridge is to be cooked, stir in gradually the required quantity of cold water; stir well to make it smooth. Turn on the steam full, and bring to the boil. Cook for at least half an hour at a heat of about 210 deg. Fah. Be careful to stir the contents of the copper frequently with a wooden spoon or bat to prevent lumps and burning.

Some cooks prefer to make porridge by stirring the oatmeal into boiling water. This method is not recommended, as it is then more apt to make the porridge lumpy, and when cooked it is not nearly so digestible.

Note.—As the oatmeal is not always of uniform quality, it may be found that some meal will require a little more water than others. *Coarse* oatmeal is considered best for porridge.

Where steam is not employed in cooking, the porridge or gruel is to be cooked in convenient cooking vessels over the fire, the time required being about the same as for steaming, but the simmering heat (slow cooking) must be carried out where so indicated, and the heat of the fire must be regulated accordingly.

MILK PORRIDGE.

When milk porridge is ordered, mix $\frac{1}{4}$ pint of boiled or scalded milk with the porridge prepared as directed in the foregoing recipe, the only exception being that instead of using $1\frac{1}{4}$ pints of water, only 1 pint should be used.

The milk must not be added until the porridge is cooked, and should then be allowed to cook for another 10 or 15 minutes.

CHAPTER VI.

HOSPITAL DIET.

INSTRUCTIONS AND MODES OF PREPARATION OF DISHES.

It is essential and important that special care should be taken in preparing and cooking food for the sick; and also that it should be nicely served. Everything, utensils as well as materials, used for sick diet must be perfectly clean and fresh. Greasy cooking dishes should be avoided, and all food, unless intended for convalescents, must contain but very little seasoning. Great pains should be taken to see that dishes to be served hot are so kept. Half warm food, or partially cold food, is distasteful to people in health, and much more so to the sick.

BEEF TEA.

In making beef-tea it must be remembered that the heat of 150 deg. Fah. will coagulate the albumen in the meat, and thus prevent the juices of the meat from which beef-tea is made being drawn out. For this reason all beef-tea must be heated very slowly, but it must never be allowed to reach boiling heat, i.e., 212 deg. Fah., else the beef-tea becomes void of actual food value, or nutriment, which it is so essential it should contain.

When beef-tea is to be made in large quantities, it is desirable to prepare it in a specially constructed beef-tea cauldron, made on the principle of a double lined stock-pot, such as is now used in most hospitals. The outer lining is filled with water, and the beef-tea is introduced in the inner vessel or inner division. In this way the water can be kept simmering from 6 to 8 hours (being of course replenished as it evaporates), whilst the beef-tea in the inner vessel will cook very gently without being unduly heated. All fats and sinews of the meat should be removed, and if any should float on top of the beef-tea it must be carefully removed before it is served.

HOW TO MAKE BEEF-TEA.

INGREDIENTS.—1 lb. lean beef (topside or gravy beef), free from bones, skin, gristle and fat, water sufficient to issue 1 pint, a pinch of salt.

METHOD.—Shred the meat finely, or pass it twice through a mincing machine; put it into the beef-tea pan with the water and a pinch of salt, allow it to stand for about one hour, and then cook as above directed in a double lined beef-tea cauldron, or 4 or 5 hours in an ordinary pan or stock pot. Time required for cooking 6 to 8 hours.

VEAL BROTH.

INGREDIENTS.—1 lb. knuckle of veal, 2 oz. sago, 1 gill milk, 2 quarts cold water, 1 yolk of egg (optional).

METHOD.—Put the sago in a basin with a little warm water to soak, while the broth is cooking. Break up the veal bone; and cut the meat into pieces, put both into a stew-pan with 2 quarts of cold water and a little salt; let it just boil up and skim it well, draw it off the fire and let it simmer gently with the lid on for 4 hours. Then strain it, and put it back in the stew-pan with the sago, and let it simmer for half an hour longer. Draw the broth off the fire, and let it cool a little. Beat up the yolk of an egg with the milk, and stir them into the broth, stir it over the fire again for a minute to cook the egg, but do not let it boil or it will curdle.

MUTTON BROTH.

INGREDIENTS.—1 lb. mutton (scrag end of neck), 1 oz. pearl barley or sago, 1 quart water, salt to taste ($\frac{1}{4}$ to $\frac{1}{2}$ teaspoonful).

METHOD.—Remove all the meat from the bones, free the meat from all fat and skin, and cut into small pieces. Put the meat and water (cold) into a saucepan, boil it very gently for two or three minutes and remove the scum. Wash the barley or sago, drain, and stir into the broth. Simmer the whole very gently for 2 hours, skim occasionally, season with salt. Serve as it is, or strain according to directions received.

CHICKEN BROTH.

INGREDIENTS.—$\frac{1}{2}$ chicken (an old bird will do, but it must be fresh), 1 quart water, $\frac{1}{4}$ teaspoonful salt, 1 oz. rice or pearl barley.

METHOD.—Pluck, singe and truss the chicken as for boiling, cut it into very small joints. Wash the giblets (remove the gall carefully), and put the pieces of chicken and giblets into a saucepan with the water (cold), add the salt. Bring this slowly to the boil, and remove the scum. Wash the rice or barley, drain, and put with the chicken; let the whole simmer very gently for 2 hours. Take out the pieces of chicken and giblets, and serve the broth with or without rice or barley—in the latter case it must be strained. The cooked chicken can be utilized for stew or chicken balls (see recipes for these).

VEGETABLE FLAVOURING

When this is allowed, both Mutton and Chicken Broth will be much improved in flavour. In such case use a small onion (peeled) and half a carrot (scraped), and cook with the meat in the broths.

DIRECTIONS FOR FRYING FISH.

METHOD SUITABLE FOR PLAICE, COD, HADDOCK, OR SKATE.

Wash the fish, wipe it thoroughly with a cloth, and cut up into even sized pieces, each weighing as near as possible $\frac{1}{4}$ lb. Prepare a batter (see recipe below). Dip each piece of fish into the batter so that it is completely covered, and drop into deep fat (clarified suet and dripping)—the fat must be smoking hot. Fry for about 5 minutes, or until the fish has acquired a nice light or golden brown. Drain well on paper and serve.

Note.—The fat used for frying must be clean, and there must be enough of it to well cover the fish which is to be fried in it. It should be strained every time after using it. Do not attempt to fry too many pieces of fish at one time.

BATTER FOR FRYING FISH, ETC.

INGREDIENTS.—$\frac{1}{4}$ lb. flour, $\frac{1}{2}$ oz. fat (dripping), 1 gill tepid water, $\frac{1}{2}$ teaspoonful salt.

METHOD.—Melt the fat. Mix the flour and salt in a basin, add the fat, and by degrees the water. Beat well, and let it stand for 1 hour or longer.

E

This will make enough batter for frying about one pound of fish. If the batter is found too stiff add a little more water to it just before using it.

BOILED FISH.—COD, HADDOCK, HAKE, ETC.

Wash and wipe the fish, put it in a fish kettle with strainer, and pour over enough warm water to well cover the fish. Add salt and vinegar in the proportion of 1 teaspoonful to 1 pint. Bring the fish slowly to the boil, then move on one side and let it cook slowly till tender. Fish must *not* on any account be allowed to boil fast. The time allowed for cooking is 10 minutes to the pound in weight, and 15 minutes over.

SAUCE FOR FISH.

INGREDIENTS.—$\frac{1}{2}$ oz. dripping, $\frac{1}{2}$ oz. flour, $1\frac{1}{2}$ gills water and milk, 1 teaspoonful vinegar, $\frac{1}{2}$ teaspoonful salt.

METHOD.—Melt the fat, stir in the flour, and fry for a few minutes without browning, then add gradually the liquor (water and milk). Stir till it boils, add the vinegar and salt, and cook for ten minutes. The sauce is then ready. It must be frequently stirred else it will be lumpy.

FISH STEW.

INGREDIENTS.—$\frac{1}{2}$ lb. fish (haddock, cod, or other white fish), 1 oz. butter, $\frac{1}{2}$ oz. flour, 1 gill water, salt and nutmeg, 1 teaspoonful lemon juice.

METHOD.—Cut the fish from the bones, remove the dark skin, and divide the flesh into inch sized pieces. Put the bones and skin in a saucepan with $\frac{1}{2}$ pint water, cook this till reduced to about half the quantity, then strain and use instead of water for the sauce. Melt the butter in a saucepan, stir in the flour, cook for a minute or two, then add the milk, boil up whilst stirring, and add the prepared fish liquor (1 gill). Cook for 10 minutes, season with a little salt, nutmeg, and pepper if allowed; then put in the filleted fish, cook for about 15 minutes; add the lemon juice and cook a little longer. The contents of the pan must be frequently stirred else the sauce will stick to the bottom of the pan and burn. A little chopped parsley may be sprinkled over the fish when it is served.

FISH CAKES.

INGREDIENTS.—$\frac{1}{2}$ lb. cooked fish (any kind of white fish) free from skin and bone, salt and pepper, fat for frying, $\frac{1}{4}$ lb. cooked potatoes, 1 oz. butter or dripping, 1 egg, breadcrumbs.

METHOD.—Chop up the fish rather finely; rub the potatoes through a sieve. Melt the butter in a saucepan, add the fish and potatoes, season with salt and pepper, and stir over the fire till the mixture is hot, and turn on to a plate. When cold divide it into four portions, shape each to a round flat cake, dip in beaten egg and cover with bread-crumbs. Fry in deep fat (very hot) till a golden colour, drain on paper and serve.

CHICKEN STEW.

INGREDIENTS.—Pieces of cooked chicken (see chicken broth), $\frac{1}{2}$ pint milk or chicken liquor, a few drops of lemon juice, $\frac{1}{2}$ oz. flour, $\frac{1}{2}$ oz. dripping, salt and pepper.

METHOD.—Melt the fat in a clean saucepan, stir in the flour and cook for a few seconds, taking care

E 2

that it does not get brown. Stir in the milk or stock (liquor) cold, and let it come to the boil whilst stirring,—this must be carefully done else the sauce will be lumpy. Cook gently for 10 minutes, add the lemon juice and put in the pieces of chicken. Cook for another 10 minutes and serve hot.

CHICKEN BALLS.

INGREDIENTS.—$\frac{1}{2}$ lb. chicken meat, free from bone, 1 gill stock or milk, salt and pepper, fat for frying, 1 egg, 1 teaspoonful chopped parsley, $\frac{3}{4}$ oz. flour, $\frac{3}{4}$ oz. dripping, bread-crumbs.

METHOD.—Chop the chicken finely. Make a sauce as follows:—Melt the fat in a saucepan, add the flour, and stir for a few minutes over the fire, taking care that it does not get brown. Stir in the stock or milk (cold) and boil up,—stir constantly till it boils. Let this cook for about 15 minutes, then add the chopped meat and parsley. Season to taste, re-heat, and turn on to a plate or dish. When cool take a tablespoonful of this mixture and shape into a ball, dip it in beaten egg mixed with half a tablespoonful of water or milk, and cover with bread-crumbs. Continue thus till all the mixture is used up. Fry the balls in deep fat, which must be very hot but not burning. When of a nice golden colour take up, drain on paper and serve.

Note.—Any kind of cooked meat can be thus treated. Mutton and beef balls are particularly nice and suitable for sick diet.

MINCED CHICKEN.

Minced chicken, beef, or mutton, can be made by following the foregoing recipe for chicken balls, by allowing 2 gills of stock or milk instead of only

1 gill.   Cook the mixture very gently for about 15 minutes (shaping and frying being of course omitted) and serve very hot.

BOILED RABBIT.

INGREDIENTS.—1 rabbit, 1 onion, 1 carrot or turnip.

METHOD.—Wash the rabbit thoroughly in tepid water, cleanse out the blood near the head and neck, wipe it and truss into shape. Prepare and clean the vegetables. Have ready a saucepan large enough to hold the rabbit, and enough water to cover it; add enough salt to taste, and boil up. Put in the rabbit, allow it to boil, then remove the scum, add the pre-pared vegetables, either whole or cut into slices, and boil all gently for about 1 hour.

Prepare a parsley or onion sauce, according to the directions given, using the liquor from the rabbit. Cut the rabbit into portions and pour sauce over.

ONION SAUCE.

INGREDIENTS.—One large onion, 1 gill milk, 1 gill liquor, 1 oz. flour, 1 oz. dripping, salt and pepper.

METHOD.—Use the onion cooked with the rabbit, and chop it finely. Boil up milk and liquor toge-ther. Melt the dripping, add the flour, and stir for a few seconds over the fire, then add the stock (milk and liquor), stirring all the while; boil up, add the onion, and simmer for about 15 minutes. Season with salt and pepper.

BATTER PUDDING.

INGREDIENTS.—3 oz. flour, 1 egg, $\frac{1}{2}$ pint milk, 1 pinch salt.

METHOD.—Sift the flour, beat up the egg, and mix with the milk, add the salt and stir this gradually into the flour, beat well with a wooden spoon, and see that the mixture becomes perfectly smooth. Allow it to stand for about 1 hour, then pour it into a well greased baking tin, or greased pie dish, and bake for $\frac{1}{2}$ hour.

Note.—The same mixture can be poured into a greased pudding basin, the top covered with greased paper, and be steamed for 40 minutes. This is called steamed or boiled batter pudding, and may be served with castor sugar, treacle or golden syrup.

FRIED CHOP.

Trim a mutton chop, by removing the skin and the superfluous fat. Put it in a clean frying pan with $\frac{1}{2}$ oz. of fat (previously heated before the chop is put in), broil over a quick fire for about 4 minutes, then turn and cook the other side, allowing from 10 to 12 minutes in all, according to the thickness of the chop. Take up the chop, put it on a plate, pour off the fat in the frying pan, put in a couple of tablespoonfuls of stock or gravy, season this with salt and pepper to taste, boil up, and pour round the chop.

STEWED CHOP OR CUTLETS.

Take a mutton chop or two mutton cutlets (cut from the neck, best end), free the meat from skin and fat, and put it in a saucepan with half a pint of cold water or cold milk; season with salt and pepper to taste (1 saltspoonful of salt and $\frac{1}{2}$ of pepper); bring it to the boil and skim, then add a small slice of onion (if allowed) and 1 tablespoonful ($\frac{1}{2}$ oz.) of rice or pearl barley. Cover the pan, and stew gently for about $1\frac{1}{2}$ hours, or until the meat is done.

Note.—Rice or barley which is used for this dish should, before being stewed with the meat, be first washed and blanched in slightly salted water.

CORNFLOUR CUP.—(Low Diet.)

INGREDIENTS.—1 oz. cornflour, 1 pint milk, 1 oz. sugar.

METHOD.—Mix the cornflour with $\frac{1}{4}$ of a gill cold milk. Boil up the remainder of the milk, add the sugar, and stir this gradually into the mixed cornflour. Return the whole to the stew-pan, and cook for 15 minutes. Stir frequently to prevent burning.

ARROWROOT.

INGREDIENTS.—1 oz. arrowroot, 1 pint milk, 1 oz. sugar.

METHOD.—Mix the arrowroot with a small quantity of the milk to a smooth paste. Boil the milk, and pour it slowly on to the arrowroot paste. Return to the saucepan in which the milk was boiled, add the sugar, stir with a wooden spoon until it boils, and cook for about 10 minutes longer. The above quantity produces 1 pint of arrowroot.

RICE PUDDING.

INGREDIENTS.—2 oz. rice, $\frac{1}{2}$ pint milk, 1 oz. sugar, 1 egg, nutmeg for flavouring.

METHOD.—Wash the rice and boil it in water, drain it as soon as it boils, return it to the saucepan with the milk, and cook till quite tender. Add the sugar and the egg previously beaten. Pour this into a greased pie dish, grate a little nutmeg on top, and bake in a moderate oven for 20 minutes.

A very good and more digestible pudding can be made by omitting the egg and by following the above directions.

TAPIOCA OR SAGO PUDDING.

INGREDIENTS.—2 oz. tapioca or sago, ½ pint milk, 1 oz. sugar, 1 egg, nutmeg or lemon rind for flavouring.

METHOD.—Pour the milk over the tapioca or sago, and let soak for 10 minutes, then boil slowly for another 15 minutes. Beat up the egg and stir into the above, add the sugar, and pour into a greased pie dish. Sprinkle some grated lemon rind or grated nutmeg over the pudding, and bake for 15 minutes in a moderate oven.

ORDINARY CUSTARD PUDDING (BAKED.)

INGREDIENTS.—1 egg, ½ pint milk, 1 tablespoonful sugar.

METHOD.—Beat up the egg with the sugar, add the milk, and mix well. Grease a pie dish and pour in the above, place it in the oven and bake slowly for about 40 minutes.

CUSTARD PUDDING.

INGREDIENTS.—¾ pint milk, 2 eggs, ½ oz. sugar.

METHOD.—Break the eggs into a basin and beat up well, add the milk and the sugar, mix thoroughly, and pour into a greased pie dish. Bake in a moderate oven for 30 minutes. Great care must be taken not to bake this pudding too quickly, else the eggs will curdle.

CORNFLOUR MOULD.

INGREDIENTS.—1 pint milk, 1½ oz. cornflour, 1 oz. sugar, a strip of lemon rind for flavouring.

METHOD.—Mix the cornflour with a little cold milk to a smooth paste. Boil up the milk with the lemon rind, and pour on the mixed cornflour. Return to the saucepan, and stir over the fire for quite 10 minutes. Remove the lemon, and pour the mixture into small moulds, previously rinsed in cold water. Allow them to stand in a cool place for 1 hour or longer, then turn out and serve.

STEWED FIGS.

INGREDIENTS.—1 lb. figs, 1 pint water, 4 oz. sugar, 1 tablespoonful lemon juice.

METHOD.—Boil the water and sugar in a saucepan, put the figs into a stone jar, pour over the syrup (water and sugar) and the lemon juice, and cook in the oven till tender. It will take about 2 hours.

STEWED PRUNES.

Proceed in the same manner as above directed, using 1 lb. of prunes in place of figs, and cook for 2 hours in a stone jar (covered) in the oven.

APPLE JELLY.

INGREDIENTS.—1 lb. sour cooking apples, $\frac{1}{2}$ pint water, 3 oz. sugar, the thin rind and juice of 1 lemon, $\frac{1}{2}$ oz. gelatine.

METHOD.—Peel the apples thinly, cut them into quarters and core them. Slice them thinly, and put them in a clean saucepan with the lemon rind, sugar, water, and lemon juice. Simmer till the apples are quite tender, and rub the whole through a fine sieve. Put the gelatine to soak for 10 minutes in about $\frac{1}{2}$ gill of water (cold). Melt this over the fire, and strain when dissolved into the apple pulp. Re-heat the latter before the gelatine is added. Pour the mixture into small moulds, place them in a cool place to set, and serve when wanted. The moulds are dipped in warm water for a second, when the shape will come out easily.

Note.—Gooseberry or rhubarb jelly can be made in the same way, by allowing an extra $\frac{1}{4}$ oz. of gelatine and 1 oz. more sugar in addition to the above given quantities.

MILK JELLY.

INGREDIENTS.—$\frac{1}{2}$ oz. gelatine (good weight), $1\frac{1}{2}$ oz. sugar, 1 pint milk, lemon rind or cinnamon to flavour.

METHOD.—Put the gelatine to soak in a small quantity of water (about $\frac{1}{2}$ gill). Boil up the milk with a thin strip of lemon rind or an inch stick of cinnamon, add the sugar and then the soaked gelatine, omitting the water. Re-heat and strain, stir occasionally till the mixture begins to thicken, then pour into some moulds previously rinsed in cold water. Set the moulds in a cool place till the jelly is firm.

CHAPTER VII.

BREAD AND BREADMAKING.

INTRODUCTORY OBSERVATIONS.

Bread is so extensive an article of diet that too much attention cannot be paid by Bakers to the scientific principles of its manufacture.

Properly prepared and well-baked bread should contain the following in a 100 parts:—

Water	40.0	per cent.
Gluten	7.0	,,
Starch, Sugar, and Gum	51.0	,,
Salt and other Mineral Substances	2.0	,,

The Chemical Composition of Coarse Brown Bread (Wholemeal—Prison Bread) is estimated as follows:—

Water	40.0	per cent.
Albumen (Gluten)	7.5	,,
Fat	.5	,,
Hydrated Carbon Compounds, Starch, Sugar, etc.	49.5	,,
Cellulose, Salts, etc.	1.5	,,
Ash	1.0	,,

And its caloric value as 2384, that is the measure of its potential energy as a food.

Part of the water is contained in the flour itself, in the proportion of about 15 per cent., while the rest is taken up by the bread in the process of making. Thus 145 lb. of bread contains usually about 45 lb. of added water. If bread be kept it becomes stale and consequently drier. This result is accounted for by a change in the internal molecules and from loss of moisture (water). If, however, a stale loaf is placed in a closely covered tin and exposed for half-an-hour to a heat not exceeding that of boiling water, *i.e.* 212 degrees, the loaf will regain the appearance and properties of new bread.

Wholemeal bread is composed of wholemeal flour, water, yeast, and salt. In some cases a small quantity of potatoes is added to the yeast, especially so when leaven is used in place of yeast.

All bread, when well-made, should be sweet, properly baked, and of proper texture; the flour or meal, from which bread is made, must be dry (not damp), clean and free from grit or other injurious admixtures.

RULES & INSTRUCTIONS FOR BREADMAKING.

FLOUR.

The wholemeal flour provided for Prison Bread contains a certain proportion of sharps and pollard. This fact must be borne in mind by the Bakers, and they must use every precaution to have the bread thoroughly baked, so that all the essential food-properties are obtained. Great care and special precautions must be taken to keep the flour stored in a dry and well ventilated place, and on no account must it be placed in a damp or close room. It should be at least a week in store before being used. The sacks should be on wooden racks. If they are stood on a concrete floor it may give the flour a musty flavour.

Sweetness and strength of bread are the most essential points to consider, and these have necessarily much to do with the quality of the flour used, and the place where it is stored till required for use.

Meal and flour of the standard quality should produce the following quantities of bread, viz. :—

A sack of 280 lbs. flour, known as "best seconds" or "best household," produces 362 lbs. of bread.

A sack of 280 lbs. wholemeal flour (consisting of all the products of the wheaten grain, with the exception of the coarser bran) should yield at least 370 lbs. of bread.

YEAST.

The flavour of bread and its sweetness depend largely upon the yeast used in its preparation. There are several types or classes of yeast, and whatever kind is used, the Baker should make himself well acquainted with its nature and strength before using it for the manufacture of bread. Patent and compressed yeasts, distiller's and brewer's yeasts, are those mostly in use at the present time. Of these the former may be regarded as the most popular. The difference between compressed and brewer's yeast, is that the former is a spirit or distiller's yeast compressed, and of much lighter colour than brewer's yeast, whilst brewer's yeast is a liquid of paste-like consistency; it is obtained from the brewhouse, it is coloured and flavoured as the beer from which it is obtained at the time of brewing. Half a pound of dried or compressed yeast is equal to $1\frac{1}{2}$ pints of brewer's thick yeast.

The result obtained by the use of the various types of yeast is practically the same, provided that the yeast selected be properly treated and manipulated, and the correct proportion or percentage of yeast be used.

Yeast is known as a fungus, and produces a ferment, because its cells are, as it were, living beings; when immersed in fresh water of a suitable temperature, the cells of yeast give out carbonic acid, so that when the yeast is mixed with the dough it acts as a ferment.

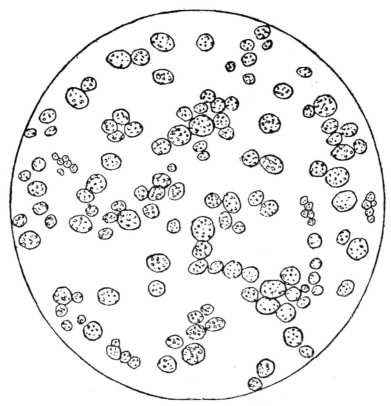

COMPRESSED YEAST.   MAGNIFIED 440 DIAMETER.

Yeast is composed of a large number of round and oval cells resembling little bladders. The preceding diagram shows a section of compressed or patent yeast examined by means of a microscope, the little cells shown are filled with an albuminous substance known as " protoplasm."

The Chemical Composition of Yeast is made up as follows:—

Carbon	48.7	per cent.
Oxygen	30.7	,,
Nitrogen	11.8	,,
Hydrogen	6.4	,,
Mineral matter (ash)	2.4	,,
	100.0	

It is most essential that the yeast used should be fresh, and should be supplied daily, or at least every other day.

In setting the sponge, *i.e.* in mixing the yeast, it is well to remember that all extremes of temperature weaken and change the action of yeast. A *cold* or *slow* fermentation is most detrimental, for it makes the bread heavy and produces bad flavours. On the other hand, *hot fermentations* are equally dangerous, because the yeast becomes over stimulated, in other words acts too quickly, and the sponge becomes over ripe before the baker is ready for it. The best results are obtained by using the liquid, *i. e*, water, to mix the yeast with, at a temperature of between 78 to 85 deg. Fah. This heat must, of course, be taken as approximate, because in each case the kind and quality of yeast employed, the temperature of the bakehouse, the kind of flour used, as well as the condition of utensils and troughs and the speed of workmen, must be taken into consideration. These things must be left to the Baker, who must decide and calculate to the best of his judgment the various operations in the process of breadmaking.

SPONGES.

Sponges are made by mixing water, yeast, and flour together so as to produce a thick spongy batter, the prime object being to feed and develop the yeast, so as to allow it sufficient scope for fermentation. After allowing the sponge to rest for a time (usually from 2 to 3 hours) it will after having risen, begin to drop or fall. It is then ready for making the dough. The usual proportions of yeast (compressed or patent) and flour or meal are 2 oz. of yeast to 1 bushel of flour.

THE DOUGH.

The next stage, after making the ferment and sponge, is the mixing of the dough. Dough may however be made without prior fermentation, using the usual quantity of yeast, which should be carefully diluted, but after the dough has been made about 2 hours, it should be cut back, dusted with flour, and well kneaded. The time required for the dough to set or rise depends upon the kind of flour or meal and yeast used. It usually requires from 6 to 8 hours.

Some bakers can make a good and sweet bread without either a ferment or a sponge, or with a ferment only, whilst others will make it with both a ferment and a sponge—the latter is no doubt the most correct method. Dough is ripe and ready for manipulation when it has well risen and is full of gas. It should then come out of the trough and be worked off with as little delay as possible.

When the dough is cold and slow in rising it may be required to be covered over, so as to help it to rise; on the other hand, if it works too freely, and is cracking all over the top, it requires to be worked up, so as to keep it more steady and prevent too speedy rising.

SALT.

Salt must in all cases be used with judgment, as this will guide the fermentation and gives flavour to the bread. For the *quick process* use 10 oz. to the bushel, and for the *long process* use 12 oz. to the bushel. The natural effect of salt upon yeast is to check its growth. This will of course to some extent delay the working of the sponge or dough. It is therefore the wiser plan to add the salt towards one of the later stages in bread-making.

MOULDING.

When the dough is ready for moulding, scale it off into the required rations, place them on the floured board, and work the pieces of dough thoroughly, taking one in each hand, press down firmly, and continue to fold and press down the dough with knuckles and fingers till the desired shape and elastic texture is obtained. As soon as moulded, place them close together on the baking tins, and mark them with the stamp indicating the weight of the loaves. Allow them to prove, after this they will be ready for baking; bake off in batches. Time allowed for proving is usually half an hour.

THE OVEN AND BAKING.

The oven in connection with breadmaking plays a most important part. It is therefore imperative that it should be well managed and well looked after. There are numerous types or kinds of ovens, some are fired with wood, others with coal, and others with steam or hot air. Coals are unquestionably the best fuel for heating a baker's oven. It is rather difficult to specify the exact time needed for baking bread, as this depends to a large extent on the heat of the oven, the kind of oven used, as well as its construction. It also depends on the size and shape of the loaves, and the manner in which they are placed in the oven.

F

Ordinary ovens, viz., those which are heated by the fuel (fire) being placed inside and then withdrawn, should register from 550 deg. to 600 deg. Fah. This may appear a great heat, but it must be remembered that during the process of baking the heat will decrease considerably. Ovens which are heated by hot water, steam, or hot air pipes, should register a temperature of 400 deg. Fah. Small loaves (4, 6, and 8 oz. rations) take from 50 to 60 minutes to bake, whilst the time required for baking large loaves is as follows:—1 lb. loaf about $1\frac{1}{2}$ hours; 2 lb. loaf about $1\frac{3}{4}$ hours.

Over-heated ovens are as detrimental to bread-making as under-heated ones. When a " batch," i. e. shapes of dough placed on sheets or tins one against the other, is put in the oven, the crust on the top of the loaves is formed too soon by an over-heated oven,—that is before the dough has had sufficient time to rise fully (expand), whilst in the case of the oven being too cool, the crust is not formed quickly enough.

TESTING THE HEAT OF THE OVEN.

An oven thermometer or pyrometer, as it is sometimes called, is of very great use and aid, because by its help the baker will be able to ascertain the correct heat of the oven. Most of the modern ovens have a thermometer fitted to them for the purpose of regulating the oven heat. A smart and observant baker will however, soon become acquainted with an oven, and will with or without its aid be able to tell the heat most desirable and suitable for the purpose in view.

When no thermometer is used, the heat of the oven may be tested by sprinkling a little flour on the tiles of the oven. Should the flour remain white after the lapse of a few seconds, it may be taken as a sign that the oven is not hot enough for baking; if on the other hand, the flour becomes a dark brown colour in a few seconds, then the oven is too hot; but if it assumes a fawny colour and looks slightly scorched, the temperature is suitable for baking purposes.

CHAPTER VIII.

PRACTICAL METHODS OF BREAD-MAKING.

With the exception of preparing the yeast or ferment, which is either made with compressed, patent, or brewers' yeast, the process of bread-making adapted by most bakers is practically the same. Bread made with baking-powder, which is known as unleavened or unfermented bread, is not manufactured in Prison Bakehouses, and is therefore not dealt with in this Manual.

A certain percentage of potatoes has been introduced in the recipes for both wholemeal bread and wheaten bread.

The use of potatoes in bread making is strongly recommended for the following reasons,—

Bread will be of distinctly better flavour when potatoes of medium size and mealy, are used in its manufacture.

The action of the ferment is considerably hastened.

Cooked mealy potatoes introduced in the ferment (yeast) provide it with a prepared food ready for immediate assimilation.

Furthermore, the presence of nitrogenous substances called "Amides" and sundry salts obtained from cooked potatoes are desirable adjuncts to be introduced in the manufacture of bread of every description.

YEAST FERMENT.

(Made from Distilled Compressed Yeast, or French Yeast.)

INGREDIENTS (for one sack of flour or wholemeal).
—8 lb. potatoes (mealy), 10 quarts of water, 2 lbs.
flour, 10 oz. compressed yeast.

METHOD.—Wash, peel, and cook the potatoes in
slightly salted water; when done (thoroughly cooled),
drain them and mash them up well: a stodge bat or
potato masher should be used for this purpose. Add
enough water to make a paste.

- Dissolve the yeast in about 2 quarts of tepid
water (75 to 80 deg. Fah.) Add this to the flour,
stir well, and add the mashed potatoes and the remainder of water. Work the ferment thoroughly
in the ferment tub, and set aside to rise. It is most
essential and of the first importance that the potatoes should be well mashed, and that the flour be
well mixed, so that there is no possible chance of
any small pieces or lumps getting into the bread.

YEAST FERMENT.

(Made from THICK or BREWERS' YEAST.)

INGREDIENTS (for one sack of flour or wholemeal).
—10 lb. potatoes, 10 quarts of water, 2 lb. flour,
$2\frac{1}{4}$ lb. of thick or brewers' yeast.

METHOD.—Prepare and cook the potatoes as directed in the previous recipe. Add the flour to the
mashed potatoes and stir in the water (the temperature of the water should register from 75 to 80 deg.
Fah., according to the temperature of the bakehouse
and season) and the yeast. Stir well and see that
there are no lumps in the mixture. Work the ferment in the ferment tub thoroughly with your hands,
so as to thoroughly mix all the ingredients. Cover
it with a cloth and leave it undisturbed for about 6

hours. At the end of that time it should be ready for working the dough.

It is important that the yeast used for this ferment be *weighed*, not *measured*, as it is more certain then to obtain uniform results in the bread.

HOW TO MAKE MALT YEAST.—(ALF. SMITH'S METHOD.)

INGREDIENTS.—1 lb. malt, 2 gals. of water, 1 oz. of hops, 6 oz. of flour.

METHOD.—Put the hops in the water and boil for 10 minutes, and then strain off $\frac{1}{2}$ a gallon of the hop water, which should be cooled down, and mixed with the malt, and allowed to stand for two hours; the remainder of the hops and water to be kept warm to extract the strength of the hops. At the end of two hours the $\frac{1}{2}$ gallon of hop water is strained from the malt, to which is added a small quantity of old yeast to set it to work.

The other $1\frac{1}{2}$ gallon of hop water is now brought to boil, and strained on the malt, where it remains until cool; the malt is then strained from it and 6 oz. of flour added, and the whole mixed together, making 2 gallons.

It is covered up for 24 hours, when it is fit for use. The temperature when it is set to work is regulated by the weather.

SETTING THE SPONGE.

Ferments and sponges should always be prepared by the Baker and not be left to the men under his charge.

Once the ferment is ready for operation, the sponge must be set with as little delay as possible. A sponge is usually made by making up a portion of dough in one end of the trough, in which the prepared ferment, yeast, etc. is incorporated. A "sponge proper" is made by mixing about a quarter of the flour to be used for bread with the prepared yeast or ferment, water and salt (the latter is optional). After being well worked (kneaded), it must be allowed to rise and fall twice. It requires from 6 to 8 hours, according to the kind of yeast used for making the ferment, to obtain a perfect sponge.

This stage in the manufacture of bread is most important, for it may safely be said that at this stage of the work the quality of the bread is more or less determined. Some bakers do not take the trouble to set a sponge but make up the dough immediately after the ferment is made and ready for operation; this practice is by no means desirable as the results are far from satisfactory, and should therefore not be followed.

The sponge is generally set over night, and the time of its ripeness naturally depends upon the period of the year, the heat of the bakehouse, and the temperature at which it is put away. This must be left to the judgment of the Baker, who should know when the sponge is ready, and he must act and direct accordingly, and carefully study the circumstances and the law which govern the action of the yeast. In all cases the trough containing the sponge should be covered, either with a cloth, or, better still, with the trough lid.

MAKING THE DOUGH.

When the sponge is ready, that is, when it has sufficiently fermented, and has come up for the second time as before described, weigh the salt, about 3 lbs. to the sack of 280 lbs., put it in the ferment tub, and dilute it with water—3 pails (about 30 quarts), is the quantity required, and the water used must be of the right temperature as before mentioned. When the salt has sufficiently dissolved, pour the liquor into the trough containing the sponge, break up the sponge, that is, tear it up with the hands into small pieces, and work it until a mixture of a batter-like consistency is obtained. Use a scraper so as to mix in every particle of sponge etc. in the trough. Next strew in sufficient flour to form the dough of the required consistency and texture. "Cut it back" several times, and knead over from one end of the trough to the other. "*Knead it well, do not spare it,*" and turn up the sides so as to thoroughly clear it. Leave it then for about an hour and "pin it" up with the bag board if necessary. After this the dough should be ready for the next stage, viz., "scaling"; throw it on the board , weigh it off, and mould it ready for baking. Before putting the dough into the oven, it should be *proved* as described below.

It may be well to state here that *salt* is used in order to flavour the bread, and the water is used to bind the flour. Salt further hardens the gluten, and renders the dough sufficiently firm to support itself during the process of fermentation. It also imparts a certain firmness to the texture of the bread, and prevents, to a certain extent the loss of moisture, *i. e.,* the evaporation of water.

The quantity of water needed depends largely on the quality of the flour. The best quality absorbs far more than flour of inferior quality. New and inferior flour usually requires more salt and less water than the best and finest quality, *i. e.* "seasoned" flour.

PROVING.

After weighing or scaling the dough, it is moulded as described elsewhere (see directions for this); the loaves of dough should next be allowed to prove in the baking trays or tins for about half-an-hour, when they will be ready for baking, and should be put in the oven in batches.

BAKING.

When the loaves of dough are placed in the oven, the swelling, or what is technically known as fermentation will, owing to the high temperature of the oven, become increased during the first 10 or 15 minutes, after that the fermentation will discontinue and the crust be formed. The proper temperature of the oven, and the time needed for baking bread, is set out on a previous page and should be carefully studied.

WHOLEMEAL BREAD.—No. 1.

INGREDIENTS.—280 lb. of meal as issued, 10 oz. compressed yeast, 14 to 15 gallons of water, 3 lb. salt, 8 lb. potatoes (mealy).

METHOD.—Sift enough meal to make the sponge as directed on page 86, by mixing the yeast, potatoes, and tepid water (about 8 quarts), in a clean pail, add a little salt, and stir in sufficient meal to form a weak dough, cover and let it stand in a warm place, undisturbed for 2 to 3 hours. Next mix the ferment with flour and water to make the sponge; let this remain undisturbed from 10 to 12 hours (covered). Add the remainder of ingredients, and proceed as directed in the foregoing notes on sponges, doughs, and baking. These directions must be carefully studied and carried out accordingly, so as to obtain uniform results in the bread.

WHOLEMEAL BREAD.—No. 2 (ALF. SMITH'S METHOD).

INGREDIENTS.—560 lb. wholemeal, 6 lb. salt, 3 pints of malt (brewers' yeast—see recipe for this), 28 to 30 gallons of water, 12 lb. potatoes.

METHOD.—The wholemeal to be sifted to obtain about 140 lb. of the flour to make the sponge,—7 gallons of water and 3 pints of yeast is required for this. The sponge is mixed before leaving the bake-house in the evening, and is ready for making into dough at 5.10 a.m. the following morning, or be-between 12 and 13 hours in the sponge. The re-mainder of the ingredients are then added and mixed into dough, when it is left in the trough to rise for 1½ hours; it is then ready to be weighed, moulded into loaves, and placed in the baking tins, where it again rises before putting it in the oven.

The temperature of the water used in mixing is regulated by the state of the weather, and the nature and quality of the wholemeal, and the time the sponge is required to be ready. The salt and yeast also require to be regulated according to the nature of the wholemeal used.

The above quantity fills two ovens and takes 50 to 60 minutes to bake, but some meal takes much longer.

WHITE BREAD (HOUSEHOLD).—For Hospitals, etc.

INGREDIENTS.—1 sack (280 lb.) best seconds or household flour, 2¼ lb. thick yeast (brewers'), 10 lb. potatoes (mealy), 3 lb. salt, about 60 quarts or 15 gallons water.

METHOD.—Wash thoroughly and cook the pota-toes, peel them and break them down and mash them in the ferment tub, add about 8 quarts of tepid water (see that the temperature is correct), add the yeast, either of the above-named, and stir into the flour. Mix well, and let it stand (covered) to rise for about 4 hours. By this time the ferment ought to be ready for straining. Dissolve the salt in the water (made up to 60 quarts in all) of the required temperature; now make the dough at the end of the trough, strain the ferment into the flour, add enough water to form a fairly stiff and firm dough; pin it up at one end of the trough, cover with cloths or the lid of the trough, and leave it from 9 to 10 hours. At the end of that time cut it back, and add the remainder of ingredients; work it well and knead thoroughly, and allow it to remain for another hour. The dough will then be ready for weighing and moulding. Any desired shapes may be made after the dough is weighed.

Bake the loaves of dough in the usual manner, allowing :—

About $1\frac{1}{4}$ hour for 4 lb. tin loaves, or

1 hour for 2 lb. tin loaves.

Cottage loaves, or loaves that touch each other :—

$2\frac{1}{4}$ hours should be allowed for 4 lb. loaves.

$1\frac{3}{4}$ hours for 2 lb. loaves, and

$1\frac{1}{4}$ hours for 1 lb loaves.

See that the bread is well and thoroughly baked before the batch is drawn from the oven. Bread made by this method will prove both light and palatable, and should never be close in texture.

FAULTY BREAD.

It is often a most difficult matter to explain the reason of faulty bread, especially so when it has an unpleasant or sour flavour, but the most common complaints can be attributed to the oven, i.e., the baking. The heating of an oven must be well tried and thoroughly understood by the Baker, and he must learn by actual practice and careful observation the exact time required for baking. The making of the dough and baking are governed by fixed laws, and these, when once understood, must be faithfully followed. The lack of one or both of these essential operations in bread-making, is generally the cause of faulty bread.

The strictest cleanliness must be observed throughout the manufacture of bread, and especially so with so-called over night doughs. When doughs are constantly made at the same end of the trough, something is sure to go wrong sooner or later. The troughs must be well scrubbed out and thoroughly dried each time they are used. Special care must be taken to see that there are no cracks or holes in the wood where stale dough could accumulate and eventually become mixed with the fresh dough. The troughs must be well lined, so that no moisture or liquor can get in between the joints. The neglect of these details, and the use of dirty utensils, are very often the cause of sour bread.

DIETARY SCALES.

Extracts from Rules made on the 2nd September,
1901, by the Secretary of State, under the
Prison Act, 1898.

LOCAL PRISONS.
DIET A.

Meals.	—	Men.	Women and Juveniles.
Breakfast	Daily :—		
	Bread	8 oz.	6 oz.
	Gruel..	1 pint	1 pint
	Sunday :—		
	Bread	8 oz.	6 oz.
	Porridge	1 pint	1 pint
	Monday :—		
	Bread	8 oz.	6 oz.
	Potatoes	8 ,,	8 ,.
	Tuesday :—		
	Bread	8 oz.	6 oz.
	Porridge	1 pint	1 pint
Dinner	Wednesday :—		
	Bread	8 oz.	6 oz.
	Suet Pudding	8 ,,	6 ,,
	Thursday :—		
	Bread	8 oz.	6 oz.
	Potatoes	8 ,,	8 ,,
	Friday :—		
	Bread	8 oz.	6 oz.
	Porridge	1 pint	1 pint
	Saturday :—		
	Bread	8 oz.	6 oz.
	Suet Pudding	8 ,,	6 ,,
Supper	Daily :—		
	Bread	8 oz.	6 oz.
	Gruel..	1 pint	1 pint

NOTES—(a) Men include all male prisoners over 16 years of age. Women
include all female prisoners over 16 years of age. Juveniles include all
prisoners under 16 years of age.

(b) Juvenile prisoners may, in addition to the above diet, be allowed milk
not exceeding one pint per diem, at the discretion of the Medical Officer

Meals.	—	Men.	Women and Juveniles.
Breakfast	Daily :—		
	Bread	8 oz.	6 oz.
	Gruel..	1 pint	1 pint
	Sunday :—		
	Bread	6 oz.	6 oz.
	Potatoes	8 ,,	8 ,,
	Cooked Meat, preserved by heat	4 ,,	3 ,,
	Monday :—		
	Bread	6 oz.	6 oz.
	Potatoes	8 ,,	8 ,,
	Beans	10 ,,	8 ,,
	Fat Bacon	2 ,,	1 ,,
	Tuesday :—		
	Bread	6 oz.	6 oz.
	Potatoes	8 ,,	8 ,,
	Soup	1 pint	1 pint
Dinner	Wednesday :—		
	Bread	6 oz.	6 oz.
	Potatoes	8 ,,	8 ,,
	Suet Pudding	10 ,,	8 ,,
	Thursday :—		
	Bread	6 oz.	6 oz.
	Potatoes	8 ,,	8 ,,
	Cooked Beef, without bone	4 ,,	3 ,,
	Friday :—		
	Bread	6 oz.	6 oz.
	Potatoes	8 ,,	8 ,,
	Soup	1 pint	1 pint
	Saturday :—		
	Bread	6 oz.	6 oz.
	Potatoes	8 ,,	8 ,,
	Suet Pudding	10 ,,	8 ,,
Supper	Daily :—		
	Bread	8 oz.	6 oz.
	Porridge	1 pint	—
	Gruel..	—	1 pint

NOTES—(a) Men include all male prisoners over 16 years of age. Women include all female prisoners over 16 years of age. Juveniles include all prisoners under 16 years of age.

(b) Juvenile prisoners may, in addition to the above diet, be allowed milk, not exceeding one pint per diem, at the discretion of the Medical Officer.

Meals.	—	Men.	Women and Juveniles.
Breakfast	**Daily :—**		
	Bread	8 oz.	6 oz.
	Porridge	1 pint	—
	Tea	—	1 pint
	Sunday :—		
	Bread	6 oz.	6 oz.
	Potatoes	12 ,,	8 ,,
	Cooked Meat, preserved by heat..	5 ,,	4 ,,
	Monday :—		
	Bread	6 oz.	6 oz.
	Potatoes	12 ,,	8 ,,
	Beans	12 ,,	10 ,,
	Fat Bacon	2 ,,	2 ,,
	Tuesday :—		
	Bread	6 oz.	6 oz.
	Potatoes	12 ,,	8 .,
	Soup	1 pint	1 pint
Dinner	**Wednesday :—**		
	Bread	6 oz.	6 oz.
	Potatoes	12 ,,	8 ,,
	Suet Pudding	12 ,,	10 ,,
	Thursday :—		
	Bread	6 oz.	6 oz.
	Potatoes	12 ,,	8 ,,
	Cooked Beef, without bone	5 ,,	4 ,,
	Friday :—		
	Bread	6 oz.	6 oz.
	Potatoes	12 ,,	8 ,,
	Soup	1 pint	1 pint
	Saturday :—		
	Bread	6 oz.	6 oz.
	Potatoes	12 ,,	8 ,,
	Suet Pudding	12 ,,	10 ,,
Supper	**Daily :—**		
	Bread	8 oz.	6 oz.
	Cocoa..	1 pint	1 pint

NOTES—(a) Men include all male prisoners over 16 years of age. Women include all female prisoners over 16 years of age. Juveniles include all prisoners under 16 years of age.

(b) Juvenile prisoners may, in addition to the above diet, be allowed milk, not exceeding one pint per diem, at the discretion of the Medical Officer, and one pint of porridge in lieu of tea for breakfast.

The terms to which the foregoing diets shall be severally applied shall be those set forth in the following table :—

Term.	Diet A.	Diet B.	Diet C.
Seven days and under	Whole term	—	—·
More than seven days and not more than four months	Seven days	Remainder of term	—
More than four months	—	Four months	Remainder of term

The diet for special classes of prisoners, viz. :—

(a) Prisoners on remand or awaiting trial who do not maintain themselves ;

(b) Offenders of the 1st Division who do not maintain themselves ;

(c) Offenders of the 2nd Division ;

(d) Debtors ;

shall be Diet B : provided that they shall receive for breakfast one pint of tea in lieu of gruel, and for supper one pint of cocoa in lieu of porridge or gruel; and that when detained in prison more than four months they shall receive C diet at the expiration of the fourth month.

The diet for prisoners of both sexes, irrespective of age on the day of first reception, whether on remand, to await trial, or on conviction or otherwise, shall be :—

Breakfast .. { Bread	8 oz.	
Cocoa	1 pin	
Dinner .. { Bread	12 oz.	
Cooked meat preserved by heat..	4 ,,	
Supper .. { Bread	8 oz.	
Porridge	1 pin	

The foregoing diets shall be prepared as follows :—

Bread	To be made with whole-meal flour, consisting of all the products of grinding the wheaten grain, with the exception of 12 per cent. of coarse bran and coarse pollards.
Porridge	To every pint, 3 oz. coarse Scotch oatmeal, with salt.
Gruel	To every pint, 2 oz. coarse Scotch oatmeal, with salt.
Tea	To every pint, $\frac{1}{6}$ oz. tea, 2 oz. milk, and $\frac{3}{4}$ oz. sugar.
Cocoa..	To every pint, $\frac{3}{4}$ oz. Admiralty cocoa, 2 oz. milk, and $\frac{3}{4}$ oz. sugar.
Milk	To be fresh unskimmed milk ; to be served hot with the breakfast and supper of juveniles.
Suet pudding ...	To every pound, 2 oz. suet and 8 oz. white or whole-meal flour.
Soup	In every pint, 4 oz. clod (or shoulder), leg, or shin of beef ; 4 oz. split peas ; 2 oz. fresh vegetables ; $\frac{1}{2}$ oz. onions ; pepper and salt. From May to September inclusive the soup to consist of the following ingredients :— 4 oz. clod (or shoulder). leg, or shin of beef ; 1 oz. pearl barley ; 2 oz. fresh vegetables ; 1 oz. onions ; $\frac{1}{8}$ oz. flour ; pepper and salt.
Cooked meat, preserved by heat.	Colonial or American beef or mutton of approved brands and of best quality. This meat should not be cooked or heated in any way ; it should always be served cold as it leaves the tin.
Meat liquor or broth.	The liquor in which the beef is cooked on Thursdays should be thickened with $\frac{1}{6}$ oz. flour, and flavoured with $\frac{1}{2}$ oz onions to each ration, with pepper and salt.
Beans	Haricot beans, or broad or Windsor beans dried in the green state and decorticated.
	SUBSTITUTES.
Cooked beef without bone.	Colonial or American beef or mutton, preserved by heat, may be substituted for cooked English beef, weight for weight. Cooked fresh fish, 8 oz., or cooked salt fish, 12 oz., may occasionally be substituted for 4 oz. cooked English beef without bone, and in like proportion for other quantities.
Potatoes	Fresh vegetables may be substituted for potatoes, weight for weight after cooking ; rice, also, may be substituted in the same proportion after cooking ; rice, however, should be sparingly used as a substitute for potatoes, and when so used should, if possible, be combined with fresh vegetables in equal proportions.
Fresh vegetables	If fresh vegetables are not procurable, $\frac{1}{4}$ oz. preserved mixed vegetables may be used, in lieu of 1 oz. fresh vegetables, for ordinary prison diets.

G

CONVICT PRISONS.

DIET C.

For **MALE** Convicts undergoing separate confinement.

Breakfast	Daily :—		
	Bread	8 oz.	
	Porridge	1 pint	
	Sunday :—		
	Bread	6 oz.	
	Potatoes	12 ,,	
	Cooked meat preserved by		
	heat	5 ,,	
	Monday :—		
	Bread	6 oz.	
	Potatoes	12 ,,	
	Beans	12 ,,	
	Fat Bacon..	2 ,,	
	Tuesday :—		
	Bread	6 oz.	
	Potatoes	12 ,,	
	Soup	1 pint	
Dinner	Wednesday :—		
	Bread	6 oz.	
	Potatoes	12 ,,	
	Suet Pudding	12 ,,	
	Thursday :—		
	Bread	6 oz.	
	Potatoes	12 ,,	
	Cooked Beef, without bone	5 ,,	
	Friday :—		
	Bread	6 oz.	
	Potatoes	12 ,,	
	Soup	1 pint	
	Saturday :—		
	Bread	6 oz.	
	Potatoes	12 ,,	
	Suet Pudding	12 ,,	
Supper	Daily :—		
	Bread	8 oz.	
	Cocoa..	1 pint	

DIET D.

For MALE Convicts after period of separate confinement when engaged in Industrial Employment.

Breakfast	**Daily :—**	
	Bread	8 oz.
	Gruel, sweetened with ½ oz. sugar	1 pint
	Sunday :—	
	Bread	8 oz.
	Potatoes	12 ,,
	Cooked Meat, preserved by heat	5 ,,
	Monday :—	
	Bread	8 oz.
	Potatoes	12 ,,
	Beans	12 ,,
	Fat Bacon	2 ,,
	Tuesday :—	
	Bread	8 oz.
	Potatoes	12 ,,
	Cooked Mutton, without bone	5 ,,
Dinner	**Wednesday :—**	
	Bread	8 oz.
	Potatoes	12 ,,
	Pea Soup (Pork)	1 pint
	Thursday :—	
	Bread	8 oz.
	Potatoes	12 ,,
	Cooked Beef, without bone	5 ,,
	Friday :—	
	Bread	8 oz.
	Potatoes	12 ,,
	Vegetable Soup (Beef) ..	1 pint
	Saturday :—	
	Bread	8 oz.
	Potatoes	12 ,,
	Suet Pudding	12 ,,
Supper	**Daily :—**	
	Bread	8 oz.
	Cocoa..	1 pint

A convict on attaining the third stage may have 1 pint of tea and 2 oz. additional bread in lieu of gruel for breakfast.

DIET E.

For MALE Convicts after period of separate confinement when employed at certain prescribed forms of Labour.

Breakfast	Daily :—	
	Bread	8 óz.
	Butter or Margarine* ..	½ ,,
	Porridge	1 pint
	Sunday :—	
	Bread	8 oz.
	Potatoes	16 ,,
	Cooked meat preserved by	
	heat	6 ,,
	Monday :—	
	Bread	8 oz.
	Potatoes	16 ,,
	Beans	12 ,,
	Fat Bacon	2 ,,
	Tuesday :—	
	Bread	8 oz.
	Potatoes	16 ,,
	Cooked Mutton, without	
	bone	6 ,,
Dinner .. ••	Wednesday :—	
	Bread	8 oz.
	Potatoes	16 ,,
	Pea Soup (Pork)	1 pint
	Thursday :—	
	Bread	8 oz.
	Potatoes	16 ,,
	Cooked Beef, without bone	6 ,,
	Friday :—	
	Bread	8 oz.
	Potatoes	16 ,,
	Vegetable Soup (Beef) ..	1 pint
	Saturday ;—	
	Bread	8 oz.
	Potatoes	16 ,,
	Suet Pudding	16 ,,
Supper	Daily :—	
	Bread	12 oz.
	Cocoa..	1 pint
	Wednesday and Friday :—	
	Cheese	2 oz.

* Butter or margarine to be given for six months in the year, October to March (inclusive). During the remaining months, April to September, (inclusive), milk, ¼ pint for each convict, to be substituted for butter or margarine, and to be given in the form of milk porridge.

A convict on attaining the third stage may have 1 pint of tea and 2 oz. additional bread in lieu of porridge for breakfast.

DIET F.

For FEMALE Convicts undergoing separate confinement.

Breakfast	**Daily :—**	
	Bread	6 oz.
	Tea	1 pint
	Sunday :—	
	Bread	6 oz.
	Potatoes	8 ,,
	Cooked Meat, preserved	
	by heat	4 ,,
	Monday :—	
	Bread	6 oz.
	Potatoes	8 ,,
	Beans	10 ,,
	Fat Bacon	2 ,,
	Tuesday :—	
	Bread	6 oz.
	Potatoes	8 ,,
	Soup	1 pint
Dinner	**Wednesday :—**	
	Bread	6 oz.
	Potatoes	8 ,,
	Suet Pudding*	10 ,,
	Thursday :—	
	Bread	6 oz.
	Potatoes	8 ,,
	Cooked Beef, without bone	4 ,,
	Friday : —	
	Bread	6 oz.
	Potatoes	8 ,,
	Soup	1 pint
	Saturday :—	
	Bread	6 oz.
	Potatoes	8 ,,
	Suet Pudding*	10 ,,
Supper	**Daily :—**	
	Bread	6 oz.
	Cocoa	1 pint

* 2 oz. golden syrup may be given with the suet pudding to those female convicts who desire it.

DIET. G.

For FEMALE Convicts after period of separate confinement.

Breakfast	**Daily :—**	
	Bread	6 oz.
	Tea	1 pint
	Sunday :—	
	Bread	6 oz.
	Potatoes	12 ,,
	Cooked meat preserved by heat	4 ,,
	Monday :—	
	Bread	6 oz.
	Potatoes	12 ,,
	Cooked Mutton, without bone	3 ,,
	Tuesday :—	
	Bread	6 oz
	Potatoes	12 ,,
	Cooked Beef, without bone	3 ,,
	Wednesday :—	
Dinner	Bread	6 oz.
	Potatoes	12 ,,
	Cooked Mutton, without bone	3 ,,
	Thursday :—	
	Bread	6 oz.
	Potatoes	12 ,,
	Suet Pudding*..	10 ,,
	Friday :—	
	Bread	6 oz.
	Potatoes	12 ,,
	Cooked Beef, without bone	3 ,,
	Saturday :—	
	Bread	6 oz.
	Potatoes	12 .,
	Vegetable Soup (Beef) ..	1 pint
Supper	**Daily :—**	
	Bread	6 oz.
	Cocoa..	1 pint

* 2 oz. golden syrup may be given with the suet pudding to those female convicts who desire it.

The foregoing diets shall be prepared as follows :—
(CONVICT.)

Bread...	To be made with whole-meal flour, consisting of all the products of the wheaten grain, with the exception of 12 per cent. of coarse bran and coarse pollards. This may be varied for female convicts at the discretion of the Governor and Medical Officer.
Porridge	To every pint 3 oz. coarse Scotch oatmeal, with salt.
Milk Porridge ...	To every pint 3 oz. coarse Scotch oatmeal, $\frac{1}{4}$ pint milk, with salt.
Gruel	To every pint 2 oz. coarse Scotch oatmeal, $\frac{1}{2}$ oz. sugar.
Tea	To every pint $\frac{1}{6}$ oz. tea, 2 oz. milk, $\frac{3}{4}$ oz. sugar.
Cocoa...	To every pint $\frac{3}{4}$ oz. Admiralty cocoa, 2 oz. milk, $\frac{3}{4}$ oz. sugar.
Milk	To be fresh unskimmed milk.
Butter or Margarine.	To be of approved brands of best quality.
Suet pudding...	To every lb. 2 oz. beef suet, 8 oz. white or whole-meal flour.
Pea Soup for Male Convicts.	To every pint 4 oz. salt pork, 4 oz. split peas, 1 oz. onions, $\frac{1}{4}$ oz. vinegar, pepper and salt.
Vegetable Soup	To every pint, clod or shoulder, leg or shin of beef in the proportion of 8 oz. for male convicts on E diet, and 6 oz. for male and female convicts on D and G diets ; and, in addition, the soup to contain 1 oz. pearl barley, 2 oz. fresh vegetables, 1 oz. onions, $\frac{1}{8}$ oz. flour, with pepper and salt.
Meat Liquor ..	The allowance of cooked mutton to be served with its own liquor, flavoured with $\frac{1}{2}$ oz. onions, and thickened with $\frac{1}{8}$ oz. flour, with pepper and salt.
Ditto	The allowance of cooked beef to be served with its own liquor, flavoured and thickened as above.
Cooked Meat, preserved by heat.	Colonial or American beef or mutton of approved brands and of best quality. This meat should not be cooked or heated in any way. It ought to be served cold as it leaves the tin.
Beans...	Haricot beans, or broad or Windsor beans, dried in the green state and decorticated.

SUBSTITUTES.

Cooked Beef, without bone.	Colonial or American beef or mutton, preserved by heat, may, if necessity arises, be substituted for cooked English beef or mutton, weight for weight. Cooked fresh fish 8 oz., or cooked salt fish 12 oz. may occasionally be substituted for 4 oz. cooked English beef or mutton, and in like proportion for other quantities.
Potatoes	Fresh vegetables or rice may be substituted for potatoes, weight for weight after cooking. Rice, however, should be sparingly used as a substitute for potatoes, and, when so used, should, if possible, be combined with fresh vegetables in equal proportions.
Fresh vegetables	In the event of fresh vegetables not being procurable, $\frac{1}{4}$ oz. preserved mixed vegetables may be used in lieu of 1 oz. fresh vegetables for ordinary prison diets.

HOSPITAL DIETS.

LOCAL AND CONVICT PRISONS.

—	Ordinary Diet.	Pudding Diet.	Low Diet.
Breakfast ..	Bread, 8 oz. Tea, 1 pint, containing $\frac{1}{8}$ oz. tea $\frac{3}{4}$ oz. sugar, and 2 oz. milk.	White Bread, 6oz. Milk, 1 pint	Bread, 6 oz. Tea, 1 pint ; ingredients as in ordinary diet.
Dinner ..	Meat, 5 oz. (cooked). Potatoes, 8 oz Vegetables, 4 oz. Bread, 6 oz. Salt, $\frac{1}{2}$ oz,	Rice Pudding, containing 2 oz. rice, 1 egg, and 10 oz. milk ; or, Batter pudding, containing 3 oz. flour, 1 egg, and 10 oz. milk ; or, Custard pudding, containing 1 egg, and 10 oz. milk.	Cornflour, containing 1 oz. cornflour, 1 pint milk, 1 oz. sugar ; to produce 1 pint.
Supper.. ..	Bread, 8 oz. Tea, 1 pint.	White Bread, 6 oz. Milk. 1 pint.	Bread, 6 oz. Tea, 1 pint.

Notes on the Hospital Dietary.

Cooked meat to consist of fresh beef or mutton, which may be roasted, baked, stewed, or boiled ; when boiled, the allowance of cooked meat to be served with its own liquor, thickened with $\frac{1}{8}$ oz. of flour, and flavoured with $\frac{1}{4}$ oz. of onions, with pepper and salt.

Fowls, rabbits, or fish may be substituted for 5 oz. cooked meat, at the rate of 8 oz. (uncooked), or bacon, 4 oz. (uncooked), per diet. Sago or tapioca may be substituted for rice.

$\frac{1}{2}$ oz. to 1 oz. sugar may be used to sweeten the puddings.

Beef tea, 16 oz. lean beef, without bone, $1\frac{1}{2}$ pints of cold water, to make 1 pint.

Mustard and pepper will be issued to each convict when required.

Extras and medical comforts may be given to patients when considered necessary by the Medical Officer.

The following are the maximum allowances of uncooked food to produce the authorized quantities of cooked food, viz. :—

Bacon...............	$1\frac{1}{5}$ oz.	to produce		1 oz.			
Beans...............	1	,, ,,	,,	2 ,,			
Beef and Mutton, including bone	11	,, ,,	,,	6 oz. without bone.			
,, ,,	9	,, ,,	,,	5 ,,	,,		
,, ,,	7	,, ,,	,,	4 ,,	,,		
,, ,,	$5\frac{1}{3}$	,, ,,	,,	3 ,,	,,		
Potatoes...........	110 lbs.	,,	,,	100 lbs.			
Rice	5 ozs.	in lieu of		1 ,, Potatoes			

Notes

Abbreviations:
PP—Parliamentary Papers;
RCP—Report of Commissioners of Prisons;
RIP—Report of Inspectors of Prisons;
NAO—National Audit Office.

1.   PP, 1899, *Report of Departmental Committee on Prison Dietaries*, p. 22.
2.   PP, 2005–6, National Audit Office: *Serving Time: Prisoner Diet and Exercise*, p. 1.
3.   Peters, 1995, p. 8.
4.   Walmsley, R., *World Prison Population List* (8th ed., 2009).
5.   Peters, 1995, pp. 5–6.
6.   *War with Catiline* (LV).
7.   Forsyth, 1994, pp. 67–68.
8.   25 Edward III, s5, c2.
9.   Webb, 1922, p. 4.
10.   Brodie et al, 2002, p. 11.
11.   Peters, 1995, p. 31.
12.   Brodie et al, 2002, p. 11.
13.   Ibid., p. 14.
14.   *Oxford English Dictionary*, 2nd ed., 1989.
15.   Brodie et al, 2002, p. 13.
16.   Coppack, G., 1993.
17.   Verse 1 of Psalm 51 in the Authorised Version. Prior to the seventeenth century, the equivalent verse of Psalm 50 in the Latin Vulgate Bible was used.
18.   Briggs et al, 1996, p. 74.
19.   Harding, 1985, p. 11.
20.   Pettifer, 1939, p. 128.
21.   Dobb, 1964, p. 91.
22.   Briggs et al, 1996, p. 75.
23.   Ibid.
24.   McLynn, 1898, p. 263.
25.   Briggs et al, 1996, p. 24.
26.   Pettifer, 1939, p. 102.
27.   Acts 16, v. 24.
28.   Pettifer, 1939, p. 109.
29.   Ibid., p. 124.
30.   Ibid., p. 125.
31.   *A tour thro' the whole island of Great Britain, divided into circuits or journies*, vol. 2, letter 5.
32.   Dobb, 1964, p. 89.
33.   *Encyclopaedia Britannica*, 2008.

34. Bassett, 1944, p. 394.

35. Allen, 1829, p. 149.

36. Dobb, 1964, p. 90.

37. Bassett, 1943, p. 233.

38. Ibid., p. 236.

39. Ibid., p. 239.

40. Riley, 1868, p. 677.

41. Barron, 2005, p. 166.

42. Leonard, 1965, p. 99.

43. Ungerer, 2002, pp. 182–91.

44. Brodie et al, 2002, p. 17.

45. Neild, 1812, p. 603.

46. Pugh, 1968, p. 59.

47. Tower of London Press Office, 2008.

48. Bassett, 1943, p. 240; Pugh, 1968, p. 189.

49. Shaw, 1947, p. 371.

50. Pugh, 1968, p. 191.

51. Webb, 1922, pp. 6–7.

52. Dobb, 1964, p. 95.

53. Webb, 1922, p. 25.

54. Dobb, 1964, p. 96.

55. Langley, 1724, p. 42.

56. *The Gentleman's Magazine*, 1804, p. 199.

57. Ibid., p. 5.

58. Bassett, 1944, p. 396.

59. Dobb, 1964, p. 96.

60. Acts of the Privy Council, 1592, p. 306.

61. Dawson, 1597, p. 3.

62. Grey, 1653, p. 83.

63. Ibid., p. 89.

64. Langley, 1724, p. 11.

65. Dobb, 1964, p. 96.

66. Harding, 1985, p. 89.

67. Webb, 1922, p. 11.

68. Stow, 1603, p. 392.

69. Jones, 1979, p. 9.

70. Pugh, 1968, p. 357.

71. Langley, 1724, p. 44.

72. Ibid., p. 45.

73. Pitcher, 2003, p. 168.

74. Webb, 1922, p. 21.

75. Howard, 1784, p. 9.

76. *Penny Cyclopaedia of the Society for the Diffusion of Useful Knowledge*, 1835, p. 477.

77. Veall, 1970, p. 144.

78. *Cry of the Oppressed: Being a True and Tragical Account of the Unparallel'd Sufferings of Multitudes of Poor Imprison'd Debtors.*

79. *An Essay Towards the Reformation of Newgate and Other Prisons in and about London, 1702.*

80. Pitofsky, 2000, p. 97.

81. Brodie et al, 2002, p. 79.

82. Howard, 1929, p. 15.

83. Howard, 1777, p. 8.

84. Ibid., p. 206.

85. Norgate and Lee, 2004.
86. *The Gentleman's Magazine*, 1804, p. 801.
87. Zedner, 1995, p. 298.
88. De Haan, 2004.
89. 39 Elizabeth I, c4.
90. Harding, 1985, p. 65.
91. Ekirch, 1985, pp. 184, 188.
92. Ibid., p. 184.
93. Ekirch, 1987, p. 90.
94. Ibid., p. 100.
95. Campbell, 2001, p. 8.
96. 16 George III, c43.
97. 19 George III, c74.
98. Campbell, 2001, p. 33.
99. Ibid., p. 20.
100. Howard, 1784, p. 466.
101. Ellis, 1750, p. 202.
102. Campbell, 2001, p. 35
103. 24 George III, c56.
104. Mellick, 2000, p. 877.
105. Adapted from Corke, 1986.
106. Crosby, 2004, p. 205.
107. Griffiths, 1900, p. 27.
108. PP, 1838, *Report from the Select Committee on Transportation*, p. vi.
109. Campbell, 2001, p. 62.
110. PP, 1812, *Third Report from the Committee on the Laws Relating to Penitentiary Houses*, p. 139.
111. Quoted in Hughes, 1988, p. 265
112. PP, 1812, *Third Report from the Committee on the Laws Relating to Penitentiary Houses*, p. 139.
113. PP, 1831–2, *Report from Select Committee on Secondary Punishments*, pp. 12–15.
114. PP, 1847, *Inquiry into the state of the convict establishment at Woolwich*, p. xvii.
115. Brodie et al, 2002, p. 54.
116. Johnson, 1957, p. 51.
117. Ibid., p. 55.
118. PP, 1780, *Report from Committee Appointed to Enquire into the State of the Health of the Prisoners Consined in the King's House, at Winchester*, p. 5.
119. Bradley, 1762, p. 271.
120. Glasse, 1758, p. 239.
121. PP, 1818, *Select Committee on State of Prisons in the City of London and Borough of Southwark, and on Dartmoor Prison*, p. 237.
122. Thomson, 1907, p. 48.
123. Ibid., p. 54.
124. Ibid., p. 18.
125. Ibid., p. 59.
126. Brodie et al, 2002, p. 38.
127. Ibid., pp. 44–52.
128. Bentham, 1830, p. 133.
129. Brodie et al et al, 2002, p. 60.
130. Griffiths, 1884, p. 27.
131. Ibid., pp. 49–50.
132. PP, 1862, *General report on the Convict Prisons*, p. 62.
133. *The Times*, 28 November 1843, p. 4.
134. PP, 1849, *Seventh report of the Commissioners for the Government of the Pentonville Prison*, p. 4.

135. Harding, 1985, p. 153.
136. 55 George III, c50.
137. 4 George IV, c64.
138. County gaols plus those in London, Westminster, Bristol, Hull, Norwich, Canterbury, Leicester, Nottingham, Chester, Lichfield, Portsmouth, Coventry, Lincoln, Worcester, Exeter, Liverpool, York, Gloucester and Newcastle upon Tyne.
139. PP, 1841 RIP I. Home District, p. 168.
140. Edwards & Hurley, 1981, p. 33.
141. Brodie et al, 2002, pp. 98–9.
142. Mayhew, 1862, pp. 331–5.
143. Anonymous, 1832, p. 526.
144. PP, 1840, *Reports Relating to Parkhurst Prison*, p. 4.
145. Ibid., 1844, p. 5.
146. *Good Words*, 1866, p. 283.
147. PP, 1800, *Papers Presented to House of Commons, Relating to His Majesty's Prison in Cold Bath Fields*, p. 86.
148. PP, 1812–3, *Report from Commissioners Appointed to Enquire into … His Majesty's Prison the Castle of Lancaster*, p. 22.
149. PP, 1818, *Select Committee on State of Prisons in the City of London* etc., p. 197.
150. Ibid., *Second Report*, p. 260.
151. PP, 1837, *RIP I.* Home District, pp. 482–91, table 22.
152. PP, 1837, RIP II. N & E District, p. 9.
153. Johnston, 1985, pp. 158–9.
154. PP, 1837, RIP II. N & E District, p. 46.
155. PP, 1842, RIP II. N & E District, p. 51.
156. PP, 1843, RIP. *Relative to the System of Prison Discipline*, p. 3.
157. For example, Gilbert Blane, *Observations on the Disease Incident to Seamen*, 1785, p. 57.
158. Lancet, vol. II, p. 789, 3 September 1842.
159. *London Medical Gazette*, 1843, pp. 699–703.
160. Priestley, 1985, p. 155.
161. Carpenter, 2006, p. 2.
162. Chapman, 1967, p. 14.
163. Smith, 1864, p. 218.
164. Smith, 1859, p. 287.
165. Guy, 1863, p. 258.
166. Ibid., pp. 266–8.
167. PP, 1863, *Select Committee of the House of Lords, on the Present State of Discipline in Gaols and Houses of Correction*, p. iii.
168. 28 & 29 Victoria, c126.
169. Morris, 1995, p. 94.
170. PP, 1864, *Report of Committee to inquire into Dietaries of County and Borough Prisons*, p. 28.
171. Ibid., p. 72.
172. PP, 1864, *Dietaries of County and Borough Prisons*, p. 75.
173. Brodie et al, 2002, p. 146.
174. PP, 1887, RCP, p. 61.
175. PP, 1878, *Report of Committee to inquire into Dietaries of Prisons in England and Wales*, p. 9.
176. Ibid., p. 7.
177. Tempest, 1950, p. 203.
178. PP, 1878–9, *Report of Commissioners Appointed to Inquire into Working of the Penal Servitude Acts*, p. xxxvii.
179. Ibid., p. 355.
180. Priestley, 1985, pp. 160–1.
181. Drummond, 1939, p. 494.

182. WBN, 1903, p. 111.
183. Mitchell, 1968, p. 148.
184. PP, 1878–9, *Report into Penal Servitude Acts*, p. 352.
185. Brocklehurst, 1898, pp. 123–4.
186. Foote, 1886, p. 130.
187. WBN, 1903, p. 111.
188. Dr Alexander McCook Weir, quoted in Priestley, 1985, p. 151.
189. Priestley, 1985, p. 152.
190. Brocklehurst, 1898, p. 119.
191. Cooper, 1897, chapter 22.
192. WBN, 1902, p. 106.
193. Lovett, 1876, p. 227.
194. Priestley, 1985, p. 289–90.
195. PP, 1863, *Discipline in Gaols*, p. 360.
196. Balfour, 1907, p. 191.
197. Priestley, 1985, pp. 169–75.
198. Ibid., p. 152.
199. Housden, 2006, para. 8.
200. Blom-Cooper, 1987, p. 291.
201. PP, 1895, *Departmental Committee on Prisons*, p. 1.
202. Ibid., pp. 16–8.
203. Ibid., p. 42.
204. PP, 1899, *Report of Departmental Committee on Prison Dietaries*, p. 3.
205. Ibid., p. 10.
206. PP, 1895, *Departmental Committee on Prisons*, p. 35.
207. PP, 1899, *Departmental Committee on Prison Dietries*, p. 34.
208. PP, 1878, *Dietaries of Prisons*, p. 32.
209. *The Manual of Workhouse Cookery*, 1902, Local Government Board.
210. 1899, RCP, p. 22.
211. PP, 1900, RCP for 1899–1900, p. 23.
212. *Report of the Committee of the Society for the Improvement of Prison Discipline*, 1820, p. 8.
213. PP, 1902, RCP for 1900–1, pp. 62–5.
214. Ibid., pp. 6–8.
215. PP, 1819, *Report from the Select Committee on Criminal Laws*, p. 127.
216. PP, 1902, RCP for 1900–1, p. 6. PP, 1945–6, RCP for 1939–41, p. 27.
217. PP, 1922, RCP, 16, 72.
218. Brodie et al, 2002, p. 173.
219. Ibid., p. 196.
220. Ibid., p. 227.
221. Ibid., p. 212.
222. House of Commons Library note SN/G/4334 Prison Population Statistics, 2009.
223. *Report of Departmental Committee on Diets,* 1925, p. 1.
224. Ibid., p. 6.
225. PP, 1945–6, RCP for 1939–41, p. 62.
226. PP, 1946–7, RCP for 1942–4, pp. 69–71.
227. PP, 1952–3, RCP for 1951, p. 120.
228. PP, 1950–1, RCP for 1949, p. 65.
229. PP, 1962–3, *Report of an Inquiry held by the Visiting Committee into Allegations of Ill-treatment of Prisoners in HMP Durham*, Appendix B.
230. PP, 1971–2, *Report on the Work of the Prison Department*, 1971, p. 53.
231. PP, 1931–2, *Report on the circumstances connected with the recent disorder at Dartmoor Convict Prison*, p. 12.
232. Brown, 2007, p. 282.

233. Erwin James, http://www.guardian.co.uk/lifeandstyle/wordofmouth/2008/jul/07/prisonfood1

234. PP, 1990–1 *Prison Disturbances,* April 1990. Report of Inquiry by Rt Hon. Lord Justice Woolf & His Honour Judge Stephen Tumim, p. 398.

235. Ibid., p. 452.

236. PP, 1989–90 *Report of Her Majesty's Chief Inspector of Prisons 1989*, p. 13.

237. Ibid., p. 24.

238. PP, 1997–8 NAO: HM Prison Service: *Prison Catering.* Report by Comptroller and Auditor General, p. 27.

239. PP, 1990–1 *Prison Disturbances* report, p. 399.

240. PP, 1997–8, NAO, *Prison Catering*, p. 29.

241. Ibid., p. 30.

242. *Prison Services Catering Manual*, 2008, p. 4.

243. PP, 2006, NAO, *Serving Time: Prisoner Diet and Exercise*, p. 1.

244. Ibid., p. 14.

245. Ibid., p. 13. Table reproduced by kind permission of NAO.

246. PP, 1906, RCP for 1905–6, p. 249.

247. PP, 1910, RCP for 1909–10, p. 340.

248. PP, 1933–4, *Report of Departmental Committee. Part I. The Employment of Prisoners*, p. 47.

249. PP, 1953–4, RCP for 1953, p. 96.

250. PP, 1992–3, HM Inspectorate of Prisons: *Doing Time or Using Time*, p. 80.

251. *Prison Service News*, no 242, December 2005.

252. Tempest, 1950, p. 44.

253. Prison rules and orders 323(3).

254. *The Sun*, 30 October 2008.

Bibliography

Allen, T. (1829) *A History of the County of Surrey*

Anonymous (1588) *The Good Hous-wives Treasurie*

Anonymous (1832) 'The Schoolmaster's Experience in Newgate' (in *Fraser's Magazine*, p. 526)

Balfour, J. (1907) *My Prison Life*

Barron, C. (2005) *London in the Later Middle Ages: Government and People 1200–1500*

Bassett, M. (1943) 'Newgate Prison in the Middle Ages' (in *Speculum* vol. 18, pp. 233–46)

Bassett, M. (1944) 'The Fleet Prison in the Middle Ages' (in *University Toronto Law Journal*, vol. 5, no 2, pp. 383–402)

Bateson, C. (1958) *The Convict Ships*

Bentham, J. (1830) *The Rationale of Punishment*

Blom-Cooper, L. (1987) 'The Penalty of Imprisonment' (in *The Tanner Lectures on Human Values*, pp. 279–350)

Bradley, R. (1762) *The Country Housewife, and Lady's Director for Every Month of the Year ... Containing the Whole Art of Cookery*

Briggs, J., Harrison, C., McInnes, A. and Vincent, D. (1996) *Crime and Punishment in England*

Brocklehurst, F. (1898) *I Was in Prison*

Brodie, A., Croom, J. and Davies, J. (2002) *English Prisons – an Architectural History*

Brown, A. (2007) 'The Amazing Mutiny at the Dartmoor Convict Prison' (in *Brit. J. Criminol*, vol. 47, pp. 276–92)

Cadoux, T.J. (2008) 'The Roman Carcer and its Adjuncts' (in *Greece & Rome*, vol. 500, no 2, pp. 202–21)

Campbell, C. (2001) *The Intolerable Hulks*

Carpenter, K. (2006) 'Nutritional Studies in Victorian Prisons' (in *Am. Soc. Nutr. J. Nutr.*, vol. 135, pp. 1–8)

Chapman, C. (1967) Edward Smith (1818–74) 'Physiologist, Human Ecologist, Reformer' (in *J. Hist. Med.*, vol. 22, pp. 1–26)

Cooper, T. (1897) *The Life of Thomas Cooper*

Coppack, G. (1993) *Fountains Abbey*

Corke, D. (1986) *They Came to Botany Bay*

Crosby, A.W. (2004) *Ecological Imperialism*

Dawson, T. (1597) *The Second Part of the Good Huswifes Jewell*

De Haan, F. (2004) 'Fry , Elizabeth (1780–1845)' (in *Oxford DNB*)

Dobb, C. (1964) London's Prisons (in *Shakespeare Survey* XVII)

Drummond, J. and Wilbraham, A. (1939) *The Englishman's Food*

Edwards, A. and Hurley, R. (1981) 'Prisons Over Two Centuries' (in *Home Office, 1782–1982* by Rawles, J.)

Ekirch, A. (1985) 'Bound for America: A Profile of British Convicts Transported to the Colonies, 1718–1775' (in *The William and Mary Quarterly*, vol. 42, no 2, pp. 184–200)

Ekirch, A. (1987) *Bound for America: the Transportation of British Convicts to the Colonies, 1718–1775*

Ellis, W. (1750) *The Country Housewife's Family Companion*

Encyclopædia Britannica (2008), from *Encyclopædia Britannica Online*: http://www.britannica.com/EBchecked/topic/592715/Arthur-Thistlewood

Foote, G. (1886) *Prisoner for Blasphemy*

Forsyth, W. (1994) *History of Trial by Jury*

Glasse, H. (1758) *The Art of Cookery, Made Plain and Easy*

Grey, E. (1653) *A Gentlewomans Delight*

Griffiths, A. (1884) *Memorials of Millbank*

Griffiths, A. (1900) Prisons Over Seas (in *The History and Romance of Crime*, vol 5)

Guy, W. (1863) 'On Sufficient and Insufficient Dietaries, with Especial Reference to the Dietaries of Prisoners' (in *J Stat Soc*, London, vol. 26, pp. 239–80)

Housden, M. (2006) 'Oscar Wilde's Imprisonment and an Early Idea of 'Banal Evil'' (in *Forum Historiae Iuris*, http://www.forhistiur.de/zitat/0610housden.htm)

Howard, D. (1960) *The English Prisons*

Howard, J. (1777) *The State of the Prisons in England and Wales* (Further editions in 1780, 1784 and 1791)

Howard, J. (1929) *The State of the Prisons in England and Wales* (Reprint of 1784 edition)

Hughes, R. (1988) *The Fatal Shore: A History of the Transportation of Convicts to Australia, 1787–1868*

Johnson, W.B. (1957) *The English Prison Hulks*

Johnston, V. (1985) *Diets in Workhouses and Prisons 1835–1985*

Jones, W.T. (1979) 'The Foundations of English Bankruptcy' (in *Trans. Am. Phil. Soc.*, vol. 69, pp. 1–63)

Langley, B. (1724) *An Accurate Description of Newgate*

Leonard, E.M. (1965) *The Early History of English Poor Relief*

Mayhew, H. and Binny, J. (1862) *The Criminal Prisons of London and Scenes of Prison Life*

McGowen, R. (1995) *The Well-Ordered Prison* (in *Morris and Rothman*)

McLynn, F. (1989) *Crime and Punishment in Eighteenth-century England*

Mellick, S. (2000) 'John White and Matthew Flinders, Voyageurs Avantureux, in New South Wales 1788–1799' (in *Aust. N.Z. J. Surg.*, vol. 70, pp. 875–82)

Mitchell, H. (1968) *The Hard Way Up*

Morris, N. and Rothman, D.J. (eds) (1995) *The Oxford History of the Prison*

Neild, J. (1812) *The State of the Prisons in England, Scotland and Wales*

Norgate, G. and Lee, S. (2004) 'Neild, James (1744–1814)' (in *Oxford DNB*)

Peters, E.M. (1995) 'Prison before the Prison' (in *Morris and Rothman*)

Pettifer, E.W. (1939) *Punishments of Former Days*

Pitcher, J., Lindsey, R. and Cerasano, S. (2003) *Medieval and Renaissance Drama in England*

Pitofsky, J. (2000) 'The Warden's Court Martial' (in *Eighteenth-Century Life,* vol. 24, no 1, pp. 88–102)

Priestley, P. (1985), *Victorian Prison Lives*

Prison Service Catering Manual, 2008 edition (online at: http://pso.hmprisonservice.gov.uk/PSO_5000_prison_catering_services.doc)

Pugh, R.B. (1968) *Imprisonment in Medieval England*

Richardson, J. (2001) *The Annals of London*

Riley, H.T. (1868) *Memorials of London and London Life*

Shaw, P. (1947) 'The Position of Thomas Dekker in Jacobean Prison Literature' (in *PMLA*, vol. 62, pp. 366–91)

Smith, E. (1859) 'Contributions to a News Scheme of Prison Dietary' (in *Dublin Q J Med. Sci.*, vol. 27, pp. 281–94)

Smith, E. (1861) 'On the Elimination of Urea and Urinary Water …' (in *Phil. Trans. Roy. Soc.* London, vol. 151, pp. 747–834)

Smith, E. (1864) 'On Private and Public Dietaries' (in *J. Soc. Arts*, vol. 12, pp. 212–24)

Stow, J. (1603) A *Survey of London*

Tempest, P. (1950) *Lag's Lexicon*

Thomson, B. (1907) *The Story of Dartmoor Prison*

Tower of London Press Office (2008) *Fact Sheet: Prisoners at the Tower*

Ungerer, G. (2002) 'Prostitution in late Elizabethan London' (in *Medieval and Renaissance Drama in England* vol. 15, pp. 138–223)

Veall, D. (1970) *The Popular Movement for Law Reform, 1640–1660*

W.B.N. [Lord William Nevill] (1903) *Penal Servitude*

Webb, S. and Webb, B. (1922) *English Prisons under Local Government*

Zedner, L. (1995) 'Wayward Sisters' (in *Morris and Rothman*)

Prison and Punishment Index

Prison Food Index

Note – the contents of the *Manual of Cooking & Baking* are listed on pages 138–140.

Acknowledgements

Thanks to Bev Baker and the National Galleries of Justice Museum, Nottingham, for their kind assistance with access to the Prison Service archives. Thanks also to Cate Ludlow at The History Press for her continual encouragement and enthusiasm.

Visit our website and discover thousands of other History Press books.

www.thehistorypress.co.uk